THE
SCOTS

THE
SCOTS

CLIFFORD HANLEY

DAVID & CHARLES

NEWTON ABBOT LONDON

THE SCOTS is for my dear friends
the Scotts

British Library Cataloguing in Publication Data
Hanley, Clifford
    The Scots.
    1. Scotland—Biography
    I. Title
    920'.0411   DA758

ISBN 0-7153-7854-6

Typeset by ABM Typographics Ltd, Hull
and printed in Great Britain
by Butler & Tanner Ltd, Frome
for David & Charles (Publishers) Limited
Brunel House, Newton Abbot, Devon

CONTENTS

ACKNOWLEDGEMENTS

My thanks are due to my friend Brian Skillen for his generous and invaluable help in compiling the Bibliography. I am also grateful to him and Douglas McKendrick for tracking down the illustrations.

C.H.

FOREWORD

N O MORTAL man may write the story of the Scots and write it entire. Countless books have been written already about a single Scot, Robert Burns. The life of one woman, Mary Stuart, has provoked dozens of books and plays. Many other great Scottish figures are viewed by present-day Scots in double vision, as heroes and villains simultaneously, and the truth is elusive.

Probably such people were both goodies and baddies. The contradictory nature of the Scot, however, is what makes him fascinating. It also makes a final analysis a delusion.

Scotland is a country of recurrent depression, betrayal, surrender, grim-faced intolerence. It is also a country of unquenchable exuberance and hope, of bubbling inventiveness and intellectual power. It is a nation of parochial isolation; it is a nation open to the world and all its wonders.

The Scots have riven themselves with fatuous squabbles over obscure doctrines, they have conscientiously smothered the life spirit; and they have demonstrated the meaning of tolerance and given poetry and colour and passion to other peoples.

How can one writer sum up this people? He cannot, except in his own way. The Scots you meet here are not the definitive Scots. They are my Scots. I can try to take an Olympian view and see the truth whole, but what will come out is a partial, an individual and a human view, distorted by cheerful prejudice. Every time I completed one subject I realised there was much more to say about it. Sometimes I went back to make amends. At other times I decided enough was enough, because the Scots are altogether too much.

The many omissions are deliberate. I will defend them to the death, however illogically, because, in spite of my name, I am a Scot.

ORIGINS

(Porridge & Whisky)

T HE SCOTS are tall, rugged people who live in the mountain fastnesses of their native land, on a diet of oatmeal porridge and whisky. They wear kilts of tartan weave, play a deafening musical instrument called the bagpipe, are immensely hospitable but cautious with money (which they call 'bawbees'). They are sparing with words, but when they speak they speak the truth. They have a hard and Spartan religious faith and regard virtually any activity on Sunday as a grave sin. When they leave their native land, they immediately rise to the top in other peoples' industries and professions.

This summary, which has a precarious basis in truth, is mostly nonsense, but it is the impression many outsiders have of the Scots; and travelling Scots are sometimes at pains to reinforce the myth. There are certainly some people in Scotland who fit the picture. For the rest, they vary quite as much as any large group of people, and at a glance they are indistinguishable from ordinary human beings. A few of them will play the bagpipes if provoked. Some play guitars or electronic organs. Most, like most people everywhere, merely listen or, as the case may be, try not to listen. On the whole, they wear clothes which would go unnoticed in Moscow or Manhattan.

Nevertheless, they are Scots, and it is a particular and peculiar thing to be a Scot, as the outside world recognises even if its impression is often based on that myth figure. This small nation, of no more than five million people in modern times, has made a mark on the world out of proportion to its size. It has a history of seething intellectual vigour, religious dissension and innovation, and technical discovery which is really quite astonishing in a country so small and often impoverished. Scotland is also rather a fun place.

The land that produced these people crams a huge variety of scene into its small area, from stark mountain and moor to lush rolling plains, tortuous sea lochs and scatters of islands.

In the beginning, it was ice and little more. When the Ice Ages passed, it was still cold and damp and miserable, but human beings moved into it for some eccentric reason of their own. Presumably they had nowhere else to go. They lived in caves, fished, hunted reindeer and seal and avoided the wolf and the wild boar. As centuries passed, they developed a kind of civilisation, left the caves and dug holes of their own with branches for roofs, and practised rudimentary agriculture. They were short people with long heads, and there are still plenty of people in Scotland who fit that description.

The Bronze Age was brought to the land by a fresh wave of immigration from continental Europe. It really is hard to guess why anybody should want to go to the bother of immigrating. We can only suppose continental Europe was fairly ghastly at the time too.

The new colonists brought a technological breakthrough in the form of earthenware beakers, where the aborigines had been content to drink from sea shells. Apart from that, and their habit of burying their dead in circular graves, we know practically nothing about them except that they were fairly bright. Even to survive in this hostile landscape, people had to be fairly bright.

But more and more astonishing, other people poured into the place. The next wave, who carried the Iron Age with them, were a branch of the Celtic people, the Britons, and their language is the first of which any record or trace remains. They had wandered across the map from eastern Europe, and their language kept drifting, or being pushed, westwards till it reached the ocean and could drift no farther. The Celtic tongue is a fringe affair, surviving or nearly surviving on the outer edges of Europe: in Brittany, Cornwall, Wales, Ireland and the West Highlands of Scotland. (Some people mistakenly imagine the Basque language belongs to this group. Basque in fact is a linguistic 'sport', like Magyar and Finnish, and apparently just grew out of the ground with no previous history and no relatives.)

The Britons were also quite bright; good husbandmen who established villages and used horses and carts. Their small communities kept themselves pretty much to themselves until they were provoked into uniting by a Roman invasion in AD 80.

The motives of the Romans in pushing north from England are another mystery. They had a perfectly good home in Italy, with plenty of sunshine and dark-eyed girls. Even in England, which is noticeably milder in climate than Scotland, they were able to produce a kind of substitute Rome and grow their own wine, a thing they couldn't hope to do north of the river Tweed. Conquest is a bit like salted peanuts: once you start you can't find the will power to give up.

The Romans had a bad time in Scotland, and their expedition is the first evidence of the Scottish character under stress. In a way, the invasion both revealed and shaped a notable element in the Scots personality—stubbornness, 'thrawnness', to the death and beyond in a cause. And in a way, it hammered the early Britons into something like a nation.

Julius Agricola, the commanding Roman general, was one of the empire's best. He led a steady incursion into the south of Scotland and plastered the area with fortresses to maintain control of it. In AD 83 he started to mop up the country farther north with a naval force as a start. This did frighten the natives, but it frightened them into savage opposition. An army of Britons swooped on the camp of the Ninth Legion by night, and slaughtered and scattered the sleeping Romans. Agricola rushed reinforcements and the natives fled, but they fled in good order and vanished in the natural cover of the country they knew so well.

The Legions pushed on, and extended the empire as far north as Perth. But they never conquered the whole country, and they didn't conquer the Scottish Britons. The outposts were always in danger. In AD 115 there was a mass attack on them. The Ninth Legion was sent north to put down the rebellion and vanished without trace. A few years later the Emperor Hadrian decided that the country wasn't worth the trouble. He had a wall built along a line which is roughly the modern border between Scotland and England. The greatest military power in the world had decided that Scotland was unconquerable, and the best it could do was put up a barricade to keep the savages out.

What they did north of the Wall we don't know. But in the fourth century, when Rome was having its own troubles, the northerners started to invade Roman England. In the end they reduced it to ruins.

This is almost the last time the Scots, of their own volition, went out to conquer anybody else's territory. Other people went on trying to conquer Scotland. For centuries, the conquest of Scotland was a staple industry in neighbouring countries.

The very name 'Scot' was brought into the ancient land of Caledonia by invaders, the Scoti tribe from Ireland, who were infiltrating the country during those obscure centuries behind the Wall.

The invasion of Christianity came first from the south, in the person of Ninian, a Romanised Briton, and was continued by Columba, who came over from Ireland, where he had conducted bloody war against the king over some small point of principle, or pique. He turned more placid with age, but his early belligerence might be taken as a powerful element in the Scottish character.

There is still a saying applied to some Scots, by other Scots—'He would start a fight in an empty house.'

More intruders came from Europe, the Angles and the Saxons, and pushed their way north. The natives whom they were displacing were by now known as Picts, which was just a term of insult, since neighbours and invaders regarded them as painted (*picti*) savages. This is a venerable tradition among colonisers: call the natives savages, and it becomes legitimate to rob them and exterminate them.

By the seventh century, the country was a patchwork mess of little kingdoms and conflicting languages and cultures, Scots, Picts, Britons, Angles. It was only reasonable that the rapacious Norwegians should decide it was their turn to swoop on the place. They were the dreaded Norsemen of the long ships, who wanted everything movable that anybody else owned, and who had the strength and ferocity to get it. At one point they sailed right up the river Seine and put Paris in a panic.

They came to rob Scotland, and progressed to occupying large parts of it, particularly the islands and the west coast, where they stayed as masters for centuries. The Scots, or those Scots who had not been murdered in the first place, put up with this, and in what was left of their country they began to turn into some kind of nation, first under one Kenneth McAlpin, who became the first king of both Picts and Scots. This unification was achieved by some very dirty deeds according to legend. Dirty deeds have dominated the history of Scotland, and it would be tiresome to list the catalogue of murder and treachery down the centuries as individuals jostled for the throne of this rather ridiculous little country.

It is worth citing one name, Macbeth, since at least we remember him through the very bad press he received from Shakespeare. He is not a myth. There was indeed a man named Macbeth, and he killed King Duncan and ruled in his place. Unfortunately, the details are obscure. Macbeth was of royal blood, and it is possible he was simply getting rid of a rival equally murderous. It is also a fact (insofar as anything in history is a fact) that Duncan's son Malcolm got the help of the English in overthrowing Macbeth, pursued him to the north and killed him.

In the centuries following, the land enjoyed some kind of peace. In 1263, at the Battle of Largs, the Scots were engaged in a rather messy but nominally successful clash with the Norsemen. The Norwegians now got bored with the whole Scottish thing and agreed to give up the islands for a down payment and a series of instalments.

These islands that came back into the power of Scotland, incidentally, included the Isle of Man, which is nearer England than Scotland and has no business in a Scottish kingdom. Maybe Man was the only foreign territory that the Scots captured. The little island now has its own Parliament and laws, and one of these, which has never been repealed, permits native Manxmen to kill any Scotsman found more than a mile inland. It is not enforced.

The general refusal of the Scots to push out and conquer other people's lands is worth mentioning because it is quite particular and even odd. Most other peoples in these times regarded conquest as not merely a hobby but a duty. There may be something in the Scot's character that makes him content with his own, and not too interested in what other people have.

The next enemy was England, which is still referred to in Scots parlance as the Auld Enemy. From the thirteenth century on, English kings were just as nervous of the turbulent northerners as the Romans had been, and sometimes solved the problem by claiming Scotland as an English district and appointing puppet kings to the Scottish throne. The Scots, apart from the puppets who were quite pleased with the gift, didn't like this a lot, and liberation heroes like William Wallace sprang up to get rid of English power. Wallace failed, and was executed.

Robert de Brus, himself a sort of puppet king, took up the fight for independence, and won it in 1314. But the English never quite admitted the loss. The truth is that, from the beginning, the people who chose to live in Scotland were being hammered incessantly by outsiders. Even today we can find the psychological results in many a Scot; a vague sense of being beleaguered, a suspicion that his birthright is in danger, and a complacent conviction that he wouldn't wish it any other way.

His geography is a part of his personality. Even if he lives in a city street, or a split-level house overlooking the warm gentle landscape of Galloway, he feels he is the owner and the partner of the thrusting granite mountains, the Grampians and the Cairngorms, the rugged islands and the storm-beaten shores.

His climate is part of him, and although he knows there are long summer days and magic springtimes and golden autumns, his unconscious view of his climate is of the bitter east winds and the western gales that toughen a man's skin and his soul.

His history matches the natural elements, and adds something else. The long-drawn-out skirmishing trouble with England was ended, superficially, when James, the son of Mary Queen of Scots, fell heir to the thrones of both Scotland and England, and a United Kingdom arrived. But to the really 'thrawn' Scot, that was a kind of surrender, since the monarch was taken away to London (no, hardly

13

taken; he couldn't wait to shake Scots dust from his shoes and move to the softer surroundings of the south), leaving Scotland as a mere fringe of England.

And when the Parliaments of both countries were amalgamated in 1707, the same thrawn Scot cried, 'Betrayal'. He didn't see the move as a merger, so much as a takeover, in which the smaller partner was swallowed up by the larger.

Geography, climate and history have had their share in making the Scots what they are; emigrants, for one thing. Compared with larger nations (and with some smaller nations) Scotland has gone on being poor, plunging into industries that boomed and died, weaving dreams that faded away. Energetic Scots for centuries have gone out to find fortunes elsewhere; not to colonise, but to assimilate. The Scot abroad remains a Scot, but becomes a marvellous mixer. He does not extirpate overseas cultures, he absorbs them; and he often does very, very well in them.

He is not at all an uninteresting man. And she is by no means a boring woman. I have said Scotland was poor. In its way it is immensely rich too, and the folk who people it are its prime richness.

2

YE HIGHLANDS AND YE LOWLANDS

I T IS typically arrogant of a tiny country, with a tiny population, to contain two separate nations. America gets by with one. Soviet Russia makes a stubborn attempt to claim that its millions of disparate people are all Russian; but then, Russia is a very big place and its people can be politically stupid on occasion. Belgium is more to the point, with ferocious nationalisms and separate languages locked inside its tight borders. Switzerland, with very few people inhabiting all those Alps, contrives to contain four language groups in reasonable amity and keep rich.

Scotland is particular, even so. Throughout its modern history it has been two peoples, living separate lives in separate cultures, mutually hostile or apathetic, mutually incomprehensible. There are Highlanders, and there are Lowlanders. There is no such thing as a Scot. There are various Scots, and that is the prime division.

Neither race is pure. No race is pure. But the Highlander, the Gael, is very Gaelic. He is a member of the Celtic language group which has been pushed to the outermost western fringes of Europe—the Welsh, the Irish, the Manxmen, the Cornish, the Bretons and the old Scots. His language is Celtic—the tongue, he claims, that was spoken in the Garden of Eden.

The Lowlander is a totally different mixture. Lowland Scots is a form of the English language, a member of the Germanic family. The Lowlander and the Highlander have practically nothing in common except being close neighbours and, until modern times, not all that neighbourly. The Lowlander had more in common with Englishmen just across the border than he had with the strange barbarians away up north.

When the Lowland Scots were settling in towns and thinking of cities, the Highlanders still clung to an older society, crofting a wee bit, fishing a wee bit, fighting a lot and giving loyalty to a clan chief, very often a rascal. They even wore a curious garb, pre-dating the newfangled trouser of the south; the great Highland kilt.

What makes us what we are? We are what we speak, what we sing, and what we wear. The Highlander was his kilt. It was an eccentric and immensely versatile creation; a huge length of woven wool which he put on and took off with a wearisome ritual. Naked, he would spread the thing on the ground, with a leather belt lying across it under the middle. He would then fold the cloth into pleats end to end, lay himself on top of it, pull one end over his shoulder and down his front, and then fasten the belt round his waist to secure everything. When he stood up, he was well covered against the bitter climate, and with his legs free, he could race across the heather like a hare.

At night, the great length of cloth was both bed and tent, if he was in the open. On the move, the Highlander was completely self-contained.

It was necessary, in hard mountainous country with a population widely scattered and enemies plentiful. The clans, dignified by romantic authors once they had disappeared, were little more than quarrelsome neighbours with ludicrous family pride, who turned on one another occasionally with fist or knife or sword.

But that is to belittle them too much. In the intervals of feuding, they preserved a society in which the family was supreme, and they made poetry and music. How they got on to the bagpipe does not matter much. There are similar instruments in Greece, and Brittany. The Highland bagpipe is itself. To outsiders it may sound like a head-splitting screech. To the man with the proper ear, it is immensely subtle. At its heart is an airtight leather bag, a pressurised reservoir filled by a tube leading from the piper's mouth. As he fills it from his lungs, he cuddles it in his left armpit and forces the air steadily out with his arm. The air escapes through a set of drones, providing a steady bass note, and through the chanter, with a row of holes which he fingers to produce the melody.

It is magic for dancing. It is fearsome on the battlefield. As the Duke of Wellington said in another context, 'I don't know what effect these men will have upon the enemy, but, by God, they terrify me.'

The Gaels also sing. There is no way to stop the Gaels from singing. Their music is cast in the pentatonic scale, which can be exhilarating but is oftener melancholy. It suits the proud melancholy history of the Highlanders.

Ever since they were driven out to the north and the west, and cut off from British civilisation, they have been different, they have been 'other'. Their ways seemed as alien and bizarre to the Lowlanders as the culture of the Apache seemed to the white Americans. And as the Apache were in the way of progress, the Highlander was a nuisance too.

The Highlander has survived, but his story in modern times has glum parallels with that of the American Indian. He lived in his own remote fastnesses, not bothering anybody, and that in itself was somehow offensive. He had his weird gibberish of a language and his outlandish songs, which clearly made him less than a genuine modern human being. The proper treatment of such people is extirpation.

This process began before the Napoleonic Wars, but these wars accelerated it. For centuries, the clansmen had survived—not opulently, but well enough—in the clan lands, doing an occasional murder or aggravated assault for the chief, scratching a bit of ground, milking a cow. Suddenly, England needed meat for its armies, and somebody realised that the great underpopulated acres of the Highlands could support sheep, and sheep would return a bigger profit than human beings. The clan chiefs, or many of them, had caught the English bug. They wanted to be civilised, and proper, and rich, and it was easy enough for them to claim that they owned the clan lands in their own right, rather than by consent of their kinsmen. They sold out to the sheep men.

It was a hideous episode in the history of Scotland. Some of the organisers of the great sheep boom were not content merely to drive the Highlanders from their primitive little cottages. They organised round-ups and packed the dispossessed clansmen into ramshackle hellships to be removed to the North American wilderness, to take their chances with the Indians who were suffering the same treatment. The cottages were knocked down, or burned down, to make the evictions final. One at least was burned down with an old woman still inside it.

The Highlander has never recovered from this trauma. Among his merry songs are the fierce laments for the way of life that was strewn to hell by the money men from the south.

While all this was happening, Scots in Glasgow and Edinburgh were scarcely aware of it. If they had known, they might not have cared. They too regarded the Scottish Highlander as a foreign barbarian. Today, because all Scots are mawkish and sentimental, the Lowlander joins in the Gaelic laments for the vanished golden age, and vaguely blames the English. Blaming the English is a passionate Scottish hobby. But at the time, nobody south of the Highland line gave a damn.

The Highland line does not appear on maps. It is an imaginary division between the two Scotlands, running roughly from Argyllshire in the south west to Ross in the north east. It is a state of mind rather than a row of posts.

But the Highlands persist. The people are stubborn, and accommodating, and devious, and kindly, and always polite. And they are various. The Highlander in Sutherland feels himself quite different from the folk in Skye or the Isle of Lewis. He speaks the divine Gaelic tongue with a totally different accent. Every Scotsman is his own Scotsman.

The Lowlanders are even more different, because there are more of them. The Aberdonian is one animal, the Ayrshireman is another. Sometimes they have difficulty in understanding each other. In the Lowlands, there is no such thing as a Scots accent. There are hundreds.

Down there, below the Highland line, the race is a wild mix. There were all those early incursions from Europe. There were the Scots from Ireland. The border between Scotland and England was a vague conception and people drifted back and forth over it. In modern times came Jews and Poles and a sizeable number of Italians. The Lowland Scot is a rich compound; aggressive and sentimental, cautious, recklessly generous. He probably has a bit of Highland blood in him, or Irish blood.

He doesn't give a damn.

3

FREEDOM AND WHISKY

THE SPIRIT, as we have seen, moves strongly in the Scot. Sometimes it robs him of the power of speech or ambulation, but that's the other spirit. And if the Holy Spirit has to be approached with reverent caution by an explorer in Scotland, the national drink is not to be taken lightly either. Its devotees bring to Scotch a sense of awe which is both lunatic and mystical. They are certainly proud of it.

I well remember finding myself in Edinburgh, jaded and thirsty and in search of a tavern. I accosted the nearest citizen and said, 'Excuse me, Jimmy,' (I always observe the linguistic courtesies when I'm in Edinburgh) 'where is the nearest boozer?' He pulled himself up tall, focused on me and replied, 'You're talking to him.'

> Freedom and whisky gang thegither
> Tak' aff your dram!

The words are of course the words of Robert Burns who, if not an expert on whisky, was a pioneer consumer unit.

It's hard to see why hard liquor should be known as Dutch courage, when the supreme hard liquor is Scotch. More than any other drink in the world, whisky has acquired a mythology and a mystique, and it richly infuses the modern history and culture of Scotland. Strange, for it is after all merely a chemical substance that depresses the higher centres of the brain, and in some cases leads to madness, blindness and death. But to the Scot, whisky is less concerned with logic than with magic.

It can certainly be dangerous, and is even a grave social problem. A lot of people in Scotland drink an awful lot of whisky ('Do you drink a lot?' 'No, I spill most of it.') and alcoholism is commoner in the country than, say, in England. An ingenious researcher even announced recently his discovery of the M-Factor, and struck terror into the hearts of many moderate soaks in the Glasgow area.

The M-Factor he derived from studying the names of a group of alcoholics and establishing the percentage whose surnames began with M. Then he compared this with the local telephone directory, and reported that there were more 'M' alcoholics in his study group than the proportion of Ms in the phone book could justify statistically. In fact, most of the M alcoholics were Macs. This appeared to prove that people of Highland or Irish extraction were more prone to liquor problems than other people.

The proposition was strongly opposed by other researchers (some of whom might well have had names beginning with M) and petered out. At least it proved that there is a powerful and inquisitive concern in Scotland about drink and drinkers. The ordinary Scot is concerned less with the pathology of whisky than with its pleasure and its price.

In the beginning, before voracious governments in London realised that whisky was a taxman's Eldorado, everything was simpler.

Scotch whisky today may be hailed as a noble spirit, gilded with a highfalutin mythology and provoking a lot of entertaining nonsense among half-cut connoisseurs. It started as peasant firewater. The pioneer distillers were strictly back-kitchen operators who made the stuff for domestic consumption, concocting a savage dram from their own malted barley in crude pot stills, and not giving a damn for principalities or powers.

When the Scottish Parliament first imposed a tax on the stuff in the seventeenth century, it was evaded as a matter of routine, even as a matter of principle, because it represented two processes that touched the rugged Scot on the raw: tampering with his freedom, and dipping into his pocket.

There may be illicit stills working to this day. One hears tales. I have seen a beautiful little still in the hands of a man who was proposing to take it to his ancestral home in the far north and give it a try. The crime had suddenly become safe, he explained, with the development of butane gas. In earlier times, no matter how craftily a still was hidden in a hole in the mountains, the fire had to be constantly attended, the moonshiner's comings and goings could be observed, and the smoke was a sure giveaway. A gas cylinder could be left to work on its own for weeks on end without a puff of reek.

As recently as the last war, a reckless character distilled a goodly batch in the ground-floor flat of a Glasgow tenement, and I had evidence that it was everything the tippler is warned about. One glass produced dramatic amnesia. But more, when the victim came to, feeling frightful, he only had to take a glass of water to plunge back into a shambling coma. It took three or four days for the power to wear off, and some of the survivors actually signed the pledge when their fingers started working again.

Obviously, much of the illegal booze in the bens and glens was produced with more experience and tenderness and less danger to life and limb. Beating the 'gaugers' was not just a commercial enterprise, it was an art and a sport and an assertion of the rights of man.

One engaging ploy was operated between the wars by a long-sighted moonshiner who wrote anonymously to the Excise Department reporting an illicit still on an uninhabited islet off the West Coast. An inspector was dispatched to the place and spent a day and night searching. He found nothing except that the islet was not totally uninhabited. It had an ant population of millions which had not tasted human flesh for years.

A few weeks later the department received another anonymous letter insisting that the still was there and could be found. The inspector was sent back, protesting hysterically, and repeated his experience. Once he was safely home, the moonshiner rowed out to the islet and set up his still. It was the safest place in Scotland.

The manufacture of whisky is a simple industrial process, straightforward and profoundly mysterious.

The straightforward business of making a malt is easy to describe. Ripe barley, clean and dry, is soaked in water until it absorbs enough to start to germinate. The excess water is drained away, and each grain of barley starts to develop a shoot. During this time the barley is constantly stirred and turned over to expose it to the air and prevent it from building up too much heat. The process is called malting, and it converts the starch of the grain into sugars.

When the process has gone far enough, the grain is put into a kiln, where the heat stops any further development. The fuel in the kiln is either wholly or partly peat, which burns with a rich flavoursome smoke, and this is absorbed by the drying grains, to persist through all the following processes and give whisky its native tang.

The malted barley is now sifted and ground and mixed into a thick mess with hot water. The virtue of the barley passes into the water, which is eventually moved into enormous vessels and introduced to yeast. It explodes into fermentation and in due time becomes a kind of beer.

The process is more ticklish than it sounds, of course. There are pitfalls at every stage, and profound skills, human and mechanical, have to be applied at every stage. But in principle, it is a simple matter of turning the material in the original barley grain into a weak form of alcohol with some interesting impurities.

To transform this into Scotch whisky is equally simple in principle. Alcohol comes to the boil at a lower temperature than water. So if you have a quantity of alcohol-and-water mixed, and heat it gently, the alcohol will boil, turn to vapour and rise in the air at well below 100 degrees Centigrade. Trap that vapour, cool it, and it becomes liquid again, concentrated and potent.

In practice, the business is finicky and critical. The early vapours that rise in the still, pass through cooling pipes and become liquid, are a long way from the true spirit. They produce 'low wines', relatively feeble and distasteful, and these move to another still to be reprocessed nearer the heart's desire.

The trick about whisky is that unlike, say, vodka, it is pretty well adulterated. When the second distillation begins, it is watched over by the stillman, the master craftsman, who discards the early stuff and the late stuff, and chooses the exact moment to direct into the spirit receiver the high-quality liquor that comes in the middle of the run.

The discarded liquid at the beginning and the end are returned to be distilled over again. But the batch in the middle, the whisky, still contains fusel oil and other 'impurities' which make Scotch what it is.

And what makes it, apart from these? The water, in the first place. Any whisky fancier will explain that water taken from two streams a half-mile apart on the same hill will produce two totally different whiskies. Why this should be so nobody knows. The expert will prescribe river water that is both pure and peaty. I have never grasped the theory of how peat can be distilled along with alcohol, but in the whisky business it is not wise to raise carping questions of theory. It works; and that is all that matters.

The Irish make their own whiskey. They claim to have invented it, in fact. The Americans produce ryes and bourbons which are perfectly all right to anybody who fancies them. There is nothing, however, that duplicates Scotch. The Danes have tried, even the French. The Japanese are still trying, and shrewdly importing real Scotch in bulk to add bite to their home-grown reproduction. Japanese whisky, I find, is a strong drink, it doesn't seem dangerous or obnoxious, and a man in sore need of a dram would not turn it down. A sober Scots palate would not mistake it for whisky.

The liquor bought and drunk in such cheery quantities by the natives is sold at 70 proof, a term which is worth explaining. Before the days of precise analytical chemistry, somebody stumbled by accident on a crude and efficient system of testing whisky's strength. If it was mixed with gunpowder and lit, and the gunpowder went off, the liquor was strong enough. This happens when the whisky-water mixture reaches a strength of 57 to 43, and that proportion is 'proof'. So our 70 proof whisky is about forty per cent alcohol. Exported Scotch is often at higher strength because, as a distiller explained, there is no sense in spending money shipping a lot of water.

The whisky I have described in the making is a single malt, the original, basic Scotch. The overwhelming proportion of modern Scotch is blended, using some malt liquor and a lot of grain whisky, which is easier to turn out in large quantities by the patent continuous still invented by Aeneas Coffey. The advantage of blending is that it can produce a consistent flavour year after year, and justify the promotion of individual labels as distinct and unique. This has produced the thrustful, competitive and enormously profitable Scotch whisky industry of our times, and given rise to much hilarious *snobisme* and added to the gaiety of drinking.

The dedicated poseur will touch no brand but his chosen brand, and if he is very silly indeed, he will affect to recognise it at the first sip, or even whiff. It is true that different brands can be very different, and a seasoned toper can easily tell Haig from Standfast if his palate is clean and his head is clear. After two or three, the most that mortal man can manage is probably to declare, 'That is *not* Haig. It must be one of two hundred others.'

This was demonstrated in a television programme about the stuff, which included a tasting trial by three enthusiasts, of which I became one with a spurious show of reluctance. The game was to nominate, unlabelled, a single malt, a blend, a pure grain liquor. The results were a pure catastrophe; but quite fun at the time.

There is, all the same, good reason for the variety of brands. Without them, Scotch would probably have remained the eccentric taste of low-class Caledonians, instead of conquering the world. It must be remembered that until the eighteenth century, even Scotsmen of any standing and discrimination tended to favour claret and cognac, long established in the land through the Auld Alliance of Scotland and France.

It was not until the mid-nineteenth century that blending was practised at all. There are vague and competing legends of how the new brand products infiltrated civilised society, and the tale of Thomas Dewar is as good as any.

The legend is that his was a single-handed invasion of the apathetic London market. Dewar was the kind of Scotsman (not too untypical) who only had to see an impossible challenge to take it on. But he was too shrewd to try to saturate the sprawling masses of London pubs with the new potion. He obtained introductions, and aimed at the gentlemen's clubs of the capital, mixing blunt Scots aggression with cajolery and a touch of the snob; a combination which has simply got to be irresistible.

The success of Scotch in high places was helped by the disastrous failure of France's vine crop in the 1860s, and later through the ravages of phylloxera. The gentlemen of London had to get smashed on something, and Scotch whisky was there to fill the breach.

The cunning distillers of Scotch have stuck to that tradition, of aiming in their export drives at the top, the high fashion, the status-symbol markets. Whisky is an intensely 'in' drink, all over the world. The Americans, a well 'in' people, drink three times as much of it as the British.

If freedom and whisky gang thegither, Hogmanay and whisky are one. They are twin phenomena that the Scots have presented to the world at large, and of course both tend to be misunderstood, and abused, and hurried. It is worth pausing to explain Hogmanay, to remind Scots of their shifting traditions and to bring other peoples to a proper appreciation of a magic ceremony, which should not be trampled on, and should certainly not be taken lightly, because the old dark gods are watching it, and their vengeance can be horrible.

Hogmanay, New Year's Eve, is older than most things in human affairs. The midwinter festival, filtered down to modern times through the Scots, has a much longer pedigree than the Christmas feast. Recent scholarship has suggested, in fact, that Christ was born some time in April. It is not important. Long before Christianity spread through Europe, there was already a traditional festive time at the bottom end of the Northern winter, and it was wise and reasonable of the early Christians to borrow the ancient rite and inject the new faith into it. It was equally wise not to choose a precise date, but to set up in near opposition. The result, certainly, has been confusing, with two December feasts tumbling over each other. But the Scots don't mind too much.

So far above the equator, the peoples of Europe needed a celebration to assert their survival against the dark misery of winter, when the earth is dead, the sun scarcely rises before setting, and the notion of a spring sowing is hard to believe. Thus, Hogmanay. The origin of the word becomes more obscure the more it is investigated. It may well be a corruption of the old French, *au gui menez*, 'lead on to the mistletoe'. Why not? What it is about is man's ludicrous determination that he will survive, and conquer, winter.

Mistletoe. Mistletoe itself is a powerful myth, which has been borrowed and rendered harmless by the English Christmas ceremony of kissing under a mistletoe bough. It was big magic to the Druids, who held it in superstitious awe. Shakespeare called it the 'baleful mistletoe'. One reason (I quote *Brewer's Dictionary of Phrase and Fable* with deep Scottish scepticism) is that it was once a tree from which the wood of Christ's cross was formed. There is, more credibly, the Scandinavian legend of Balder, the Norse god of light, who was killed by an arrow made of mistletoe. His mother, Frigg, had sworn all things on earth not to harm him, but had overlooked mistletoe as unimportant. Oh well, Achilles had the same kind of trouble.

Mistletoe has been credited with powers both poisonous and curative. And Balder, like other gods, did not die permanently, but rose again in season. So with the earth, with the Scots, with Hogmanay and all the splendid nonsense that goes with it.

'The world is dead. Long live the world.' The Scots go to great and particular pains to make sure of that. But dichotomously, it goes without saying; we are dealing with the schizoid nation.

Until recent generations, the Presbyterians in Scotland scarcely celebrated Christmas at all. They regarded it as a newfangled, or old-fangled, Romish rite, for reasons mentioned elsewhere in this book. They did celebrate Hogmanay, in their various ways, from place to place, and the ritual varies from place to place. But some things are fixed and enduring.

The day itself, the day before the New Year dawns, is a time of reckoning, of atonement even, of balancing the books of life. The fervent Scot will go to much trouble to settle his debts before the year ends. Debts and dirt belong to the old time, and should not be carried into the new time to sully it.

By the same token, his wife engages in a fierce ritual of cleansing. Every speck of dust is banished from the household, every smooth surface is polished to death, every garment is cleaned for its new life. If the family takes the tradition in dead earnest, it is a day of sobriety too. The ceremonial bottle of whisky stands sealed and inviolate on the kitchen dresser. It is all quite solemn.

A few minutes before midnight, the ashes are raked from under the fire and removed from the house. It has become harder to do this with gas-fired central heating; but if it can be done, it is done.

Then, time stretches unbearably as the old year interminably breathes its last, and the man of the house tries not to let his eyes flicker to the bottle standing so enticingly on the dresser, for it contains Next Year's Dram.

When, finally, the bells strike, Balder has risen from the dead. Old hardships are cast aside. The world is renewed. The bottle is eagerly opened. The moment of joy is often infused with sadness and mawkish sentiment, the Scots being what they are. They suddenly remember friends long gone, and hopes abandoned, and vanished youth, and all the stuff that makes all mankind kin. In damp happiness they broach the bottle and drink to the renewal of everything.

With the dram, they take a bite of shortbread, which cannot be too ancient a symbol; and a mouthful of Black Bun, which must be older than Europe itself by the rich dark magic flavour of it. It is a concoction with the whiff of ambrosia and the specific gravity of platinum, and it *matters*.

This brief maudlin ceremony is merely the curtain raiser, however. It must be followed, sooner rather than later, with the advent of the First Foot. Soon after midnight, other Scotsmen are venturing into the black night as emissaries of the ancient gods, to bring the benison of prosperity to their neighbours. Some of them disappear for days on end, with any luck.

Our New Year family, kissing awkwardly and putting all dissension behind them, have ears cocked for the arrival of their own First Foot, who may come by prearrangement or by chance. He must be male, and he should be dark haired. Why?

Ask the dark gods.

He must also be bearing the proper gifts, for they betoken the prosperity of the household for the next twelve months. In the first place, he must bear a good dram. He will give this to the family and be given a good dram in return. He should also carry Black Bun, or something equally solid. By some pathetic misreading of the runes, there are English people who imagine that a First Foot needs nothing more in his hand than a piece of coal. Well, nobody will refuse a piece of coal; but it is a mere trimming, an adornment, of the proper ritual gifts of drink and food.

The First Foot may be an old enemy. No matter. At New Year, there are no old enemies and no old enmities. These too were cleansed by the observance of Hogmanay, and from now on, there will be peace and happiness among men and women.

The ceremony will now go on and on, except among abstemious, insensitive, or exhausted households. The men of the house may themselves have obligations as First Foots to other families, and once they have crossed those thresholds, no man may chart their paths. In small communities it is still true that a lighted room is an invitation to any passing stranger, and there is a welcome there. I have stood in a bar in a West Highland village on the second day of January when the landlord brusquely announced, 'Ladies and gentlemen, you know the licensing laws. It is now half past two and the pub is closed. You can't get out.'

That particular Hogmanay was very durable, but not unheard of. The Scot may make jokes about his native drink, and his drink-fired annual festival. But he takes them seriously.

Strangers within his gates are advised to do likewise.

4

BRAINS

W HEN SCOTSMEN are not knocking back big drams (and sometimes more so when they are) they often contemplate the universe and ponder on questions like the meaning of meaning. Several of them have even come up with answers, and many others are still hard at the job.

These are also accepted as archetypal Caledonians. In some moods we see ourselves as the gem-hard intellects of the world, reaching out on behalf of ignorant mankind into the uncharted mysteries of the human condition, wrestling with the enigma of creation and winning by three falls or a submission. It is a pretty conceit, and gives us a proper sense of superiority over grosser breeds.

Do not sneer too glibly, or dismiss the pretention as mere vanity. I once encountered, in a grubby inn among the tenement back streets of working-class Glasgow, a shabby individual who on visual inspection would not have fetched £2 fully clothed on the open market, and while I was making the calculation, he said, 'The basic fallacy of Freudian theory is the silly old trout's assumption of his own clinical rationality, when in fact he was a suppressed doorknob fetishist, and it's your turn to buy the next drink.'

And he was (he existed, I assure you) merely a part-time, amateur student of Truth. When we consider the full-time operators, it's clear that for its size, Scotland has thrown up more than its share of mental giants, and started a goodly number of philosophical hares bounding across the world of thought. They are men who lived in a perfect fever of ratiocination. They couldn't stop thinking things up.

Among the early runners, the Laird of Merchiston stands well out. At first glance, he was a religious philosopher and even a bit of a bigot. John Napier was known to a wide public, in his own day, as the author of *A plaine discovery of the whole revelation of St John*. Today, nobody would read a page of it, unless he had run out of material for basket weaving. But in the sixteenth century it was a huge popular success.

It was translated into several languages, and accepted as the final refutation of the Roman Catholic Church. Napier, a strict Presbyterian, really disliked Rome. As quite a young man he served as Edinburgh Commissioner to the General Assembly of the Church of Scotland, and worked on committees to persuade the king to punish the Roman Catholic nobility for the crime of being Roman Catholic nobles.

The Catholic Church has survived the onslaught of Napier. Mathematics is another matter. In the intervals between tirades against the papacy, he invented the full stop in decimal notation.

To anybody who has used decimals it must seem incredible, insane, that the system ever existed without that little dot. The whole decimal system depends on it and can hardly mean anything without it. Well, decimals did exist without the dot. They were doubtless in a state of chaos, but they existed. We think the dot is as fundamental as . . . as the wheel. But somebody had to invent the wheel, and Napier had to invent the full stop. It is fair to say that the world has never been the same since.

In 1614 he published his *Mirifici logarithmorum canonis descripta*, a slightly teasing learned work which included the first table of logarithms ever seen, but with no explanation of how to use them. He also devised novel systems of calculation using Napier's Rods. In the end, or rather, after the end, because he was already dead, his book describing the use of logarithms appeared.

To the non-mathematician, all this may sound obscure and even pointless. To any schoolchild who has endured their study, logarithms are a stupendous contribution to the business of counting. This is a crude description of how they work.

In simple arithmetic there is a thing called *the power*, which is seen when a number is multiplied by itself, once, or twice, or any number of times. For instance, 4 is 2 to the power of 2; and 32 equals 2 to the power of 5, because we get it by multiplying five 2s—$2 \times 2 \times 2 \times 2 \times 2$.

Innumerate readers who are prone to headaches may skip the next few paragraphs. I had a severe attack of dementia praecox in trying to write them. Courageous souls will read on.

If we have absorbed the idea of *the power*, we can understand that, say, 10^9 (the mathematical way of writing ten to the power of nine) is a convenient shorthand for 1,000,000,000. The little figure ^{9}, which describes the power, is called the index.

If 10 is the only number we ever have to deal with, there is no difficulty. We can raise it one power by simply adding a nought. But if we have to calculate, say, 349^9, we have long laborious drudgery ahead of us.

Napier's blinding flash of insight was this: any number can be expressed as the index of a power of another number. And when this truth was simplified for practical purposes by sticking to the number 10 as a universal base, common logarithms had blazed into life.

Any number at all can be expressed as the index of a power of 10. That index is called its logarithm. The logarithm of a million, for instance, is 6; because 1,000,000 equals 10^6.

The logarithm of 7 is more difficult to work out by wearisome calculation. But if some patient scholar does work it out, the answer is there permanently, for everybody who comes later. If the same scholar goes through a long list of numbers, he has made up a table that can be used by anybody, for all time.

The advantages are not obvious to the layman, but they are big advantages. What an index achieves is to convert multiplication into simple addition. To multiply 349^5 by 349, we just add 1 to the index and get 349^6.

So if we want to multiply 349 by *another* awkward number, say 8,923, we can look up the tables and find the logarithms of both numbers. Those logarithms are indices. We add them together, and the result is the logarithm of the answer we want. We then look up another table—a table of anti-logarithms—and translate back into plain figures; and the job is done in a trice.

It gets better. If we want to multiply a number by itself many times—say 13 times—we simply find its logarithm in the tables, multiply that by 13, look up the result in the anti-logarithm tables, and we have a quick answer instead of a tiresome chore. All the logarithms and anti-logarithms we need are already there, in the tables produced by Napier's genius. Nobody has to go through all that drudgery again. Ordinary students have been given a computer by which they can make other, enormously complex, calculations in seconds.

They can discover, for instance, what number has to be multiplied by itself 13 times to produce the answer 1,594,323. How would you go about that sum? There is virtually no way in the world of doing it, short of trying every number from 1 upwards. The answer is 3. I confess I myself checked it on an electronic calculator. But I couldn't have worked it out on the quite sophisticated calculator I used. It didn't have that talent. Common logarithms have.

Only in our century has it become possible to make such abstruse calculations by electronic machinery. Napier's work of genius still stands. It doesn't need batteries, it is unbreakable, it will not malfunction. He gave power over the universe of numbers to any ordinarily intelligent youth with a sheet of paper and a pencil. This is no small gift to the storehouse of man's discoveries.

Adam Smith, even from the distance of two and a half centuries, also has the authentic blaze of genius, and the very Scots habit of scattering it in every direction that took his fancy. He was stolen by tinkers, incidentally, when he was three. A relative traced them and rescued the child. With that escapade, the turbulence of his life was over, and everything that followed was calm, rewarding and curiously un-Scots.

Born in Fife and raised by a widowed mother, he studied mathematics and natural philosophy at Glasgow, spent seven years at Oxford, and became professor of Logic at Glasgow University when he was twenty-eight. At forty, he spent three years travelling Europe as tutor to a young Scottish nobleman, meeting the lively minds of the time, and collecting notes for a major work.

Smith's life was a huge outpouring of words and ideas. It may be just as well that masses of his papers were destroyed on his own instructions. He has left posterity quite enough for one man. His first publication was the *Theory of Moral Sentiments*. There is also a hefty work based on lectures on jurisprudence, including police, revenue, justice and arms. Other lectures, often given without notes and transcribed at speed by listeners, cover the field of human and social behaviour. An accomplished linguist, he was passionately in favour of 'pure' English. The language then, as always, was in transition, and Smith knew best where it should be going, or staying. He brought an impressive knowledge of other languages to his prescriptions for good English, but it must be added that his notion of pure language would be dismissed as short-sighted heresy by modern linguistics men.

The truth is that, as a man of Europe and the world, he had a wee trace of shame about his own Scottishness—another rather common Scottish failing. He and his intellectual friends produced the short-lived *Edinburgh Review* with the intention of making Scottish literature 'respectable'. North Britain, he felt, couldn't make cultural progress without a refined standard of language, and when he reviewed *Johnson's Dictionary*, he was even more hysterical than the great Doctor about the importance of excluding any 'improper' words. In the grip of this odd obsession, Smith was capable of quite hilarious pomposity.

'It is the duty of a poet,' he proclaimed, 'to write like a gentleman!' And: 'Humour is something which comes upon a man by fits, which he can neither command nor restrain, and which is not perfectly consistent with true politeness. A man of wit is as much above a man of humour as a gentleman is above a buffoon.' I have read that a dozen times. I still don't get the joke.

31

But never mind. There was true greatness, and great work, in the man, and it came out in *The Wealth of Nations,* which founded the science of political economy at a stroke.

His prescription for national wealth combined individual free enterprise with cooperation, specialisation and the division of labour that went with it. He also foresaw dangers in free enterprise and envisaged some degree of state control. In spite of some contradictions, he sketched the groundwork for the new industrial society, and every economist since has had to start from Adam Smith. Considering what political economy has done for, and to, the world, he has a good deal to answer for.

David Hume, a contemporary and friend of Smith, was the Edinburgh man who transformed philosophy and woke Kant from his dogmatic slumber. (The testimonial came from Kant himself.) His mother too was widowed early. He too moved restlessly about in search of his destiny. After an inconclusive period at Edinburgh University, he took an unrewarding job as a merchant's clerk in Bristol, then spent three years in France, writing. He had the splendid arrogance to complete his *Treatise on Human Nature*—a three-volume essay wrapping up the entire condition of mankind—when he was twenty-six years old. It was not a total flop, but it failed to set the world alight.

Still, he adventured into any field that took his fancy, with *Essays Moral and Political, Political Discourses*—which were concerned with economics—and the *Natural History of Religion.* His writings on religion were not respectful. Hume was one of the great sceptics. In a sense, he rejected everyday logic and questioned the idea of cause and effect as a mere imposition of human ideas on the natural universe. Ordinary mortals are convinced that if they throw a stone in the air, it will come down again, but that is merely because it has happened so often before, and Hume wasn't sure that it was bound to go on happening just because people have got used to it.

This view—and it is a nice, categorical, you-can't-convince-me-of-anything view—also made mincemeat of historical miracles. If we can't be sure of natural laws, we can't say they have been broken.

The existence of a Deity was equally impossible to prove. A lot of earnest theologians of the times had convinced themselves that they had completely rational proof of God. In simple terms, their argument went thus: if we see a chair, our experience entitles us to presume that there was a carpenter. So, if we see an orderly universe, we can presume a Creator of the universe. Hume swept all that aside. We have seen thousands of chairs (he said in effect) and know

When Mary Queen of Scots arrived in Edinburgh in 1561 to take the throne, she was a beautiful, naive Roman Catholic nineteen-year-old. She and John Knox were like creatures from different planets (*François Clouet c 1558, Bibliotheque Nationale, Paris*)

Queen Victoria's Scotland: (*above*) 'They wear kilts of tartan weave, play a deafening musical instrument called the bagpipe'; torchlight dance of Highlanders, 1852, the fifteenth year of the Queen's reign; (*below*) 'a cat may look at a queen. A Scot may go much, much further than looking.' The Queen on Fyvie with John Brown at the pony's head

all about carpenters. But we haven't seen any other universes to compare with our own. The apologists' argument collapses.

As well as wakening Kant from his dogmatic slumber, Hume was able to write an English history, serve as a tutor for a year to an insane young nobleman and travel on diplomatic missions as secretary to General St Clair. He worked at the British Embassy in Paris and had an unrewarding friendship with Jean-Jacques Rousseau. He predicted the American Revolution, and his political essays inspired the Founding Fathers. In his sixties, he resolutely retired from writing, in spite of pleas from the publisher of his English history.

'I must decline not only this offer,' he said, 'but all others of a literary nature, for four reasons; because I'm too old, too fat, too lazy and too rich.'

He can be forgiven. He had done more than most thinkers ever do to stir up his times and launch good arguments.

The American novelist Sinclair Lewis once threw off the following little parody:

> Lives of great men all remind us
> We can make our lives sublime
> If we nag the kids and neighbours
> And look noble all the time.

It's hard to believe he wasn't thinking of Thomas Carlyle. Many books have been written on the prophet of Ecclefechan, in the unanimous conviction that he was 'great'. He was also impossible, and it is difficult to approach this Victorian monument without exasperation. A life of spiritual torment may well be the stuff of nobility. For people who have to live beside it, it must be fantastically boring too.

In the intervals between wrestling with his soul, his indigestion, and the reality of the invisible universe, Carlyle was driven by a simpler demon familiar to many a Scottish village lad o' parts: the lust to be as famous as hell. At fourteen, he walked a hundred miles to enrol in Edinburgh University. He didn't like it. He tried teaching. He didn't like it. He had been reared to conventional religion. He didn't like it. At the same time, when he contemplated a Creation without God, he didn't like it.

It is astonishing that anything worth a button came out of this carnaptious egocentric. But I have not mentioned his fierce, crackling intellect, which led one historian to describe him as the greatest man by force of wit and character in a generation of great men. The word 'wit' here refers to wisdom rather than snappy wisecracks.

He married the delightful Jane Welsh when he was thirty, a move which was good for Thomas, miserable for Jane. She had met him three years earlier and grown fond of him, but determined never to be his wife. Her first instinct was certainly right. For forty years she put up with a cantankerous neurotic, angelically but without much fun of any kind.

But he obviously had something, in addition to his frenzied literary energy. The English philosopher John Stuart Mill became his good friend, and Mill has been retrospectively diagnosed by psychologists as having an intelligence quotient that went right off the Richter scale.

Success and fame came to Carlyle with his enormous history of the French Revolution, which took three years to write and now takes almost as long to read. It is beautifully written and packed with good stuff. It also embodies one of his lifelong obsessions: hero worship. This preoccupation is probably entangled with his interminable search for God, which he managed to sort out in *Sartor Resartus* (The Tailor Reclothed) describing in allegory his exploration of his own soul. His guardedly happy conclusion was that there is indeed Something, a Divine Idea, an invisible Force, and that the universe is fundamentally a good thing.

The Carlyle view of the universe, and of British society, is an intriguing mixture of conflicting notions. He was hooked on the hero principle. He was horrified by materialism and the prospect of a mechanical age which would crush man's spiritual nature. He believed that industrial workers, oppressed and angry, might one day be given a sort of partnership in industry. But he also thought democracy was fatuous. 'It is the everlasting privilege of the foolish,' he wrote, 'to be governed by the wise.'

Underlying all this, all the same, was a genuine sense of idealism and hope. Like that other crotchety genius, Wagner, he put his hope in giants. If he lived today, he might not be so certain. But he was a man of his own time, as we all are.

And he put his mark firmly, dramatically, on his own time. The irascible temper, the nightmarish soul searching, could not entirely subvert the huge intellectual power; and his absurd dreams of all-powerful, all-beneficent father figures could not entirely blind his insights into the problems of society as it was. He was vindicated in his own life by becoming a Great Man. But we get the impression that he didn't get much exhilaration from it. Rather a Scotch thing, that.

James Clerk Maxwell stands in amiable contrast. He was even-tempered and witty, and wrote light verse, and everybody enjoyed his company. But the little grey cells always crackled with electric force. As a schoolboy, he struck on a system for drawing oval curves, the magic of which I personally do not understand, but it was surprising enough to be published by the Royal Society of Edinburgh. He had an effortlessly brilliant academic career at Cambridge and occupied various university chairs till his first retirement in 1865. This leisure he spent in having an agreeable time and writing a treatise on electricity and magnetism, after which he went back to work as professor of experimental physics at his old alma mater.

Clerk Maxwell is remembered by people who know for his study of colour vision and his work on the viscosity of gases, but mostly for his work on the theory of electromagnetic radiation. Rays and waves and suchlike phenomena were still mysterious things in the middle of the nineteenth century when the English giant Faraday found that light could be affected by a magnetic field. Clerk Maxwell translated Faraday's work into mathematical terms and showed that electromagnetic waves, though much longer than light waves, travel at the same speed. Among other things, this prepared the world for Einstein, that other amiable man who changed everything.

There was a mason in Cromarty who found sermons in stones, and they were the death of him. Hugh Miller, a man torn by inner conflicts, would hardly credit the honour that has surrounded him. He was born in 1802, the son of a sea captain who was lost in a storm when the boy was five years old. He was gifted or burdened with the powers of observation and analysis and imagination, and encountered a ghost in his boyhood. He might have had a distinguished academic career, but he wilfully chose to be a stonemason, and was rightly proud of his skill and talent. In later life he worked variously as a bank accountant and a journalist.

He was a journalist of some distinction, and an essayist of modest success. He was also profoundly and passionately religious, in a totally Scottish way. The passion first burst forth in a controversy over patronage—the appointing of parish ministers by aristocratic landlords, as opposed to the Knoxian principle of election by the congregation. A brilliant and bitter tract against patronage attracted the attention of the Evangelical Party, and he was invited to be editor of their journal, *The Witness*. He gave the job all the fervour of his very Scottish soul, and spent his life in public argument and debate. He also wrote poetry, and a rich and sensitive autobiography which crystallised the vanished country society of his youth.

But throughout this time he had also been obsessed by stones. When he worked as a mason, he uncovered fossil remains in the Old

Red Sandstone of the county. Virtually singlehanded he exposed the ancient secrets of the stone, working in total isolation from the mainstream of geological study. He made a prodigious collection of fossils. When he first wrote about them, he was surprised by the response from complete strangers. Darwin consulted his work. Thomas Henry Huxley wrote with respect of his contribution to science.

His gift was an agonising burden. Miller did not accept the Old Testament as completely and literally factual, but it was ingrained in him and he couldn't discard it either. Darwin had not yet published *The Origin of Species*. It was a confusing time for students of the past and Miller, who laid the groundwork of modern palaeontology, was more deeply confused than most. The effort of reconciling the evidence of ancient fossil forms with the six-day Creation brought him private and public pain. Geology itself was under attack from conservative Christians, and Miller's attempts to find a synthesis of religious and scientific belief merely angered both sides in the conflict.

His work made it possible for people after him to accept the real message of the prehistory around them. He himself couldn't. On Christmas Eve 1856 he shot himself. He was a victim of the Scottish hunger for belief.

5

THE
SNATCHERS

(*Criminal Compendium 1*)

REELING from the contemplation of these intellectual Titans, we may soothe ourselves by recognising that there are other, earthier pursuits to which the Scots have brought passionate energy and sometimes skill; and it's for my own ease as well as the reader's that I have decided to slip down from the Olympian heights from time to time and punctuate the recital with a relaxing look at more homely things, like violent death. The Scots, like other peoples, are quite attached to violent death, as long as it's happening to somebody else, and preferably long ago. But rather than wallow over-long in gore, I am scattering the proud history of Scottish mayhem through the rest of this book as brief appetisers.

Readers who actually prefer a good wallow may leaf through the succeeding chapters and take the Criminal Compendium at a single gulp.

Here is a question that has always interested me. How long does it take for a hideous event to become acceptable as a joke? At the time, it would have been unthinkable for respectable people to joke about a great marine disaster. Today, the incident is far enough away for us to enjoy the story of the sailor stranded on an iceberg who shouted to his mates, 'We're all right now—here comes the Titanic!'

The question I asked is particularly relevant to my native land, because the Scots tend to find the joke in any disaster almost synchronously. They deeply believe in death. The Presbyterian faith has taught them that man groweth as a flower, and like a flower he is cut down in his prime. It is a fact at which we have to weep, and when nobody is looking we also have to laugh. Laughter proves to us that we, at least, are still alive. It is the survival kit.

In this chapter, I have a dread tale to tell, of unmitigated evil and brutality and the callous pricing of precious human life. If the story were unfolding today, I should be wrung with grief and horror. It is a terrible story.

Since we are discussing death, and the Scots, let me fortify myself with a contemporary report, first told in the hard realistic context of Aberdeen, and therefore nearly certainly true.

An old lady called upon her friendly neighbourhood undertaker, or mortician, or comfort consultant, or whatever the trade description may be this year. She had an ordinary sad tale to tell. Her husband had passed away, full of years and wisdom, after sixty years of happy marriage.

'And never a hard word in sixty years, Mr Johnson,' she insisted. 'And I want to do the best for him, because he deserves it. But I've only got the pension and the wee bit insurance, and it's not much.'

'I entirely understand, Mrs Banff. I knew Charlie well, and a respected man he was throughout the community. Don't worry, even if the funeral is economical, it will be dignified.'

This was all very well, but as he was leading the old lady off the premises, they walked through the showroom, where one of his current clients was laid out in a spectacular coffin of afrormosia with platinum handles, red silk lining and reckless ornamentation; and inside, the dear departed, dressed in a clawhammer-coat, pinstripe trousers and patent leather pumps. A tile hat sat on his chest, and the cosmetic department had done a triumphant job on his face.

'Oh!' she cried. 'It's beautiful! If only I could do that for Charlie! But I've only got the pension and the wee bit insurance, you understand.'

Mr Johnson nodded gravely and assured the widow that she would not be disappointed at his scenario for Charlie. When she went back next day, Charlie was lying in an identical box of the same rare African hardwood, with red silk lining. He wore a clawhammer-coat, pinstripe trousers and patent leather pumps, he had a similar tile hat on his chest, and somebody had worked a piece of cardboard into his mouth to force a smile on him, and daubed his ancient cheeks with rouge.

'Mercy me!' cried Mrs Banff, 'He looks better now than he did the day I married him! But the price, the price!'

'Stop worrying, my dear. For you, forty pounds.'

'Never, never. I know it's worth thousands, and I don't believe in debt or charity. Mr Johnson, I will pay every penny, if it takes a hundred years.'

'Ach, be quiet, wummin,' he muttered, 'I just changed the heads.'

If we can accept this everyday experience, we are ready to contemplate the true history of Burke and Hare.

The names are inseparable, like Hengist and Horsa, Fortnum and Mason, Sears and Roebuck, Laurel and Hardy. History is made by partnerships. Burke and Hare are also seriously misunderstood. Mention the company, and the lay listener immediately thinks of body-snatchers. They were not body-snatchers. Body-snatchers, like hyenas, spend their lives looking for a convenient corpse. Burke and Hare were manufacturers of death. They are entitled to be recognised as creative artisans.

The highfalutin name for body-snatchers, in a country as educated as Scotland, was 'resurrectionists'; and these men plied a dangerous but useful trade. In the early days of scientific medicine in Scotland, teachers needed human cadavers as demonstration pieces, and—although the Scots were given to killing one another quite as vigorously as other people—there was a continuous shortage of corpses available for dissection.

The legal authorities did what they could to supply the lack. A law of 1505 permitted the surgeons the use of 'one condemned man after he be dead'. It was less than enough for a growth industry. The supply was increased in 1694 by an Act that gave them the bodies of people who died in the correction house, foundlings, suicides and people put to death by order of a magistrate.

The demand was still racing ahead of supply. The Scots, always at the front of any scientific advance, needed endless queues of corpses. By the early eighteenth century, little ships were bringing carcasses from London to the Port of Leith, and the resurrectionists were robbing fresh graves for laboratory specimens. The common people of Scotland were outraged. A tourist in Scotland today may find plenty of old cemeteries with massive stone slabs lying on every lair, and spiked iron railings built round it. Scottish mourners looked forward to the day when the last trump would sound, and the graves give up their dead to face divine judgement. They did not want their dear ones to be marked absent when that joyful sound was heard.

In 1742, a pair of sedan chairmen in Edinburgh were stopped and found to have a dead body as a passenger. It was not a paying passenger, but a piece of merchandise for sale to the medical schools. They were banished from the city. The harder penalty of flogging and transportation was given to a gardener discovered with a bag containing the body of a child which he had stolen from Pentland cemetery.

As recently as the middle of the eighteenth century, a pair of female ogres, Helen Torrance and Jean Waldie, were convicted of kidnapping and murder. They were in the business of supplying bodies for dissection, and when they failed to find a dead child, they stole a live child, killed it and sold it to a surgeon. The price was a drink and a half-crown.

This, then, was the age that was ready to spawn Burke and Hare. The time was ripe, the characters fitted, and the *deus ex machina* was already there: the great anatomist Robert Knox, brilliant, extroverted, obsessional, and able to pay £10 for a good-quality body.

Neither Burke nor Hare (and no Scot will let anybody forget this) was a Scotsman. William Burke was born in County Tyrone, Ireland, in 1792. He married, deserted wife and family, and migrated to Scotland in 1818, where he took up with one Helen McDougal, and drifted towards the capital city of Edinburgh.

William Hare was already there, another Irish exile, who had taken lodgings in an Edinburgh hovel and married the landlady after her husband died. The place (the names give a dark colour to the history) was Log's lodging house in Tanner's Close.

From this distance in time, it is difficult to choose between the partners in villainy, but a contemporary described Burke as a neat little man, light on his feet, and appearing to have a conscience; but, after all his crimes, impenitent as a snake. Hare, it seems, had no redeeming features at all. He was an animal; even worse than an animal, 'the most brutal man ever subjected to my sight'.

The two were clearly destined for each other. When an old man died in the lodging house, owing Burke £4, they fell spontaneously into a partnership, almost without discussion. They took the body from its coffin, replaced it with a bag of stolen tanner's bark, and sold the corpse to Doctor Knox.

That was as near as the couple ever got to the dirty, cold and inconvenient business of robbing a grave. Obviously, there were easier ways of finding human bodies than scrabbling in a cold cemetery at night. When an old miller fell sick in the lodging house, they hurried him to his end by holding a pillow over his face. A young Englishman who contracted jaundice was helped out of his discomfort by the same method.

In 1828, the partnership encountered an elderly pauper, Abigail Simpson, who had come to Edinburgh to collect a small pension allowed her by an old employer. They got her drunk—obviously never a difficult thing on Abigail's social level in Scotland—and took her to the lodging house, where she spent the night. Why they omitted to dispatch her before bedtime is not clear. Perhaps they were too drunk themselves. At any rate, they left her in peace for her last night on earth, got her drunk again in the morning, and held her nose and mouth until she expired. On viewing the corpse, Doctor Knox was much impressed with its freshness.

Somewhere around this time, a couple of undated and undocumented victims creep in. The legal authorities and later historians have found it hard to be exact, since Burke and Hare didn't keep accurate books of the company's transactions. But they then came to a dramatic and significant enterprise: the case of Mary Paterson.

There was nothing vague or anonymous about Mary Paterson. She was eighteen years old, and although she was already a confirmed wanton, she was enchantingly beautiful. Nobody who saw her could forget her. She was, in her way, an institution in the *demi-monde* of Edinburgh, and altogether the wrong choice for a business that depended on obscurity. Obviously, the partners were too confident and too greedy to let this give them pause.

In company with a friend, Janet Brown, Mary Paterson met Burke in a tavern, and he invited them home; home, in fact, to the house of his brother Constantine, a scavenger employed by the city. More drink was taken, an alcoholic squabble broke out, and Janet Brown left. Mary was drunk and unconscious. The hour was ten in the morning.

Miss Brown, perhaps intuitively, was not happy about her friend. She found another friend to back her up, and went back to Constantine's twenty minutes later. By that time, Mary Paterson was dead. Her body was hidden in the house, Mr Burke was already on his way to Surgeons' Square to negotiate the sale, and Janet Brown was invited to come in for a drink and wait for him.

She herself was now on the dangerous edge. But her landlady, to whom she had described the previous experiences, sent a maid to fetch her, and William Burke lost the chance of a double sale.

When the Paterson body was brought to the lecture room for dissection, at least one student recognised her and was horrified. He wanted to know how this beautiful young girl had died, and Burke's answer was 'the drink'. Even in death, the victim was so appealing that several students made sketches of her before Doctor Knox demonstrated his skill. The anatomist's lack or wilful suppression of curiosity about Mary Paterson would tell against him when justice overtook his suppliers.

Burke's next prize, in the meantime, was literally snatched from the hands of the police. Two officers were taking a drunken vagrant into custody when he told them he knew her, and could take her to her lodgings. They were happy enough to get rid of an awkward customer, and Burke earned £10 for his neighbourly gesture.

There are fresh horrors to come. The enterprising pair met an Irishwoman, with her deaf-mute grandson, a child of twelve, wandering the streets of Edinburgh in the hope of finding friends who lived there. They took the wanderers home, poured drink into the woman till she was insensible, and killed her. When they considered what to do with the boy, some distorted sort of conscience affected them, and they thought of taking him out and abandoning him to roam the streets.

But even though deaf and dumb, the lad might be dangerous, if he had enough intelligence to remember where he had been. Rather than take the risk, Burke took the child on his knee and broke his back.

The murderer later claimed that he had been haunted by the expression on the victim's face as he looked up at the instant of his death. He was crammed into a herring barrel and transported to Surgeons' Square by horse and cart.

Apart from their offhand attitude to the population at large, the team suffered some internal dissensions. At one point, Mrs Hare tried to induce Burke to murder his doxy McDougal, apparently on the grounds that McDougal was a Scotswoman and therefore eligible for death. Burke refused to see the point, and instead took his lady to visit her relatives in the town of Falkirk. When they came back to Edinburgh they discovered that Hare had done a job on his own during their absence, and pocketed the full fee. The Burkes took umbrage and actually left Tanner's Close for other lodgings. But the business was too good to abandon over a minor quarrel, and they soon resumed the joint practice. In an oblique way, Mrs Hare was to have satisfaction in her dislike of the McDougal clan, for a relative of Helen's, Anne McDougal, paid a visit to Edinburgh and was promptly smothered to death.

The next victim was an inoffensive charwoman, Mrs Hester. She was followed by Mrs Haldane, a prostitute, and when her daughter Peggy Haldane called at Tanner's Close in search of her, she was added to the list.

The case of Daft Jamie is of special interest for the light it throws on Doctor Knox's state of mind during this eventful year. Daft Jamie was a harmless halfwit and something of an Edinburgh institution, regularly badgered by children and familiar to every adult who walked the streets of the capital. He was easily enough lured into the deadly lodging house, but he didn't like alcohol and it was impossible to get him fuddled. He fought his killers heroically before they overpowered him. His body, even in death, was quite unmistakable, and the doctor's students recognised it at once. Knox declared positively that it was not Daft Jamie, and when the boy was reported missing, he decided to begin dissecting the body at once, clearly to remove the evidence.

The end of the enterprise was not far away, however, and it arrived symbolically on All Hallows Eve in 1828, just nine months after the formation of the partnership.

Mrs Docherty, an old pauper begging in a tavern, was taken to Tanner's Close. There was a fairly confused drinking party to celebrate Hallowe'en, with neighbours and lodgers coming in and out. Towards midnight, one of these heard the cry 'Murder!' and went to find a policeman, but failed. Others, not too drunk to be suspicious, noticed that Mrs Docherty had vanished, and asked where she had gone. Naturally, they got no clear answer, but one of them, Mrs Gray, who had been in the drinking company earlier, roused Burke to fury when she innocently started to look for her stockings under a bed. She was convinced that something was very wrong, and at the first chance she moved the straw that was under the bed and found the old woman, naked, bloodstained and dead.

When Mrs Gray and her husband said they were going to the police station, the killers threatened, pleaded and finally offered them a fat bribe, but they broke away and got to a police station. The game was over.

In the end, justice was incomplete. The authorities found themselves pathetically short of evidence and decided to accept Hare as a Crown witness and proceed only on the Docherty case, and only against Burke and McDougal. Since Doctor Knox wasn't involved in the Docherty case, he wasn't involved in the trial. It was left to enraged public opinion to ruin him and drive him from his brilliant career.

The citizens of Edinburgh soon knew more about the history of Burke and Hare than was ever revealed in court, and there was a wave of revulsion all over the country. Even so, on the evidence that was laid before the jury, two of the jurors voted to acquit Burke; and a verdict of 'Not Proven' was brought in on the charge against Helen McDougal. This verdict is peculiar to Scottish law, and means in effect, 'We believe you did it and refuse to find you innocent, but the evidence isn't enough for a conviction.'

In passing the death sentence on Burke, the judge said, 'If it is ever customary to preserve skeletons, yours will be preserved, in order that posterity may keep in remembrance your atrocious crimes.'

The skeleton has indeed been preserved and remains in the Anatomical Museum of the University of Edinburgh. After execution, the body was publicly dissected and anatomised; not by Doctor Knox.

6

THE
CAPRICIOUS MUSE

B URKE AND HARE were men of action, men of few words, most of these obscene ones. There are Scots who fit the stereotype of the dour northerner, even if they don't sell corpses. There are those who husband their words, who ration them stingily, as if every spoken statement were an expenditure that could never be recovered.

But just as typically, the Scots are articulate to the point of madness. The nation has a long tradition of literacy and an endless procession of natives intoxicated with the language. I believe, though I have rigorously avoided testing the report, that we still have ministers of religion in Highland churches who think a sermon is giving short weight if it runs to less than three hours.

We are concerned here with less terrifying wordsmiths. And if it is true that poets and dramatists help to create a nation as well as reflecting it, then the nation they have created is a lively compound of merriment, bawdry, drink, wild hopes and, in the words of a sympathetic Irishman bearing my own surname, 'blood, feud, betrayal and battered spirituality'.

All the same, the early 'makars' looked out as well as inwards. Scots in earlier times were passionately European, and even British, and it is probable that before Robert Henryson wrote his swash-buckling patriotic drama *The Wallace* in 1470, he had already read and absorbed the early work of England's seminal bard Geoffrey Chaucer in manuscript. Quite apart from his narrative inventiveness, Chaucer pioneered the process of converting English-English from a sprawling collection of dialects into a national language, as did Dante for Italian and Pushkin for Russian. But although he admired the great Englishman, Henryson was carving out verses in his own, Scots-English tongue. In the centuries that followed, the two English forms would diverge widely and help to create curious traumas in the Scottish psyche.

It's easy to see the resemblances between medieval English and

44

Scots from a glance at Henryson's 'Taill of the Uponlandis Mous and the Burges Mous'.

> Esope, mine author makis mention
> Of twa rnyis, and they were sisteris dear,
> Of wham the eldest dwelt in ane boroughis toun
> The other wynnit upon land weill neir . . .

But the differences are just as important, and even more obvious in Henryson's young contemporary William Dunbar, whose 'Dance of the Sevin Deidly Synnis' begins:

> Of Februar the fifteen nicht,
> Full lang before the dayis licht,
> I lay in-till a trance;
> And then I saw baith heaven and hell;
> Methocht, amangis the fiendis fell,
> Mahoun gart cry ane dance
> Of shrewis that were never shriven,
> Aganis the feast of Fasternis Even,
> To mak their observance;
> He bade gallantis go graith a guise,
> And cast up gamountis in the skies,
> That last came out of France.

Dunbar is a good archetype for the Scottish genius in letters, since he had a wee touch of the manic depressive, which is maybe a peculiarly Scottish hobby. He said savage things about Edinburgh, but he loved it at the same time. When he was merry, he was very very merry. When he was down, he was desperate. A sensitive reader of our time can still get the shudders from his long, his very much over-long, 'Lament for the Makaris, Quhen he was Seik'.

> I that in heill [health] was and gladness,
> Am troublit now with great seikness,
> And feeblit with infirmity;
> Timor Mortis conturbat me.

The poem goes on for ever about the futility of human existence, with a long list of splendid chaps now dead, and every verse ends with that dark clang, *Timor Mortis conturbat me* (I am wracked with the fear of death).

The same man was capable of penning the cheerfully blasphemous 'Ballad of Kynd Kittok', the alewife who had a tussle with St Peter at the golden gate, and the 'Seven Deadly Sins', which he turned into a sly dig at the Scottish Highlanders.

45

Dunbar, unusually for a Scottish poet, was a sturdy non-democrat. He was comfortably born and had a nurse in infancy, and he didn't hold with any nonsense about egalitarianism or a man being a man for a' that. He brooded a lot over not being awarded a good clerical living by the king, but that was because he knew he was superior, and entitled to favours. His 'Complaint' is all about the deplorable habit of poor humble people, of rising to positions of comfort and profit.

King James was less impressed by poets than by administrators, warriors and scientists; and Dunbar was particularly incensed at his patronage of one John Damian, a smooth-talking European who made up dances, toyed with gold production and theorised about aviation. When this confidence trickster was presented with the Abbey of Tongland, the poet was really sick, and never forgave the man. But in the end, Dunbar did well enough with a Royal pension in 1500 of £10 a year, rising to £80 by 1510. Considering the value of money, few modern poets do as well.

With Allan Ramsay, born in Lanarkshire in 1684, we leap into a new situation with the language. By the time he was born, Shakespeare had already soared aloft and stayed there. The crowns of England and Scotland had been united in 1603 under James VI, who promptly moved to London and put his Scottish connections behind him. By the time Ramsay began to write, the English Parliament had absorbed the Scottish Parliament, and the psychic situation of Scotland was quite odd. Its attitude to its own language was schizophrenic, for instance. Literary people reacted to the Union of Parliaments with a mixture of patriotism and romantic Jacobitism, thinking nice thoughts about Bonny Prince Charlie.

But Ramsay's early poems were firmly in English, because English was proper and polite. When he published his first slim volume, in 1721, half of the eighty poems were in English, and the others in varying mixtures of English and Scots. The curious thing is that he used English for 'serious' work, and Scots for funny verses.

For a poet, he had an agreeably comfortable life. He served an apprenticeship in Edinburgh and became a successful wigmaker. But once he had tasted the vivacity of the literary set in the capital's taverns and coffee houses he abandoned the wigs and opened a bookshop which became a kind of salon for the poetry crowd. He even launched a circulating library, probably the first in Britain, and in 1736 opened a theatre in Carruber's Close. He and his friends might well have railed at the evil tyranny of the remote Parliament in London, because in 1737 it brought in the Licensing Act, which prohibited the performance of plays for profit outside London.

The Edinburgh Presbytery, or federation of the city's churches, reacted to his new theatre with the spirit that has so often inspired the Scottish Kirk: if folk are enjoying something, it must be sinful and it must be stopped. They cited the Licensing Act and called for the theatre to be closed. Ramsay fought back expensively for a couple of years, but inevitably he lost, and lost money. But he wasn't ruined. (The Kirk was probably rather sad to learn that.) He built himself a nice eccentric octagonal house on Castlehill for his retirement, and called it Goose Pie. And there he happily lived out his sunset years.

I find in Ramsay's poetry a sweet gentle quality that reflects what seems like a pleasant prosperous life. His longest work, *The Gentle Shepherd*, is a rustic verse play, blatantly sentimental but full of life. He also produced the obligatory patriotic piece, *The Vision*. This affects to be a Latin manuscript dated 1300, the time of Scotland's hardship and oppression, and translated in 1524. It is very Scots, fairly opaque, and rather conventional (though it is in a very durable convention).

> Bedoun the bents of Banquo Brae
> Milane I wandert waif and wae
> Musand our main mischaunce;
> How be they faes we are undone,
> That staw the sacred stane frae Scone,
> And leids us sic a daunce . . .

And so on and so on. There is more bite and fun in 'The Monk and the Miller's Wife', a ballad with strong Chaucerian undertones. In the story, the simple miller Hab is flattered by the parish priest, who then privately enjoys the favours of Hab's wanton young wife. A student sees the sinful couple at their capers, and confounds them by a display of Rosicrucian magic.

> An honest miller wond in Fife
> That had a young and wanton wife
> What sometimes thol'd the partish priest
> To make her man a twa-horned beast . . .

Sentimentalists who like a bard to die tragically young will prefer Robert Fergusson, whose creative life was over almost as soon as it began. He was a brilliant child, born in Edinburgh in 1750. At St Andrews University he shone in mathematics, adored the classical poets, sang well and caricatured his professors. The family fortunes collapsed with his father's death and he became an ill-paid drudge in an Edinburgh office. Briefly, he enjoyed the literary life of Edinburgh tavern society, and was one of the truly gifted members of a sodality called the Knights Companions of the Cape.

His early poems were derivative works in the English language, but he soon found himself in Scots, and wrote affectionate and savage satires on his native city; like 'The Daft Days':

> Now mirk December's dowie face
> Glours our the rigs wi' sour grimace
> While, thro' his minimum of space
> The bleer-eyed sun
> Wi' blinkin' light and staling pace
> His race doth run
>
> And thou, great god of Agua Vitae!
> Wha sways the empire of this city
> When fou we're sometimes capernoity
> Be thou prepar'd
> To hedge us frae that black banditti
> The city Guard . . .

There were graver things to be protected from. His own periodic depressions, when he read the Bible and wrote despairing letters about his life and his health. What ailed him physically we don't know, but it was no doubt compounded by a fall in which he injured his skull. A brief time he spent in squalid lodgings, crazed and destitute, till he was removed to the Edinburgh Bedlam as a pauper lunatic. He died there a month after his twenty-fourth birthday.

In death at least he was not forgotten. Robert Burns, a young Ayrshire genius who acknowledged his creative debt to Fergusson, had a decent stone placed on his grave in Canongate churchyard.

And with Burns we come to the towering peak of Scottish balladry, and something extra. There is still controversy about Burns. Hugh MacDiarmid, the outstanding Scottish poet of the twentieth century, dismissed him, in a fit of typical impishness, as second rate. Some academics insist his work is not of university standard, whatever that means.

He is not to be dismissed. He will simply not go away. Alone among these early makars, he is more read and more discussed today than in his lifetime. Over 4,000 books have been written about him, in virtually every language. In dozens of countries, in thousands of towns, his birthday is solemnly or hectically celebrated every January; and in proposing the Immortal Memory, orators speak more

David Hume, *c* 1776, the Edinburgh man who transformed philosophy and woke Kant from his dogmatic slumber (*Scottish National Portrait Gallery*)

Hugh Miller, the Cromarty stonemason, who became editor of *The Witness*. His writings on fossils were respected by Darwin and Huxley. He could not reconcile his prehistorical findings with religion and shot himself in 1856, 'a victim of the Scottish hunger for belief' (*D. O. Hill, Scottish Portrait Gallery*)

sense and nonsense than has been spoken of any other man in history except Jesus Christ.

This must mean something. Shakespeare was doubtless an incomparably better poet, but there is no Shakespeare cult to approach the sheer weight of the Burns industry. People do not hold thousands of Goethe suppers. Burns is unique.

His story is simply told, and will go on being told as long as men write. He was born in a farm cottage in Alloway, Ayrshire, son of William Burness, an honest and desperately struggling tenant farmer. In boyhood, he contracted rheumatic fever which was never diagnosed and which was to kill him before his prime.

He had a sound elementary education for his time, though his brother Gilbert was regarded as a better scholar.

Burns himself worked on the farm, and other farms, and talked, and dreamed; but he was in his early twenties before the poetic urge inflamed him, and he wrote, till his death, like a man possessed. He fell in love constantly, he enjoyed the hard-drinking male company of his time, he scandalised the unco' guid church elders. He fornicated cheerfully and successfully and had more than one bastard child.

His first collection of poems, printed in Kilmarnock, made him instantly famous. He travelled to Edinburgh to meet the aristocracy and the intelligentsia and was lionised, and cheated by a local bookseller. He fell in love—platonically—with a prissy grasswidow, Mrs McLehose, who had literary conversations with him and tried to elevate him above the drawback of his Scottishness. She did persuade him to write some insipid verses in English.

Edinburgh finally discarded him. He got a job as an exciseman near Dumfries, married the childhood sweetheart Jean Armour who had already borne children to him, and settled to a well-regulated life. Illness overtook him and he died, destitute, at the age of thirty-seven. He was given a magnificent funeral in Dumfries, followed by thousands of admirers. On the day of the funeral his wife Jean, about to give birth to their last child, was without a shilling.

The bare recital scarcely hints at the magic that has gone on dazzling the generations. The poetry is at the heart of it, of course. It can be argued that 'My Love is like a Red Red Rose' is the greatest joyful love lyric, and 'Ae Fond Kiss' the greatest sad love lyric, in the English language. Millions would agree. They are only two gems in a prodigious outpouring. His genius was to transform the most ordinary impulses and experiences of the most ordinary people into something ecstatic and unforgettable.

The polite world of literary Edinburgh viewed Burns as a novelty, even an oddity, doing unexpectedly well for an unlettered ploughman. They had it completely wrong, as polite people usually do. He was not unlettered, and his verses would still have sung if they had come from the most eminent scholar of the day.

Their simplicity is deceptive. Apart from anything else, he was a master craftsman. Even in his less inspired work, everything fits—every word, every line, dances with sweet precision. And they are pregnant with feeling and insight. As he said, 'The heart ay's the part ay that makes us right or wrong.' His poetry speaks to the heart. It also cuts to the bone. 'Holy Willie's Prayer' is the most deadly thrust at Presbyterian hypocrisy that will ever be written, and twice as deadly because it is irresistibly funny.

We may doubt that 'man to man the world o'er shall brithers be for a' that.' But we needed somebody to say it and give us the courage to hope for it. James Burke, the Scottish novelist who wrote Burns's life as inspired fiction and edited a notable edition of his work, has declared without qualification:

> He is the first poet to transcend poetry. Just as there can be no greater musician than Beethoven, there can be no greater poet than Burns. Before either can be surpassed, a new race will have to be born—a different and greater species than the homo sapiens hitherto known to history.

But there is more than the poetry, there is the man. Or rather, the man and the poetry are one. Burns held back nothing of himself. His most private thoughts were public, his life was a visible drama bigger than the lives of ordinary men. His virtues and his failings were on the heroic scale. Like Gavin Hamilton in 'Holy Willie', he drank, and swore, and played at cards. It may be he drank no more than the average boozer of his time, but he did it openly, with a flourish. He loathed meanness and cruelty, but he loved mankind, and womankind, regardless, with more passionate enthusiasm than most of us can muster. He loved women, certainly. Some of his admirers wish he hadn't loved quite so many, or quite so actively. But although he enjoyed carnal lust for its own sake, he did love every girl he embraced in lust. He fathered fifteen children, six of them out of wedlock. We can find no evidence that any of the girls ever complained.

The truth is that Burns the man is revered because both his strengths and weaknesses are those that men admire, or envy. His disappointment and frustrations, even his tragically early death, are the stuff of epic heroism. He was the fierce tender lover, the overpowering wit, the dazzling thinker, the proud rebel, the reckless roisterer. Other men, humouring the boss, balancing the budget, pandering to the wife, wish they had the nerve to be such a man. And women wish they had met such a man.

This helps to explain the international Burns cult. Everybody wants a piece of him. At its best, the cult is a hearty celebration of a great man. At its worst it is the kind of boring nonsense that Burns would have laughed out of existence. Burns orators all over the world tie their brains in knots to claim him as their own. He is painfully diagnosed as a chauvinist, an internationalist, a conservative, a communist, a *macho*, a champion of women's rights, a puritan, a libertine, and for all I know a flat-earth enthusiast.

Not all his idolaters have given his works too close a study. As 25 January approaches each year, many worthy citizens who have agreed to deliver the Immortal Memory find themselves scrambling through lending libraries for a copy of the Collected Works, only to find they have been beaten to it by other worthy citizens, and some of them are capable of feats of memory like this:

> We cannot but respond to Burns' love of the lassies, so well expressed in 'Jeannie with the Light Brown Hair', and 'Annie Laurie'; in his appreciation of nature, as when his heart with pleasure fills and dances with the daffodils; his patriotism, when he cries, 'Breathes there a man with soul so dead, who never to himself hath said, This is my own, my native land', and his deep pity for the sufferings of mankind, so eloquently described in 'The Great Tay Bridge Disaster'. Gentlemen, I give you the Immortal Memory of . . . eh . . . oh aye. Robert Burns.

They can be forgiven. In the presence of Burns they are out of their depth.

They are to be found, among more knowledgeable bardolaters, everywhere from Tokyo to Pernambuco. Burns belongs to all mankind. But the Scot, however ignorant of his poetry, claims true descent and blood kinship with the great man. In many cases, the claim may be accurate.

After Burns, it was nearly impossible for any lesser man to follow. Sir Walter Scott did indeed write poetry, and wrote it well; but he is not remembered primarily as a poet. It was as if Burns had used up the Muse for the next century.

But it would be a pity to omit our great bad poet, William Topaz McGonagall, the inspired Victorian simpleton who consciously inherited the mantle of Burns, and Shakespeare for that matter, and evoked an incredulous joy among his admirers that has never faded.

McGonagall was born of Irish parents in Edinburgh, and later moved to Dundee where, in the best poetic traditions, he fell on hard times, through a recession in the hand-loom weaving industry. It is possible to suspect, by reading between the lines of his autobiographical notes, that he was a heavy drinker in his time, took the cure, and acquired the convert's fanatical hatred of the booze. At any rate, he was forty-seven before the Muse called to him—literally. During the Dundee holiday week, 'in the bright and balmy month of June, when trees and flowers were in full bloom, while lonely and sad in my room', as he recalls, a strange feeling stole over him, and in his mind he heard a voice crying, 'Write! Write!'

He grabbed pen and paper and immediately wrote his first poem, which is terrible:

> Rev. George Gilfillan of Dundee,
> There is none can you excel;
> You have boldly rejected the Confession of Faith,
> And defended your cause right well.
>
> The first time I heard him speak,
> 'Twas in the Kinnaird Hall,
> Lecturing on the Garibaldi movement
> As loud as he could bawl . . .

There is a beautiful, a divine simplicity in McGonagall that silences all critical analysis. He wrote like a man possessed. He *was* a man possessed. His poetry did not actually get worse. It maintained its early standard.

A Tribute to Mr Murphy and the Blue Ribbon Army

> All hail to Mr Murphy, he is a hero brave,
> That has crossed the mighty Atlantic wave,
> For what purpose let me pause and think—
> I answer, to warn the people not to taste strong drink.
>
> Strong drink to the body can do no good;
> It defiles the blood, likewise the food,
> And causes the drunkard with pain to groan,
> Because it extracts the marrow from the bone.

Inspired, besotted by his gift, McGonagall became a full-time bard. He tramped to Balmoral Castle to present a poem to the queen, was rebuffed by an insolent Pooh-Bah at the gate, and beaten up by wandering thugs on his way home. He gave performances of his works in public houses and was treated to abominable contempt and abuse—on one occasion the customers threw peas at him. He bore this all with Christian forbearance. He was the butt of every oafish prankster. He maintained his dignity and his belief in his Muse. He travelled to New York and was shabbily treated. He was guyed in Glasgow by a student audience, but he remembered principally their generosity to him.

Like a demented laureate, he combed the daily papers and wrote poems about every event that moved him. He wrote a eulogy on the magnificent Tay Railway Bridge. He wrote an epic on its collapse. He wrote a hymn of praise to the new bridge that replaced it. He was unstoppable.

Oscar Wilde said, of the death of Little Nell, that only a man with a heart of stone could read it without bursting into hysterical laughter. He might have said as much about 'The Tay Bridge Disaster'. But it would take a harder man to laugh at McGonagall himself, following his constant star, tilting at the windmills of poesy, in total innocence and total courage; at the holy fool who prefaced a collection of poems thus:

Since this Book of Poems perhaps will be my last effort:—

> I earnestly hope the inhabitants of the beautiful
>   city of Dundee
> Will appreciate this little volume got up by me,
> And while they read its pages, I hope it will fill
>   their hearts with delight
> While seated around the fireside on a cold winter's night;
> And some of them, no doubt, will let a silent tear fall
> In dear remembrance of
>   WILLIAM MCGONAGALL.

Poetry, as well as verse, flourishes furiously in Scotland today. Any writer with a public face is constantly put to the shamefaced duty of explaining to correspondents that he is not in a position to publish their fine verses, or their uncle's collection of pastorals. This doesn't stop them. It is rumoured that the town of Paisley contains more poets than the rest of Europe put together.

Among the dense strata of earnest doggerel, fortunately, there are bright seams of true metal. Norman MacCaig, Alexander Scott, Edwin Morgan, are imposing themselves on the literate Scottish public, fairly arrogantly, and there is the new crop of Stephen Mulrine, Liz Lochhead, Tom Leonard and others. It is their misfortune, which they accept without complaint, that every twentieth-century Scottish poet is overshadowed by Hugh MacDiarmid. It will come as no surprise that that is not his real name. He was Christopher Grieve.

Chris Grieve, who died in his eighties, was excessively Scots; a communist who was an antimaterialist, an internationalist who listed his hobby as 'Anglophobia'; a kindly husband, father and friend who lashed out savagely at everything and everybody who offended his sense of perfection. He also had the insensate productivity of so many Scots. The work he turned out between 1920 and 1940 fills almost 1,500 pages.

A Drunk Man Looks at the Thistle is a huge poem which, according to another poet, clearly surpasses anything ever written in the Scots language, including Burns. It is about the Scots, the Scots' glories and the Scots' absurdities, about the universe, about the nature of the human race. Taken in one gulp, it is stupefying.

One of MacDiarmid's passions was to restore Scots-English, which had been swamped by polite education, to its rightful place, even if it meant coining new words. His own use of the language is often too rich and dense for ordinary contemporary Scottish people to understand it without study. Yet he is the only modern Scots poet to be idolised abroad, adored by American students, and during his lifetime, sought out by enthusiasts from all over Europe. One of his contemporaries, Oliver Brown, confessed that he had never heard of the man until, in 1925, a Frenchman wrote to him about 'this great poet'.

Well, really, it wouldn't do to admit the existence of a Titan among our own folk. He might get above himself.

7

FAR
FLUNG

THE RESTLESS spirit that moved the makars' minds also works on other men's bodies. There are two types of Scot: the stayer, and the goer. The stayer is either indolent and comfortable, or committed to a land so rich in variety that a man could travel it for a year without seeing the same view twice. The goer finds the little peninsula claustrophobic. And since few spots are more than twenty-five miles from the sea, the sea has always been Scotland's main street.

If he didn't like salt water, an itchy-footed man could always travel south. 'The noblest prospect that a Scotsman has ever seen,' said Samuel Johnson, 'is the high road that leads him to London.' Johnson, of course, was not in favour of sea travel, since he also said, 'No man will be a sailor who has contrivance enough to get himself into a jail; for being in a ship is being in a jail, with the chance of being drowned.'

It is true that one legendary Scot of this century was the lad who went to London and took over. An old shipyard foreman (it is said) was sent from the Clyde to London on business. When he came back, his mates asked him how he had found the English. 'I never met any,' he said, 'I was only talking to heads of departments.'

But Scots who found even London too small for their ambitions have never hesitated to cross the water; in the early days as scholars or mercenaries. One of the latter, Marshal Keith, had an impressive record in the Russian army, and commanded a small force with skill and dash to recover the town of Otchakoff from the Turks in 1737. He was appointed as Russian representative at the peace talks, and discussed terms with the Grand Vizier through interpreters. When the formal business was over, he was startled to be shaken by the hand and hear the Vizier exclaim, 'I'm happy to meet a brother Scot in your position.'

'You? A Scot?'

'Aye, man, I well remember seeing you going to school every day in Kirkcaldy. My father was the bellman there.'

Humbler soldiers had less amusing encounters. British armies were greatly taken with the Highlanders when high policy in London threw fighting men into remote lands when Britain was indulging its curious compulsion to police the world and raise the Union Jack in quite unnecessary places. Highlanders were peculiarly suitable for these adventures. In the first place, they found it harder and harder to scrape a living in the bleak northlands, so they were willing to enlist. In the second place, the north had hardened them to cold and damp, they seemed immune to temperature and pestilence in alien climates. In the third place, they accepted discipline cheerfully, never thought of mutiny or desertion, and were ideal fighting machines.

They paid highly for their virtues. Since the eighteenth century, Britain's foreign adventures depended on heroic charges by Highlanders against any enemy who was in fashion, and they died in hordes. The cost to the Highlands was dreadful. Since neighbours and relatives usually joined the same regiment, a single bloody battle could leave an entire village full of widows and orphans in a few hours.

And though it is another story, the Highlanders got no gratitude. For over a century, starting before the Napoleonic Wars, survivors came home to find that their home wasn't there any longer. It was the long, wretched era of the Highland Improvements, commonly known as the Clearances. The old clan chieftains, now calling themselves lairds and owners of the clan lands, got into the mutton boom, brought sheep and shepherds into the hills and drove their own people out to make room. Cottages were torn down or burned down to make the evictions final.

And nobody really cared. To the southern Scot, even in the nineteenth century, the Highlander was either a romantic figure of past history, or a foreign creature who spoke gibberish. His present troubles could have been happening on a remote island. He was dispossessed like the Australian aborigine, the Maori, the Apache.

So the Highlander became another kind of traveller, exiled to North America or Australia. There are probably more people of Scots descent in these places than there are in Scotland. They cut the trees, they broke the plains, they prospered. They became Americans, Canadians, Australians, New Zealanders. The process goes on into our own time.

A great assimilator, is the far-flung Scot. He doesn't impose Scottishness on his new surroundings, as the English imposed Englishness on the Indian Empire. He adapts.

But still the blood is strong, the heart is Highland, of course. Once safely settled a few thousand miles away, he founds Caledonian societies and Burns Clubs, and even buys the kilt which he would never have dreamed of wearing in Oban or Glasgow, and altogether has a fine sentimental time. If you ask him to give up his split-level ranch house in California and go back to Greenock, he will bolt for cover. But once or twice a year he has the satisfaction of being ostentatiously Scots and shedding a facile tear for vanished glories he never saw. Most of the time, his new neighbours enjoy him.

One egregious individual who put his stamp on the outside world was William Paterson, an energetic con man who founded the Bank of England. Paterson, born in Dumfries, was a born manipulator. His first success, at the age of twenty-two, was the promotion in London of the Hampstead Water Company. Then he touted two speculative banking schemes around without finding backers; or perhaps—because many of his dealings were obscure—he had backers who wanted him to hypnotise other, richer backers.

In his own ulterior way he was a Scottish patriot, and he ran into trouble when he tried to break the overseas monopoly held by the English merchant companies. It was the tail end of the seventeenth century, when the United Kingdom had one king, but two Parliaments, and the English were happy to keep it that way. It was the wrong time to set up independent colonial ventures. But Paterson was able to found the Company of Scotland Trading to Africa and the Indies in 1695 with the blessing of the Scottish Parliament.

The English East India Company panicked. It was going through a bad time and didn't need competition. English investors in Paterson's company were threatened with impeachment. The capital faded away.

The Scots in turn were outraged. Scottish pride was stung, and Scottish money poured into what was now known as the Darien company. Paterson's vision was to take over the Darien isthmus in Central America and establish a great world emporium there, based on free trade. It was a brilliant notion. He saw the world's goods being landed at Darien, transported by land between the Atlantic and Pacific, and cutting out immense voyages round South America or South Africa.

Three ships were fitted out. In the meantime, Paterson fell out with his board of directors and was removed from command, but he sailed as a private citizen with the expedition.

It was all hellish. Over a thousand hopeful immigrants found their provisions running low. They tried to buy supplies from Jamaica, but the English colonists there had been forbidden by King William to deal with them. William was up to manipulations of his own. The Spaniards resented any settlement in Darien. William hoped to keep

Spain friendly because he expected a war with France and needed allies.

Nobody had thought of fever. Yellow fever was endemic to Darien, and when its season arrived it wiped out a quarter of the settlers. A Spanish troop attacked and drove the survivors out. The fever went with them. Two thousands lives were thrown away with nothing to show.

That was the bad news in Paterson's life. The good news was that he did found the Bank of England, and with it, the idea of the National Debt. Not everybody would agree that the good news is unalloyed.

Paterson's countryman John Law was even more colourful. The son of an Edinburgh goldsmith, he migrated to London and first attracted attention by fighting a duel and killing his man. He escaped to Holland, studied banking there and, like Paterson, touted several grandiose banking schemes round governments, and finally persuaded the Regent of France to let him set up a bank there at his own risk. It was called the Royal Bank, and was entitled to issue paper money. In France in 1716, seventy years before the Revolution, this was a little revolution of its own, and some modern economists have surmised that if Law had carried on with some caution, he would have transformed the French fiscal system and averted the mess that provoked that other, bloodier affair.

He just had too much enthusiasm. He wanted, and got, a concession to exploit Louisiana, formed the Mississippi Scheme and launched La Compagnie d'Occident. It was a wild success, a *succès fou*. It poured paper out by the ton. Juggling Mississippi shares became a national frenzy, and inside four years the enormous paper house collapsed, and Law had to skip the country yet again. He died in Venice nine years later.

Mungo Park was completely respectable. All he had in common with these other adventurers was the inability to stay put. On the surface, his passion was to map Africa, and particularly the river Niger. In reality, he couldn't bear to stay at home. He was a hefty, physical man with a lot of energy, and he had already been to Sumatra, as assistant surgeon on a naval ship, when he was invited by the African Association to open up the Dark Continent.

Intelligent, literate and thorough, he spent weeks at a settlement on the river Gambia learning the Mandingo language before he set out to find the Niger. It was eighteen months before he got back to the Gambia, after a difficult journey and a lengthy illness, and he wrote a journal of his travels which became a popular classic. He married and settled to the life of a country doctor in the Scottish Borders, but a few years of this exasperated him, and he found a subsidy to let him return to the rigours of Africa and the continuation of his search. His second trip was even tougher than the first. He set out from Gambia with forty-five healthy companions. A few months later only seven were alive. With a remnant of his company left, he ran aground in a canoe on the river of his dreams, and drowned when they were attacked by hostile natives.

It was not in vain. Today we may question the arrogance of the western races in 'discovering' areas of the world which the local people have already known for centuries. But Park's explorations and his writings—a second book was compiled from his diaries and letters—did open up Africa, for good or ill, informing enlightened people at home about cultures they had never guessed at.

Even more respectable, at first glance, is the great David Livingstone, who Christianised Africa singlehanded. That is certainly how generations of Scottish schoolchildren were introduced to him. His home at the mining village of Blantyre is maintained as a museum and a memorial, and is a successful tourist attraction.

The legend is perhaps larger than life. Born in 1813, seven years after Mungo Park's death, Livingstone certainly became a Christian of fierce devotion, and qualified as a doctor purely to equip himself as a missionary. In 1841 he set up a mission in what was then Bechuanaland and spent several years at the work before he discovered (even if he failed to admit it) that exploration was his true passion. He had converted a native chief and several of his followers to Christianity; but the number of his converts is probably trivial. More importantly, he travelled north and east as far as the ocean, recording the continent's marvels, including the Victoria Falls.

The London Missionary Society, his employer, didn't approve of these secular adventures, and when he went back to Britain he resigned. But everybody else at home was enchanted; his book *Missionary Travels* was well received and he was a national hero. When he returned to Africa it was on a Government mission as head of an exploration. His eyes were open for the commercial possibilities of the continent as well as its religious potential, and his observations were successful and extensive. His wife, who was with him on his second visit, died during that time. We get the powerful impression that, to his wife and children, Livingstone was the Victorian paterfamilias, concerned with his own important affairs and taking their subservient status for granted.

His religious fervour came out most clearly in his horror at the work of the Portuguese slave traders who were busy in Africa, and his shock that the work he was doing was providing them with new areas of operations. The ambivalence was shown when the Royal Geographical Society asked him to make his third trip to Africa to establish the source of the Nile. He said he would go only as a missionary, but make what contribution he could to the exploration. He was away for eight years, moving constantly over the continent, and was actually reported dead. This was the report that sent H. M. Stanley of the *New York Herald* to Africa to investigate, and join in some of his explorations after the two men met.

He was sixty years old when his last illness took him. He was found one May morning in 1873, dead, on his knees.

Livingstone was first and last a great explorer rather than a missionary. Perhaps there is something in the Scotsman, and especially the Victorian Scotsman, that demands a high moral purpose to justify his simple ambition. Andrew Carnegie was certainly, and wonderfully, sanctimonious about the pure-minded philosophy that drove him to get his little Scots fists into a fortune in America. He even sometimes seemed to disapprove of money.

'Beyond 50,000 dollars a year,' he advised young men, 'never earn—make no attempt to increase your fortune, but spend the surplus each year for benevolent purposes. No ideal is more debasing than the worship of money.'

This is in every sense pretty rich. Carnegie was thirty-three when he was able to expect an income of $50,000, and that was in 1868; at today's values, probably a quarter of a million or more. And his advice slides over the assumption that his young man would actually *make* a lot more; just as long as he gave some away.

Carnegie really is a beauty. His father fell on hard times, and took wife and both sons from Dunfermline to the USA when Andrew was thirteen. The boy worked as a bobbin boy in a Pennsylvania cotton mill, and never forgot the ecstasy of coming home with a week's wages he had earned himself.

'Attract attention!' was another of his counsels to the young. He attracted attention. When he worked as a messenger boy, he memorised every important address in the city more thoroughly than any boy had ever done before. He attracted the attention of Thomas Scott, the superintendent of the Pennsylvania Railroad, and worked as his secretary. It was Scott who told him to find or borrow some money to buy a block of shares that had become available in the Adams Express Company. Carnegie, penniless, said that he would, of course. His father mortgaged their little house to raise the cash. The magic simplicity of that transaction changed his life.

When he took a fancy to another block of shares, he visited a bank, and was given a loan without hesitation. Nothing could stop him then. He was in the money business. For Carnegie didn't make steel, or railroads; he made money. Steel and railroads were merely the raw materials. In leisure moments he poured out improving tracts, as the evangelist of capitalism. They were well written, sharp and pithy.

'The business man,' he wrote, 'pure and simple, plunges into and tosses upon the waves of human affairs without a live preserver in the shape of a salary; he risks all. The business man pursues fortune.'

And, in Andrew's case, catches it. He met the designer of the sleeping car and introduced it to the railroad. He traded in oil. He founded the Keyston Bridge Works because he realised that wooden bridges were inadequate for rail traffic. By 1888 he controlled the Homestead Steel Mills, plus iron fields, 425 miles of railroad, and a fleet of lake steamers. When he retired in 1901 to devote himself to good works he had a personal fortune of 300 million dollars. And his good works were vast. He built and equipped 2,500 free libraries in America and Britain and set up foundations to subsidise any good causes that appealed to him, particularly peace causes.

There is no explaining a Carnegie except that some men are, and some men aren't. Like many singleminded men, he was naïve. Like many men of limited education, he had an exaggerated reverence for learning. But naïveté is not stupidity.

Two incidents in his career are worth recalling. When he was building up his steel interests, one of the smaller steel companies introduced a process for cold-rolling steel rails. It was good, it was worryingly good. Carnegie set up a rumour network to suggest that these rails would inevitably increase accidents and deaths. The company's shares slumped. Carnegie bought them up, along with the patent, and announced that he now had a *new* process for cold-rolling steel that was totally safe.

Then there was the Homestead works lockout, which has gone into the mythology of the American labour movement. In 1892 there was a strike at Homestead, and the management decided to have a once-for-all showdown with the union. They brought in a small army of men from the Pinkerton Detective Agency, and there was a pitched battle that left ten men dead and scores wounded. The state militia was brought in—on the side of the management.

In time the strike collapsed. The workers, who had been complaining about cuts in their wages, went back to work with their wages halved. It wasn't that the company was hard pushed. In fact, after the failure of the strike, its profits went to mountainous levels; and soured capital–labour relations for a generation.

All that time, Andrew Carnegie was relaxing in his 30,000 acre estate at Skibo, in Scotland, apparently unconscious of any trouble. His lieutenant and partner Henry Clay Frick was in charge of the military operations at Pittsburg. Frick always believed that Carnegie had gone into hiding to leave the dirty work to him, and the two men never spoke to each other again. Frick also calculated what the Scotsman had gained from the battle. Carnegie had considered selling out two years earlier for a few tens of millions. Ten years later, thanks to the wage cuts, his price was multiplied by ten.

There is another paradox in Frick's decision to call in Pinkerton, an act which inspired a working-class song, 'My Father was killed by the Pinkerton Men'. Allan Pinkerton, the first private eye, was himself yet another far-flung Scot. The paradox is that he left his native Glasgow because his involvement with the labour movement had become dangerous.

Pinkerton was a cooper by trade, and a Chartist by conviction at a time when the British Government was getting seriously, and sometimes brutally, worried by the upsurge of democratic agitation. He slipped out of Scotland in fear of arrest, and settled in the hamlet of Dundee, Illinois. There he worked as a cooper, dreamed some simple dreams, and demonstrated a boyish ingenuity once or twice by catching or forestalling petty criminals. These coups involved ruses such as hiding in barrels to eavesdrop, and looking out for camp fires when tracking miscreants at night.

With a few such triumphs under his belt, he realised he was much much smarter than the average cooper, and set up in business as an investigator. It was a slow trade, but after he had persuaded the railroads that they needed him, it mushroomed satisfactorily and became a big operation. Its record in halting American crime is not dramatic, but that is probably because events showed that the fastest and most profitable way for a big private police force to make a living was in curbing militant trade unionists. So, to the American working man, Pinkerton has nothing to do with brilliant investigation, and a good deal to do with broken skulls. Still, he earns his place in history.

John Paul belongs, chronologically, somewhere in the middle of that list. I keep him to the end because of a perverse affection for a travelling Scot who abandoned all sense of decency and made an international monkey of his own country. There is something irresistible about hubris and chutzpah. John had both, and more.

Like many a Scottish lad before and since, he stared out beyond his native Kirkcudbrightshire to the fascination of the New World, and clutched America to his young breast; and this was even before cowboys and Indians made America the land of legend. He had an elder brother in Virginia, whom he visited often in his youth; and when he inherited the brother's property in his twenties, he became the all-American boy. For a brief period before this, he had interrupted a respectable apprenticeship to serve as mate on a slave ship. It troubled him not. On the other hand, he had a passion for freedom. When it came to a tussle between the British Government and the American colonists, he was one hundred per cent American; and when the colonials decided to defy their remote overlords, he was in the fight at once.

For his own reasons, he changed his name to John Paul Jones. His new name is commemorated in an old-fashioned ballroom dance in which everybody changes partners when the music stops. Make what you like of that symbolism.

As a minor naval commander, he made history without waiting for grand strategies. In 1778 he roared into the Solway Firth, a few miles from his birthplace, in charge of an eighteen-gun brig, and opened a campaign of driving his previous countrymen crazy with irritation. Nobody could get near him. He fired one British ship, spiked thirty-six guns, and took Lord Selkirk's entire collection of family plate as spoils of war. It is pleasant to relate that when all the irritation was over, six years later, he returned the property like a gentleman.

In Northern Ireland he captured the sloop-of-war *Drake*, a coup which was recorded as the first American naval success in history, and made Jones an authentic American hero. A year later, at the head of a French squadron flying the Stars and Stripes, he terrorised the Scottish port of Leith, and in a desperate encounter off Flamborough Head he captured two British men-of-war.

It would be misinterpreting Jones to suggest that he had some deep-rooted hatred for the land of his birth. He simply became an American, and did so with that terrible enthusiasm that makes Scotsmen frightening when they have it. He was honoured by Congress, ennobled by Louis XVI of France, and later took service as a mercenary with Catherine of Russia. He was one of those Scotsmen who burst into exotic flower when they are far enough from home. They make explosive transplants.

8

THE DEACON
BY NIGHT

(Criminal Compendium 2)

THERE IS a theme that keeps forcing itself into view in this survey: the stayers and the goers, the grim and the gay, the puritan and the libertine; in short, the dichotomy, or if you like, the schizophrenia of the Scot. It must mean something that we gave the world the outstanding fictional studies of schizophrenia. We also nurtured the great exponent of the double life in reality.

In talking about *Dr Jekyll and Mr Hyde*, after the novel was a runaway success, Robert Louis Stevenson said that the theme and the character had come to him in a dream, and implied that they had no connection with actual persons alive or dead. He must have been deceiving himself, because he was familiar since boyhood with the original, the archetypal man of two faces; and what is more, the man, William Brodie, had lived and worked in Stevenson's own city of Edinburgh.

There is another obvious link that must have existed in the unconscious mind of R.L.S. He himself would soon write another novel, *Weir of Hermiston*, based on the ferocious Scottish judge Lord Braxfield; and Braxfield has his gruesome part to play in our tale.

William Brodie was born to good fortune, he made good fortune, and he had good fortune thrust upon him. For a young man in the late eighteenth century, he had everything that lesser men might envy. He grew up in the honourable trade of cabinet making, and became a craftsman of the highest order himself. When he was twenty-one, his father died and left him a fortune of £10,000. He was a Burgess and Guild Brother of Edinburgh, and a Deacon who from time to time dispensed justice from the Bench. He was also witty, elegant and attractive to women. We could almost say he had *more* than any young man could want.

He just wanted more.

Certainly, he had one or two expensive habits. As well as his own douce, respectable Edinburgh home, he maintained two others, one containing a young lady named Anne Grant, and the other, Jean Watt and the child he had given her. He was also a fancier of cockfighting. He gambled on everything. For the incurable gambler, there is never enough money in the world.

And suddenly, the Deacon saw more money within his reach, an extra little job, a pleasurable form of moonlighting that would be in total contrast to the mundane business of making cabinets. It would also give him secret excitement, and a wonderful sense of superiority over the stodgy middle-class establishment of the capital. He would become a master criminal.

For a man of his exuberant ingenuity, it was too easy. Edinburgh was an honest place, where people tended to take other people's honesty for granted. Merchants, for instance, had the habit of hanging their keys on the inside of their doors during working hours. Deacon Brodie found he could drop in on one of those innocent burghers for a chat, wait till the man was otherwise engaged, and then take an impression of the main key with a lump of putty concealed in his hand. The spirit of Scottish inventiveness and innovation ran strong in his veins.

He did very well. In a city lightly policed, and whose police would never suspect an eminent citizen strolling the streets at night, he had invented the perfect, the undetectable crime. His regular raids became something like a reign of terror. The merchants, panic-stricken, put together a reward for the capture of the mystery man. The Deacon went blithely on, commiserating with his prosperous friends by day and robbing them by night, and creating the legend that would be echoed in Jekyll and Hyde, Raffles, The Amazing Doctor Clitterhouse and a hundred minor imitations.

It was all so simple that he pushed himself into more exciting and more perilous extensions of the game. Most dangerous of all, he took on a team. They were a petty criminal Andrew Ainslie, a locksmith George Smith, and a convicted criminal John Brown. With this group he carried off the splendidly audacious job of stealing the silver mace from Edinburgh University. In the same period he conscientiously performed his duty as juror in a case of homicide. He planned a raid on the excise office.

This was his first real failure. While he was exploring the office, an excise official by unlucky chance came back to check on some papers. Brodie panicked, lowered his head and rushed out past the man, leaving his companions to escape any way they could. He rushed to Jean Watt's to establish an alibi.

But the thieves were falling out. John Brown was dissatisfied with his share in the company. He could get the £150 reward and a free pardon by ratting on his friends. He did. He betrayed Ainslie and Smith, and they were arrested. Brown didn't tell the authorities anything about the Deacon. He was probably saving Brodie up in the hope of blackmailing him later.

The master criminal held on to his nerve at first. He could use his authority to visit the arrested men in the Tolbooth and make sure that they wouldn't give him away. He tried it, but he was refused permission to see them, and he took fright. He needn't have. Smith and Ainslie had said nothing about their high-class accomplice. But there was no way he could know that. He fled the city and immediately brought suspicion on himself.

He escaped from the country, in fact; and when we consider how crude and slow communications were in his time, it is astonishing how efficiently he was caught. Under a false name, he travelled on a little packet for the Continent with two other passengers, a married couple. This pair were put to some inconvenience, because Brodie had arranged sealed orders for the captain to travel to Flanders, and his travelling companions were stuck with several days at sea they hadn't planned. He was so charming that they didn't object.

In a moment of insane over-confidence he gave them three letters to post to Edinburgh on their return to England. He himself left the boat at Ostend.

The letters started the hunt. He was tracked to Amsterdam and brought to Edinburgh to be tried. Facing certain conviction, he remained elegant and suave. There is a theory, quite a convincing theory, that he had arranged for the hangman to be bribed and fake the execution, so that he could be taken from the rope by waiting friends and spirited away to be revived. The theory is given colour by the fact that there were two attempts at hanging him before the process finally worked. It could be that the executioner indeed was trying for an adjustment of the length of the rope to avert Brodie's death. And his friends were indeed allowed to take possession of the body and remove it for private burial.

The remains of Deacon Brodie were rushed to a house where he was to be resuscitated; but the rope had done its work at the third attempt, and there was no cure for a thoroughly broken neck.

Apart from giving us a legend, Deacon Brodie is one of the most likeable of Scotland's bad men. He was a pretty singer, a fair dancer, he was generous to his two ladies and entertaining to his friends, and although it was naughty to rob respectable merchants, he did it with fine panache and wit. It was his misfortune that the Britain of his time was so committed to death as the cure for practically any crime. When we look back over the years at Brodie in the dock, and Lord Braxfield on the bench, we would surely prefer the company of the impious Deacon to that of the righteous and bloodthirsty judge.

9

BETWEEN COVERS

DEACON BRODIE was bold enough, and lucky enough (for a time) to live out the plot of a pretty good novel. That is only reasonable. Many of the Scots who later wrote the things did the same.

It is true that before Walter Scott rose in his majesty to conquer the world, the novel had hardly got under way among his countrymen. Tobias Smollett is even described in reference works as an *English* novelist, though he was born in Dunbartonshire and educated in Glasgow. There are descendants to this day farming near Loch Lomond.

Admittedly, the prickly, undisciplined Smollett produced virtually all his work outside Scotland, and even wrote an acceptable history of England. Perhaps he moved south because he had run out of people to quarrel with at home. He wrote his first play at eighteen, *The Regicide*. Nobody would put it on, anywhere. He was livid. He had studied medicine, and on several occasions throughout his life decided to go into practice; he did in fact sail briefly as a naval surgeon, and got angry with the navy too.

Smollett, in fact, didn't really know who he was (the Deacon Brodie syndrome again!). Like Scott, he published his first novel, *The Adventures of Roderick Random*, anonymously. There is something odd about the Scottish lust for disguise. (I have published under six names at least.) No doubt he should have taken heart from the success of *Roderick Random*, and plunged ahead as a novelist. Instead, he did nearly anything that turned up, and even established a kind of literary commune in Chelsea to produce assembly-line works. He travelled extensively in Europe, partly for pleasure and partly for his health, which was never good.

But his personality troubles, and his tendency to blame other people for them, did not diminish the quality of his writing. Some of his best work, which still bears pleasurable examination, is in the picaresque tradition of Fielding. *Peregrine Pickle* and *The Expedition of Humphrey Clinker* are still a lot of fun; and even if he lived most of his life as an expatriate, he left something for his native country to be proud of. He was at his full creative powers when he died in Italy at the age of fifty.

Scott is nearly indescribable. He is the giant. His original destiny was the law, and his success in it was more than adequate for an ordinary man. He was a good lawyer and eventually a good and respected judge. Writing was involuntary. There is a celebrated oil painting of a soirée in Edinburgh in which he appears as a boy of nine, the youngest in a group of admirers listening to Robert Burns. The scene may well have occurred as the artist describes it. Anyway, he had a lifelong respect for the works of Burns, and he was no mean poet himself. If he had written nothing but poetry he would have left a reasonable reputation, though he can hardly be accused of sustaining a magical poetic quality throughout his verse epics.

> Along the bridge Lord Marmion rode
> Proudly his red-roan charger trod
> His helm hung at the saddle bow
> Well by his visage you might know
> He was a stalwart knight, and keen,
> And had in many a battle been.

Mm. Not *quite* A-plus. But from an output as torrential as Scott's, it is obviously going to be easy to pick out some dross among the gems. *Marmion*, taken as a whole, is a verse costume-drama of splendid narrative pace and colour, though the hero himself is a bit of a stick. Scott made his real mark with the invention of a romantic Scotland nobody had noticed before, perhaps because it wasn't entirely there. It is no bad thing for a nation to be handed a romantic tradition ready-made by a master tailor. The success of his historical novels made him the darling of the world and, in a way, the first citizen of Edinburgh. And it was a deserved success. He was a master deviser of story and character. Modern schoolchildren, put to him by compulsion, always moan about his lengthy descriptive passages, but Walter knew what he was doing, he knew his public and he had them in his hand.

It was Scott who was chosen to arrange the panoply for George IV's ceremonial and hilarious visitation to the Scottish capital, where the enormous monarch, who spoke almost no English, got himself fitted into a kilt of startling size and blinding design and strutted about imagining himself the hero of *Rob Roy*. As Hollywood gave twentieth-century children the cowboy dream, Scott gave his time the fierce gallant Highlander.

Everything should have gone well for him. He was born into a comfortable condition, he did well in the law, he did miraculously in letters, he earned an enormous fortune, was an amiable man and surrounded by friends and fans. He had one small forgivable madness. He dreamed up a character for himself as a landed aristocrat, settled himself at Abbotsford in the beautiful Border country in a richly rolling estate, and felt he had arrived. But on all this lush farmland he owned, there was nothing as squalid as cattle or sheep, or earth being disturbed for crops. If he had had the place run as a business, it would still have been picturesque and beautiful, and given him a comfortable income. Maintained as a vast picture postcard, it beggared him.

He survived, but it was a bitter blow, The weaver of dreams had lost his own. His admirers forgive him for his manic outbreak. Even the Scots like a man who is prepared to think big; especially if he is punished for it.

Scott had many imitators all over the world, and hundreds of them are still at it. In Scotland, after him, the romantic tradition degenerated into the 'kailyard', with a stream of cute, kitsch sketches and novels about pawky bucolic characters, which brought delight to millions of readers and acute nausea to intelligent Scots. The national flight from reality is very interesting. Scotland in the nineteenth century, after all, was a cradle of the Industrial Revolution. Rural life itself was revolutionised, scientific farming was coming in, the countryside was being emptied of people, and a fairly grim urban society was already there, with discontent already bubbling among the industrial masses and a new kind of Scot evolving.

None of this, absolutely none, appeared in Scottish literature. Both writers and readers turned their backs on the life around them and dived into their imitation tales.

One pure oddity, one entire original, rears itself out of the period immediately after Scott. It had nothing to do with the changes in society. It was not concerned with any kind of transient social fashion. It is concerned with the dreadful underside of the human spirit, and it stands outside time. It is *The Confessions of a Justified Sinner* by James Hogg. Hogg, an unschooled rustic who became an admirer and collaborator of Walter Scott in collecting and saving traditional poetry, is presented to Scottish schoolchildren as the 'Ettrick Shepherd', author of pleasant, workmanlike poems reflecting country life and the beauty of nature. His masterpiece was quite a different matter.

It is the first nearly clinical study of schizophrenia. The narrator, a deeply religious man, is plagued by encounters with an evil figure

—his brother? an apparition? his mirror image? As the ghastly story proceeds, this Other moves more and more into the foreground; also deeply religious, but turning religion upside down and committing a series of murders and abominations. Who is he? Does he exist independently, or is he a projection of the gentle hero? The reader's puzzlement increases his horror.

'Poe,' said one critic, 'never invented anything more horrible or with so much spiritual significance.' True. After its publication in 1824, the novel virtually vanished for a century. It was left to a Frenchman, André Gide, to rediscover it and proclaim its genius. In a way, it seems like pure Hogg, a literary mutation belonging to no tradition. It belongs, in fact, to an underground tradition. Gide was told by Dorothy Bussy, his translator: 'You mustn't forget that this work is not English but very specifically Scots . . . to its very marrow; no Englishman could possibly have written it. Its whole atmosphere, the very form and substance of its Puritanism, is essentially Scottish. You will find its counterpart and predecessor in Burns . . . Holy Willie's Prayer.'

Also true. Other, minor writers, had observed the strange effects of obsessional Scottish religion. Hogg raised these horrors to a kind of awful splendour. *Justified Sinner* foreshadows that more celebrated, but not superior Scots tale of split personality, Robert Louis Stevenson's *Jekyll and Hyde*, and a little-known but quite superb tale of John Buchan's, *Witchwood*.

Stevenson was born in 1850, fifteen years after Hogg's death. If he was influenced by *Justified Sinner*, it was a solitary incident. He was not influenced, either, by the changing times around him. In Stevenson's case, there is no sense in complaining about that. He was known in Samoa as Tusitala, the teller of tales; a gentle, courageous and immensely lovable man who was constantly ill and died of tuberculosis at the age of forty-four.

Like Walter Scott, he studied law in Edinburgh and was called to the bar. He started writing in his twenties, fed his imagination with constant travel in Europe and America—once in a canoe, once on a donkey. He had the talent for writing books for children which grip adults. Is *Treasure Island* the greatest boys' adventure story ever written? Mark Twain enthusiasts might quibble. Let's call Jim, Tom and Huckleberry Finn equal firsts. And few novels have inspired more imitators than *Treasure Island*. The innocent youth marooned is a whole genre in itself, after Stevenson.

He was already and tragically dead, however, before any Scottish novelist emerged who was capable of dismissing both costume adventure and the kailyard and looking at contemporary life plainly and brutally. He was George Douglas Brown, and his novel published in 1895 was *The House with the Green Shutters*. The critic Walter Raleigh greeted it almost in hysteria. 'I love the book,' he said, 'for just this—it sticks the kailyarders like pigs!'

Brown's tale is set in a small Scottish town, but there is nothing cute or pawky about it. Gourlay, the central character, is a grain merchant, hard, arrogant and insensitive, and enjoying the prosperity that makes him king of his little castle. He brutally offends an incomer to the town. His victim, unlike Gourlay's previous victims, retaliates. He sets up in business opposition, and progressively brings Gourlay to ruin and disaster. The atmosphere of the novel is powerful, dark and savage. This seminal novel is clearly echoed in a later bestseller, A. J. Cronin's *Hatter's Castle*, which also has a paranoid megalomaniac for its central figure, and a similar sense of classic, inescapable doom. For good measure, Cronin threw in the collapse of the Tay Railway Bridge in 1879 with a trainload of passengers, to counterpoint the final disaster.

In spite of all that, many Scots still like the kailyard, a fantasy world in which nothing exists below the surface, and everything, by and large, is *nice*. It is not for nothing that the *Sunday Post* continues to be the country's bestselling newspaper by a wide margin. It mixes a little news with, nowadays (because the paper always shrewdly accommodates itself to the times), the daring admission that marriage is partly about sex, pregnancy and problems; but, most importantly, nice short stories about nice couthy people, diverting anecdotes about the ludicrous things that happen to nice Scots families, and two comic strips, 'Oor Wullie' and 'The Broons' which run for ever, unchanging and unchangeable, and take us back to a universe that never heard of vandalism, urban decay, crime or corruption. The *Post* has an enormous overseas sale. It is posted to exiles all over the world to remind them of the world that never was, and their non-Scots neighbours love it too.

Nevertheless, after George Douglas Brown, and *The House with the Green Shutters*, Scottish writers dived gratefully into realism, and even quite enjoyed the tortures of the damned. Apart from the Gothic drama of *Hatter's Castle*, Cronin chronicled the struggles of dogged doctors trapped in the miseries of poverty and industrial disease.

James Barke, who found his greatest success with a four-volume fictionalised version of the life of Robert Burns, had already tackled the absorbing plight of a working-class family moving about Scotland in the mundane process of surviving. This fine, densely packed novel, *The Land of the Leal*, will stand the test of time.

John Buchan is a different animal. It may be, as some sour

analysts have suggested, that he achieved his innermost ambition by rising from humble beginnings to speak with kings, acquire a peerage and become Governor-General of Canada as Lord Tweedsmuir; that he was beyond all an incurable snob. Snobbery is a trivial enough accusation, it can even be rather engaging. Unless one is given to envy, there is something very pleasant in contemplating a man who is kindly, intelligent, erudite and talented, who does nobody any particular harm, and who gets what he wants.

In the process, he gave us what we wanted. Richard Hannay, the hero of *The Thirty-Nine Steps*, is aristocratic, elegant, humorous, brave and resourceful; all rather agreeable things to be. His character may not be profoundly drawn, but the story's the thing and, like R.L.S., Buchan is a great spinner of tales. Something is always happening.

Walter Kerr of the *New York Times* once defined a good play as one where the audience was continuously eager to know what happened next. Buchan knows the trick.

In his adventures, he is a Scottish writer only in the sense that he exploits the Scottish scenery. Well, he would be a fool not to. It's there. His range goes far beyond 'mere' adventure stories. *Witchwood* has already been mentioned, and in the character of Ephraim Caird, the grim Kirk elder who upholds the merciless morality of Presbyterianism, and finds no inconsistency in running a Satanic cult on the side, Buchan has given us a creation larger than life. In his short stories, some of the best collected as *The Watcher by the Threshold* and *The Moon Endureth*, we find a quite dazzling and cultivated mind exploring some of the strange recesses of human experience. He has served his reader well.

A minor novelist of this century who well merits mentioning is Neil Munro, who followed the Stevenson trail with period adventures, notably *The New Road* (the road is the one being built by General Wade to pacify the Highlands after the Jacobite rebellion). A Highlander by birth, Munro evokes a sense of place and people equal to, perhaps superior to, that of Stevenson. But he is worth mentioning for another reason.

Munro was for many years the editor of the *Glasgow Evening News*. During that time he casually dashed off a series of lighthearted tales about the crew of a little Hebridean steamer under the captaincy of one Para Handy. These were ephemera, for publication in the newspaper, and he thought little of them. When they were reissued in book form, he was almost resentful that they should gain more attention than his 'serious' historical novels. He wanted to be remembered for his important work as a writer.

The truth is (or at least, the present age has decided it is) that his novels are all right. They are rich enough in colour and excitement and conviction. The Para Handy tales, however, are just marvellous. In these throwaways, Munro wrought better than he knew. The quips and the clashes are as fresh now as two generations ago. They were written for fun. They are read for fun. But then, all art from the highest to the humblest is for fun. Let us not dismiss or under-value our jokesters. Laughter is the survival kit of mankind, and in Scotland we need it constantly.

Fun is not the description that springs to mind in the case of Lewis Grassic Gibbon. Perhaps the definition of art should be widened. Let every novelist heed the writer's first commandment: Thou shalt not bore. Gibbon is many things, and never a bore.

He was born James Leslie Mitchell (again we see the odd Scottish passion for discovering another personality). In his own name he wrote prodigiously, and supremely *Spartacus*, a novel based on the slaves' revolt of Imperial Rome which predated Howard Fast's novel by some years. 'Carved from the living rock', said one critic groping for superlatives. He was fascinated by, and wrote fascinatingly about, Mexico. As an adolescent, he was fired from a menial job on *The Scottish Farmer* for padding his expenses by three shillings.

Gibbon lived out a life that is almost a caricature of the Scottish convention: the humble beginnings on a farm in Aberdeenshire, the brilliant native intellect, the greedy lust for knowledge, the frantic outpouring of words before the body should burn out exhausted. It is all wonderful and awful.

His formal education finished at sixteen, but he had always been an incurable student. At that age he had a reasonable smattering of Russian, and he absorbed other languages almost on contact. At twenty he joined the Royal Air Force as a clerk and served for eight years. It gave him the chance to see the Middle East. When he came out, he was able to visit Central America and study the Mayan civilisation. Then he wrote. He wrote in a scramble, trying to work on two or three projects simultaneously.

The major work is the trilogy known as *A Scots Quair*, a saga of life in the hard, windblown farmland of East Scotland. It is a mountain-ous novel with deep roots and a great sprawl of memorable people, with a genuinely great fictional heroine, Chris Guthrie, at the centre. It is written in an unexpected prose style, a mixture of vernacular Scottish speech and poetry, which is irritating for a few pages and then becomes hypnotic.

He was twenty-eight years old when he left the air force. He wrote sixteen books and innumerable other things. He died in 1934, at the age of thirty-five.

Scotland is not badly off for novelists. I have not even referred to the gentle, mystical Neil Gunn, who shed a curious magic light on the far north; or the sociably irascible Eric Linklater. Alastair McLean, Scots to the bone, has put that behind him and wisely become the cheerful prisoner of Hollywood. There are still the McIlvanneys and the Quigleys, George Mackay Brown, Ian Crichton Smith, Elspeth Davie, beavering away among us. Something good will come of it all. Perhaps something great.

10

KICKS AND
STICKS

Lies, lies. Of course it is all lies; or at least it is all a delusion; and regrettably, often a drunken illusion, that Scotland invented Association Football, or soccer. Natives will insist on the legend, repetitively and sometimes incoherently. The truth must be proclaimed, however. Nobody invented soccer. It simply growed.

The human race, with its unique capacity for boredom, has been doing strange and bellicose things with balls since before anybody recorded anything. The Greeks and the Romans threw spherical objects about, bounced them off their heads and kicked them. Dear old Homer mentions a ball game favoured by the lads of the village in Troy 3,000 years ago. This chapter is intended to set straight a record that hardly exists.

There is certainly some tenuous proof that Scotsmen were engaged in some kind of ball game in the fifteenth century or earlier. It had no rules, except a ferocious resolution to win. We need pay only polite and sceptical attention to a Scottish myth that the game as we know it developed out of a casual afternoon's sport in which some euphorious Scots kicked a Viking helmet about to pass the time; possibly with the Viking's head still inside it. The human-head theory of football is in fact a universal legend. Clearly, there is something about the human head that provokes exasperated people to kick it. The English claim that this diversion was first discovered at Chester, and that an unfortunate Dane donated the missile. No doubt the Mongols and the Huns had conducted tentative experiments with the same material. Nobody knows. That is the truth about football. Nobody knows.

There is a tradition, still alive in the Orkney Isles, which shows that the Scots did get into the game reasonably early. It is the massive contest of the Uppies and the Doonies; that is, the people who live in the upward half of the town of Kirkwall, and those who live in the downward half. On certain festival days, principally New Year's

Day, the population ranges itself into two camps, throws up a ball and then clashes head-on till one mob or other claims victory.

This is probably as good a way of sobering up as anybody has invented. The teams may consist of any number, from a dozen to several hundred. Some of the time, the ball itself is invisible and the game becomes a matter of one crowd pushing another crowd for no good reason. There have been moments when the ball—a stitched leather thing filled with cork dust—has been smuggled out of the mêlée and rushed to one or other end of the town while the combatants got jammed together in a narrow street and forgot why they were there in the first place.

In the heat of the moment, women have been known to join in. During the ball game reserved for young boys, fathers have been overcome with local pride and gatecrashed the fight. There was at least one incident in recent times when the ball was hurled out of the tussle into the hands of a man galloping past on a horse, and transported towards victory at the far end of the town.

None of this is greatly relevant to the known history of soccer. It is just quite interesting. Scholarly research suggests that the Kirkwall ball game itself was imported by the Norsemen, took root and went insane.

It is equally probable that mob football was brought into England by the Normans, because the French had an early form of this nonsense. One medieval tale suggests that the game was prohibited in one Breton district because enthusiastic players tended to pursue the ball into the sea and drowned. There is even a story that in another part of France, forty fanatics drowned in a single foray.

The soccer we know, with eleven players to a side and actual rules, has less than a century of formal history. It is true that the Glasgow club, Queen's Park, was probably the first on the scene, and got the whole thing going. It is also true that the first football association was formed in England, in 1863, and we have to accept that as the beginning of the modern game, with its rigid regulations, its bureaucracy and its ludicrous hold on the imaginations of quite rational people all over the world.

It would even be too much to claim that the Scots injected into the game its essential ingredient: brainless fanaticism. The Scots are certainly good at brainless fanaticism; but when we reflect that during a local game in Turkey in our time, seven spectators were shot dead by other spectators, the Caledonian contribution should not be inflated.

What distinguishes Scottish soccer, perhaps, is the permanent triumph of hope over experience. Scottish teams have certainly made their mark now and then on the international scene. But in general, they tend to set out on a wave of euphoria and sink without trace. When a Scottish side set out to win the World Cup in Argentina in 1978, sane and canny Scots actually expected a brisk conquest. One enthusiast set off from his native land to travel through the Americas on a pushbike to share in the victory. It was a hilarious catastrophe. Next time, all will be different. It is nearly always next time the Scots are looking for.

When a Scottish team travels to London to battle with the Auld Enemy, sensible Londoners shutter their windows and emigrate. Sensitive Scots adopt outlandish accents and deny their race. The passionate fans follow the team. They tend to be young, aggressive and mortally drunk, and quite a lot of them land in jail.

All in all, although the country has helped to make soccer a rude word, it is consoling to think that it was originated by somebody else.

Shinty is another matter. The origins of this game are also reasonably shrouded, and it resembles the Irish sport of hurling; but the Scot is wearily accustomed to the claims of the Irish to have started everything, from Christianity to whisky, and attaches little importance to these impudent presumptions.

At a momentary glance, shinty looks like hockey, in that the players use a small ball and lash at it with bent sticks. Shinty is rougher. Shinty is a great deal rougher.

This is not to say that hockey, which sprang out of the Indian subcontinent, is a sissy game. Strong men may play it without shame or guilt, and suffer abrasions and contusions and occasional fractures. It is a fine and aggressive pastime. The principal difference is that hockey takes formal precautions. The hockey stick, for instance, may not be raised above shoulder level. The ball must be struck by one side of the stick only. At the start of each encounter, the ball is placed on the ground at the centre of the field, where it can do no serious harm until somebody has hit it.

Shinty differs. There is no question of the Scottish Highland game having derived from hockey. It grew up independently long before the Indian Empire was established by Queen Victoria. It is loose. But in the words of the official handbook, 'it is no pastime for weaklings, or degenerates.' It is certainly very good for broken legs.

Even the size of the pitch is a matter of luck, and in one place at least, Tighnabruaich, the shinty field has quite a steep slope from one end to the other. The regulations as laid down by the Camanachd Association specify a length of 140 to 170 yards, and a width of 70 to 80 yards. The hail posts, or goalposts, are twelve feet wide and ten feet high. The stick, properly called the caman, is a length of timber curved at the end, and its striking head must be able to pass through a ring of $2\frac{1}{2}$ inches in diameter. It can be swung in any direction, horizontally or vertically, and through any arc the player can manage.

To start the game, the referee, a man with nerves of chrome steel, positions two players at the centre spot, with their camans crossed above head level. He then throws the ball straight up, to a minimum height of twelve feet, and leaps for safety. The players lash at the descending ball, usually wielding the caman edge-on. It is a perfectly terrifying moment, and the terror is sometimes justified.

Having started its career aloft, the ball spends a lot of the game well off the ground. A vigorous player is capable of driving the object from one end of the field to the other at tooth level. Spectators at shinty games bob up and down quite a lot.

Even in this freewheeling game, there are pettifogging rules, of course. No player may attempt to strike the ball, if in doing so he is liable to strike any player with his caman when the latter is unable to protect himself from the swing of the caman. And 'hacking' means deliberately hitting at any part of an opponent's body or caman. On the other hand, hooking or cleeking an opponent's caman is all right if the opponent is within striking distance of the ball.

In practice, the game goes too fast and too far for many legalistic interruptions. It is one of the most fiendish participation sports, and one of the most exhilarating spectator sports, in the world. It is by nature a Highlander's game, and therefore a minority pursuit; but its fascination is spreading into Lowland Scotland, and the incidence of minor and major fractures can be expected to rise.

The major trophy in the game is the Camanachd Cup, which has been fought for since 1896. In the cheerful Highland fastnesses, a local victory is celebrated with fiercer intensity than metropolitan societies can possibly achieve. Festivities may go on for three days or more, and the splendid cup itself is regularly refilled with whisky to be passed round the faithful. It holds nine bottles of whisky. But the enthusiasts do not throw bricks or beer bottles, they do not assault opposing fans, they do not tear up railway lines. As mayhem goes, shinty is civilised.

It is at least probable that the game gave birth to ice hockey. Exiled Scots in Canada adapted shinty to frozen lakes, and launched that other sport, which is reasonably fiendish in its own way.

Celly Paterson, a daunting shinty champion in his time and now a respected administrator, even suggests that golf is an accidental byproduct of shinty. There, he probably claims too much.

On the other hand, who knows?

78

A
LITTLE LEARNING

THERE IS an incurable nosiness in the national character. In olden days it often found its expression in theology. In the words of a modern Scottish writer, every village-born Scotsman thinks he is a born philosopher. True. Literate Scots of past times wrestled with chapter, verse, comma and semicolon of scripture to penetrate the meaning beneath the surface and blow their minds with speculation and disputation. They construed and interpreted and projected like seminary rabbis gone beserk.

In this century, when Godlessness swept the land, the natural theologian simply switched to Karl Marx, and gave *Kapital* the same analytical hammering as his grandfather might have given Hezekiah. I have listened with my own ears to street-corner discussions, penetrating and acrimonious, on minuscule aspects of great questions like the Theory of Surplus Value, going far into the night. Sometimes they would be resolved by arbitration, which meant calling at the home of Hector McTosh or some other local authority and getting him out of bed to adjudicate. The sage would rise without complaint and pronounce judgement by reference to the book itself, which was stored permanently under his pillow.

There have been less solemn moments in this dogged pursuit of Truth, luckily. One night a group of Glasgow University law students were going through the traditional performance over an obscure point in maritime law, at an intellectual soirée stimulated by plenty of beer. The point could not be settled. In the small hours, a deputation left the party and shambled to Professors' Square, found the address of the eminent Professor X, who enjoyed life and knew everything. After much knocking and bell ringing, the door was opened by a housekeeper in a dressing gown.

'Is this Professor X's house?' the spokesman asked.

'Aye,' she said wearily. 'Carry him in.'

We have always been proud, to the point of complacency, of the Scottish educational system, second to none. We continue to have an almost hysterical reverence for sheer learning. Well, it has been around us for a long time. In the sixteenth century, John Knox dreamed of universal education as a part of the religious reformation. He stimulated the founding of the 'ragged schools' where the scruffiest child could fill his mind.

But long before then, the natural passion for literacy was there. Before the universities were founded, thirsty Scots wandered all over Europe to sit at the feet of the great scholars. There was even a Scots College in Paris, because there were enough Scots to keep one going.

The first native university was established in St Andrews by a Charter in 1412. Glasgow followed in 1451, Aberdeen in 1495 and Edinburgh in 1582. Scottish alumni today are mildly amused when Oxford and Cambridge people imagine that all other British universities are redbrick *arrivistes*.

From their earliest beginnings, none of these seats of learning was exclusive to the upper classes. A poor farm boy could, and did, finish his work at the harvest and then spend the winter in higher education. What they learned was another matter. A law around 1500 compelled country gentlemen to send their eldest sons to grammar school to study the law. Latin was the international language, and the Scots imposed it on themselves with brutal enthusiasm. A grammar school boy didn't only worm his way through declensions and conjugations in the classroom. In the brief play periods he was expected to speak the language among his friends. If he slipped into Scots he could expect to be beaten into a state of classic grace by the headmaster.

Maybe it was a consolation that the play periods *were* brief. The national attitude to learning was that it was real and it was earnest. The lads put in a six-day week of twelve-hour days beginning at six in the morning, and there was no room for fun or frivolity. We got the Reformation without the Renaissance.

All the same, the system was the wonder of Europe. It worked. It did what it set out to do, however cheerless that was.

In a way, the establishment of our own universities narrowed the horizons of the student. Since it was no longer necessary to study abroad, he came into an insular system that took a long time to build up standards. When the Auld Alliance between Scotland and France was ended by the Treaty of Edinburgh in 1560, the insularity acquired legal status.

Apart from all that Latin and law, the universities were always short of money, they couldn't lure great teachers from abroad, and their libraries were pathetic little collections. There were no labora-

Tobias George Smollet, often described as an English novelist although he was born in Dunbartonshire and educated in Glasgow. Perhaps he moved south because he had run out of people to quarrel with at home (*Scottish National Portrait Gallery*)

Thomas Telford was christened by Southey 'the Colossus of the Roads' and, alternatively, *Pontifex Maximus*. He plastered the British Isles with some 1,200 bridges, laid 1,000 miles of road and built harbours, churches and the Caledonian Canal (*Samuel Lane, Institute of Civil Engineers*)

John Loudon Macadam had retired as a merchant before an obsession with roads took hold of him. Nothing could stand thereafter in the way of Macadam's roads (*unknown artist, National Portrait Gallery*)

tories at all. Scientific study was a series of dusty lectures based on Aristotle, whose work was pretty old fashioned even by then.

None of this matters, of course, as long as the Scot is learning *something*. Most other people of the time were learning nothing, wasting their lives going to theatres, looking at paintings and enjoying the decadent pleasures of the flesh.

But even if it was all work and no play, the Scottish system had a head start on nearly every other, and it held on to it for a long time. And it went right on combining egalitarianism with élitism. The door has always been open to anybody capable of absorbing education. Even in this century, stories were told of Highland lads who came down from the far north equipped with a bag of oatmeal and a barrel of salt herring to sustain them right through the university year. No names were mentioned, and as far as I know, no investigator has managed to track down one of these frugal stalwarts. But if the stories are exaggerated, they are only slightly exaggerated. And we like a good story.

The whole thing has opened out again. Scholars travel again. There are four other universities added to the original four, and Latin has slipped down the scale in favour of newfangled disciplines like nuclear physics and sociology. Every university in the western world is getting more like every other university in the western world. But the Scots passion burns on.

Even the village dominie has always been a figure of importance, ranking with the minister and the doctor. One curious effect of this long tradition of respect and reverence is that, compared with children in, say, England or America, Scottish school students *don't talk back*. Even today, visitors to Scottish schools often get the impression that the pupils have been sent out by their parents with the stern injunction to keep quiet and listen to the teacher and don't interrupt, and come home with their skulls crammed.

Behind the quiet, attentive faces, however, the brains are whirling away; as no doubt their predecessors' minds whirled on other matters when they were trying to remember the Latin for Who was that homespun philosopher I saw you with last night?

Learning is still the king of the Scots.

12

SEEING
VISIONS

MAJOR, and even minor mysteries, like the true origin of golf or shinty, remain mysteries because we are mortals, and see as through a glass, darkly. Perhaps we should resort to oracles; and if you want oracles, Scotland is your place.

In the Highlands, especially, you will find people who are in touch with universal mysteries beyond the reach of mere science or dusty research. There is never any falling-off in the distribution of second sight ('the sicht'), and if you throw a brick in the north, you're bound to hit at least one native who is fey.

Being fey is not just a matter of seeing the future. It is restricted to seeing the glum future; and this is fairly shrewd, when you think of it. Knowing that his past history is an unbroken serial story of betrayal, conflict and catastrophe, the Highland seer can feel safe in predicting more of the same. And anyway, catastrophes are more entertaining.

'Ravens will drink their fill of Mackenzie blood three times off the top of the Clach Mhor.'

'The day will come when a laird of Talloch will kill four wives, and the fifth will kill him.'

'When a magpie nests in the gable wall of the church of Ferrintosh, the church will fall while full of people.'

How much more arresting all that is, than bland maunderings about meeting dark strangers or going on a journey or finding romance 'inside a three'. There were never any such optimistic banalities in the piercing vision of Coinneach Odhar, Kenneth Mackenzie or, as he is known to his many fans, the Brahan Seer. For Mackenzie, the future was gore and disaster or it was nothing. The Brahan Seer is still mighty big juju to romantic admirers in our time, and for the best of reasons.

The mantle of prophecy descended on him while he was still an infant, and it came to pass thus:

His mother was tending cattle near her croft at Baile-na-Cille, in the Parish of Uig, on the Isle of Lewis, and chanced to be near the graveyard at the witching hour when she saw the graves open, the dead rising from them and drifting away in all directions. In another time, in another land, this might have upset a simple peasant woman, but in the Highlands, in the early seventeenth century, folk took these things as routine, and as far as we can tell, she watched the performance with bright, calm interest until, after an interval, the wandering shades came back and tucked themselves tidily into their lairs.

One grave, however, was still open and empty, and being well up in the rituals of the period, Mrs Mackenzie put the end of her distaff down into it and awaited events. Quite soon the laggardly ghost arrived, a lady of shining white, who saw at once that she couldn't get back underground, because she worked by the same ground rules as Mrs Mackenzie, and accepted that the distaff was powerful magic and absolute death to dead people.

She pleaded eloquently and frantically to be allowed back into the earth. She explained that she was the daughter of the King of Norway, who had been lost at sea just off the coast, and later found and buried in Uig. Mrs Mackenzie had nothing against the lassie, and was presumably just trying out her distaff for strength, so she removed the thing willingly enough and let the girl get back to rest. In gratitude, the princess told her where she might find a small black rounded stone, and this, when given to little Kenneth, would give him strange gifts of prevision.

It worked like the charm it was. As soon as he had the stone, the boy was on his way into the legend books. His fame spread all over the land, and no assembly of the gentry was complete without the presence of the Brahan Seer to tell his queer tales that would curdle the aristocratic blood.

When he was a young man, his gift saved his own life (but fear not, hideous things were to come later). The lad had a sharp tongue and an irreverent wit, which so exasperated the wife of a farmer for whom he worked that she decided to end his life, and stirred poison into his mid-day meal to be properly rid of him. The food was carried to him where he was working on the hill, but before he could eat it, he fell into a deep slumber. He was awakened by a fearsome pain in his breast, and found there a little white stone with a hole in it. On peering through the hole he saw not the future, but the past, and a clear vision of the farmer's wife poisoning his snack; somewhat like instant playback on television. He went hungry, and lived.

Even this early in the tale, we detect inconsistencies. Was it a black stone he got from his mother, or a white stone he got from nowhere? Well, the documentary evidence is scanty, we all know how the truth becomes confused with many retellings, and there is no sense in being detained by quibbles. He had some kind of stone, and he could see wonders. One adornment to the second version is that the stress of peering through the white stone left him blind in one eye, but we may doubt this. After all, he spent a lot of his later life squinting through it, and surely his other eye would have gone blind at the second vision; unless, of course, the stone had such power that he was able to see through it with his blind eye. These are fruitless conjectures, and I apologise for bringing them up.

From then on, he issued oracular statements which, if properly interpreted, gave a wonderfully graphic picture of the future, near and distant.

'The day will come,' for instance, 'when ships will sail round the back of Tomnahurich Hill.'

Now it was quite absurd to predict such an event, since there was no water round the back of Tomnahurich Hill. But 150 years later came the construction of the Caledonian Canal, and the vision became reality.

His biographer, namesake Alexander Mackenzie, subjects this particular prophecy to rigorous scrutiny, and points out that since the great long lochs which were later joined to form the canal were already in existence, a man of keen intelligence might well have envisaged the eventual engineering works without any supernatural help. Either way, it remains a remarkable piece of foresight.

The issue is mildly muddied by the existence of another version, in which Mackenzie forecast that 'English mares with hempen bridles shall be led round the back of Tomnahurich', in the pursuance of some ploy that would bode no good to the Highlands. It is reasonably sure that such a thing did happen at some time or other later on.

The prophet was on sound ground when he promised that big sheep would overrun the country till they reached the North Sea, because in due time the sheep did come, and helped to destroy the traditional life of the Highlands. He also saw the hills of Ross-shire 'strewn with ribbons', and his supporters can legitimately claim that he meant the roads that were later to be built on the county.

A large part of the fascination in the Seer's statements is the high incidence of people with physical peculiarities, who lend a touch of Gothic colour to otherwise routine versions. The Isle of Lewis, for example, was promised a war which would lay it waste with one side gorily pursuing the other until a left-handed Macdonald faced them with nothing more than a cabar (or cudgel) and turned them back. No such war is found in recorded history so far; but the islands are private places with a poor supply of official archivists, and the thing may well have happened already, unbeknown to complacent people on the mainland.

The ceremonial ravens were well supplied with human gore in the Brahan Seer's grave new world. The Clach Mhor, mentioned earlier, was once a great standing stone which fell and broke, and when the birds were gorging themselves on dead Mackenzies, the cause of it all was to be a cross-eyed tailor, living at a time when marriageable men were so scarce that seven women were in conflict for his heart and hand.

'The day will come when the big-thumbed Sheriff Officer and the blind man with twenty-four fingers shall be together in Barra, and the Macneil of Barra may be making ready for the flitting.'

Those eccentric physiques again. Well, there was such a man, a blind man with twelve fingers and twelve toes, who found himself on the ferry to the Island of Barra in the company of a sherriff officer who was on his way to serve notice of ejectment on the Macneil of Barra. Mackenzie has been vindicated.

Two navels may seem to be carrying a natural taste for oddity too far, and it is certainly an uncommon idiosyncracy. Nevertheless, the prophet promised that 'when there shall be two churches in Ferrintosh, and a hand with two thumbs in I-Stianna, two bridges at Sguideal, and a man with two navels at Dunean, soldiers will come from Tarradale on a chariot without a horse or a bridle, which will leave the Muir of Ord a wilderness.'

Apart from the strange mutations, Mackenzie's readers are constantly struck by his skill in seeing technical innovations undreamt of in his time. The horseless chariot is clearly a motor vehicle. Likewise, the scoffers who refused to believe that 'fire and water will run through the streets of Inverness' simply could not imagine the arrival of piped water and gas more than a century later. He also made more than one reference to 'strings of carriages' without horses, long before his fellow Scot James Watt had perfected the steam engine that would launch the railway age.

Some of the prophecies are not yet fulfilled. Some have been kept secret because they involve families still existing and are too horrible to be revealed.

Quite as grisly as any of his menacing visions was the manner of his death, provoked by a vision and avenged by a terrible prophecy. This was the way of it.

The Earl of Seaforth, greatest of all the Mackenzies, travelled to Paris on business for the king, and was away a very long time. Having no word from him, the countess summoned Coinneach Odhar and ordered him to reveal if anything ill had befallen her husband. The

Seer was easily able to see the earl in distant France, attending a party and engaging in dalliance with a beautiful Frenchwoman. Being a man of some tact, he assured the countess that all was well with her husband.

Perhaps she detected a secret smile on Mackenzie's face. She persisted in knowing more. He warned her that it would do her no good to pry, that her husband was in good health. The stubborn woman would not be put off, and she hectored him till he lost his temper and told her that the earl would not be in a hurry to come home since he was dancing with a Frenchwoman with evident pleasure, and his hand on her hip.

The countess should have been angry at her husband; but since her husband wasn't available, she turned her fury on the Seer instead:

'You have spoken evil of dignities,' she screamed. 'You have sullied the good name of my lord, you have abused my hospitality and outraged my feelings. You shall suffer the most signal vengeance I can inflict. You shall suffer death!'

One small irritant to the lady was that Mackenzie had blurted out the story in the hearing of other people. He himself imagined she was simply making a scene to dismiss his story, and that she would change her mind. But a Scotswoman scorned is probably even more furious than an ordinary woman. Without giving herself time to think twice, she ordered him to be slain at once. The method was both economical and theatrical: immersion in a barrel of burning tar. According to one version, the Seer's final discomfiture was heightened by spikes fixed inside the barrel. When roused, the Scots really go too far.

A scarcely credible footnote is that the earl himself was at that very moment on his way home, and on hearing of the incident, spurred his horse madly to arrive in time to stop the execution. The horse died under him and he ran the rest of the way, but the deed was already done. I say scarcely credible, since it was no time since Mackenzie had seen him dancing in Paris. On the other hand, the Seer might have been looking through a time warp into the less recent past, as he had done when he saw the farmer's wife at her poisoning. There are some mysteries we shall never plumb.

To omit nothing vital, there is also a totally different version of the Seer's culpability, which is that at a large meeting of the local gentry, somebody remarked that such a gathering of gentlemen's children could rarely be seen. 'I see more in the company of the children of footmen and grooms than of the children of gentlemen,' he retorted acidly, and, unluckily for him, audibly. The gentry, and not least the countess, were incensed at the implication, and pursued him in a rage to have him done to death.

What was his crime? Witchcraft, or lese-majesty? Whatever they called it, it was in fact the fatal error of being too clever for his own good, and not concealing the fact. He had not entirely finished with his social betters, however. For one thing, he threw his magic white stone into a cow's footprint and predicted that a child with two navels (or four thumbs and six toes) would find it and acquire its powers. In spite of the evidence before them of what could happen to a prophet, onlookers scrambled to recover the charm, but suddenly water was oozing from the ground to form a lake which concealed it.

As recently as the 1920s, a biographer was able to state firmly that 'it is currently reported that a person answering to the description was born in the neighbourhood and is still living. I have been credibly informed by a person who saw him several times at the Muir of Ord markets.' Walk with caution, therefore, in the vicinity of the Muir of Ord.

The Seer's final act was his final prophecy, and it was a stunner.

I see into the far future [he declaimed] and I read the doom of the race of my oppressor. The line of Seaforth will, ere many generations have passed, end in extinction and sorrow. I see a chief, the last of his house, both deaf and dumb. He will be the father of four fair sons, all of whom he will follow to the tomb. He will live careworn and die mourning, knowing that the honours of his line are to be extinguished forever, and that no future chief of the Mackenzies shall bear rule at Brahan or in Kintail.

After lamenting over the last and most promising of his sons, he himself shall sink into the grave, and the remnant of his possessions shall be inherited by a white-hooded lassie from the East, and she is to kill her sister.

And as a sign by which it may be known that these things are coming to pass, there shall be four great lairds in the days of the last deaf and dumb Seaforth—Gairloch, Chisholm, Grant and Raasay—of whom one shall be buck-toothed, another hare-lipped, another half-witted, and the fourth a stammerer. When he looks round him and sees them, he may know that his sons are doomed to death, that his broad lands shall pass away to the stranger, and that his race shall come to an end.

Few speywives have the nerve to be so specific; but few speywives are speaking from barrels of burning tar. One Sir Bernard Burke, who wrote a number of essays on the oddities of Highland families, has reported:

> With regard to the four Highland lairds, who were to be buck-toothed, hare-lipped, half-witted and a stammerer—Gairloch, Chisholm, Grant and Raasay—I am uncertain which was which. Suffice it to say, that the four lairds were marked by the above-mentioned distinguishing personal peculiarities, and all four were contemporaries of the last of the Seaforths.

All this was over a century after the Brahan Seer's sudden death. The last Earl of Seaforth in the line, born in 1754, lost his hearing through scarlet fever in his boyhood. He went on to live a full life as a soldier and a colonial governor, and had four sons and six daughters. His youngest son died in childhood. The others never lived to marry. He had lost them all by the time he died in 1815, and the chieftain-ship passed to a distant relative.

But we are not yet at an end. His daughter, the Honourable Mary Frederica Elizabeth Mackenzie, inherited the lands. She came home from the East Indies, where her husband Admiral Sir Samuel Hood had just died. The white-hooded lassie from the east had stepped on-stage for her part in the drama.

Lady Hood remarried, her husband adopted the Mackenzie name, and they were happy. But while she was one day driving her young sister in a pony carriage, the ponies bolted. The carriage overturned, and the sister died of her injuries. The play was complete.

Such notable intellects as Sir Walter Scott and the scientist Sir Humphrey Davy accepted the truth of the Seaforth legend. A contemporary of Scott's assured him that he had heard the prophecy quoted at a time when two Seaforth sons were still alive and well.

One difficulty is that there is no genuine proof that there was ever such a person as the Brahan Seer. The Highlands are full of legends, and it is quite easy for a thousand prophecies from all over the country to be fathered on to any figure who has acquired a reputation, even if that figure itself is a tale woven from nothing but legend. It is completely possible that the whole Brahan Seer story is a chimera.

In a foreword to a new edition of the story, the present Countess of Sutherland springs to his support:

> It seems probable [she says] that the great twentieth-century 'de-bunking machine', which would discredit anything which is beyond our understanding, is shortly to be let loose on Coin-neach Odhar. Folklore is to become a science and ruthless

academic minds will rend our myths and bury our legends. We are already told that many of the Seer's predictions can be found within the folklore of any European country and it is, perhaps, only a matter of time before the machine decides that he never really existed at all.

However, old legends die hard in the Highlands and I suspect it will take more than a magnetic tape or a punched card to exsanguinate the Seer in Sutherland, Easter Ross, Inverness and other parts of Scotland where his predictions have been known and marvelled at for many generations.

And the lady is absolutely right. Let us not niggle over birth certificates or parish registers or verbatim contemporary notes that can't be found. The Brahan Seer, like the Loch Ness monster, exists because we want him to exist, we almost need him to exist, because Scotland would be a duller and poorer place without him.

There is also, just off the road between Fortrose and Fort George Ferry, a great stone slab, marking the spot where Mackenzie was callously burned to death. That surely proves it. There is nothing legendary about a stone slab.

13

THE
PLAYERS

WHEN WE look back on the life and times of the Brahan Seer and the people round him, especially the people with extra fingers, navels and possibly heads, it's obvious that our ancestors occupied a time almost as terrifying, magical and melodramatic as our own. But when it comes to drama as other peoples know it, the Scots are very, very odd indeed.

There should be no theatre in Scotland. The spirit of the folk is against it. The spirit of the folk is also in favour of it, of course. Like the Irish, but in their own way, the Scots live out a noisy daily drama in their own lives. They are incurable actors, treading God's boards. But that acting is a private thing, performed by people who would get quite angry if you suggested they were acting at all. Public acting is a different matter. It is deliberately done for fun, and it must therefore be sinful.

Let us add to the confusion. A lifelong observer of the Scots, my good friend Jack House, once said to me in despair, on the subject of Scottish broadcasting, 'Maybe the truth is that the Scots are not in favour of entertainment.' He was right (as he often is). And like all Scotsmen, he was wrong at the same time. The everyday Scot, the man or woman you meet in the street or the butcher shop or the tavern, is violently engaged in entertainment, revelry and rebellion. But when rebels choose rulers, the rulers are always, but always, grim dull people. The Scottish Establishment, wherever you find it, is stupefyingly dull.

The first memorable flowering of Scottish theatre is David Lindsay's *Ane Satyre of the Thrie Estates*, whose first performance was probably part of a Christmas revel in 1540. It was not an isolated freak in its time. It is merely the only smash hit that has come down to us. For Lindsay grew up in a Scotland that loved some kind of drama. For over a century, there had been a vigorous industry of Passion and Nativity plays in the Lowlands. The Establishment, mind you, was never too happy about this outpouring of entertainment, and the religious Establishment was particularly leery. Public performances belonged by right to the clergy, with guaranteed audiences and enforced approval (if not applause). There was something dangerous, and maybe sacrilegious, about insolent laymen poaching on that holy ground.

It is important to get a smell of the times, and to understand the permanent conflict between the People, who behaved like people (and therefore inconveniently), and the Authorities, who didn't really approve of people, or behaviour. Well after the *première* of *The Thrie Estates*, the ordinary rabble of Edinburgh adopted the legendary Robin Hood as its master of mirth. The Church—the Catholic Church, as it was then—made it a legal offence to enact Robin in 1555. When the Reformed Church, the Protestant Church, came to power, it turned the offence into a capital crime, and one citizen who proposed to play Robin Hood was sentenced to death.

His friends appealed to John Knox and to the Lord Provost of the city. The Lord Provost was a deeply pious man. He conferred solemnly with Knox and decided that the hanging must proceed. The year was 1561. If I mention that five years later, the same Lord Provost, with the approval of John Knox, collaborated in the murder of Rizzio, secretary to Mary Queen of Scots, it is merely to indicate the dramatic, the melodramatic, the black-farcical quality of Scottish history.

In any event, the criminal did not hang. His friends smashed down the door of the Tolbooth where he was held, destroyed the gallows, rescued him and locked his keepers up till they were freed, not in much of a hurry, by the captain of the guard.

This was the Scotland in which Lindsay of the Mount had presented his *Satyre*. It was a bold enterprise better left to a man like Lindsay, an aristocrat and royal favourite. It is a thundering piece of work, sprawling and repetitious but both elegant and vulgar, pious and bawdy, and it did what a satire is required to do; it sliced deep into the corruption and hypocrisy of court, politics and religion. It cut so keenly that after its first performance, the king summoned his chancellor, the Bishop of Glasgow, and other court prelates and ordered them to reform.

After the Lindsay phenomenon, the history of Scottish theatre simply left off. The rise of the Protestant Church meant the suppression of anything useless and agreeable. The Scot's natural lust for life went underground into the taverns and warm corners in barns. Or maybe it is too glib to blame the Protestant Church alone. The Kirk was after all a product of the Scottish character itself, and it demonstrated the dichotomy of which Scots are almost proud. Protestantism means the equal freedom of every individual soul in the sight of God. To safeguard that freedom from corruption, we make sure everybody stays in line and that no individual has the arrogance, the blasphemous arrogance, to raise his head above the level of conformist equality.

On top of that, the Westminster Parliament brought in a law as late as the eighteenth century to prohibit theatrical performances for gain anywhere in Britain but London. The histrionic side of the Scottish character was in the wilderness; the douce, mim-mouthed side was grimly in the ascendant. Allan Ramsay might write a rustic verse romance, but it would be read and not played.

When the dramatic Muse raised her menacing head again, there was a marvellously Scots outbreak of panic and piety.

The man inspired was a Scot of spotless respectability, who actually imagined he was serving the stern Scots God by diving into the theatre. John Home was bred to the Christian ministry, and lived a good clean life in Edinburgh. But he had the secret compulsion to write. According to a nineteenth-century commentator, he couldn't see that 'Tragedy, in which are inculcated the principles of virtue, of morality, of filial duty, and of reverence for an overruling Power, could be inconsistent with the profession of a religion in which all these are in the strongest manner enjoined.' He therefore formed a dramatic piece.

The storm burst on him instantly. Elders of the Church learned that he meant to have the thing performed in public, and made urgent visitations on him. They remonstrated, they pleaded, they threatened. Home didn't give a hoot. He too was Presbyterian, with a spiritual certainty of his own as hard as granite. The moralists turned their attention to the performers and menaced them with public disgrace, banishment, anything they could dream up. The performers turned out to be just as stiffnecked as the author.

Douglas: A Tragedy was the show that did go on in Edinburgh. It was a smash. The year was 1757—just two years before the birth of Robert Burns. The ordinary people of the town went wild for it, the Kirk elders went wild. They had Home expelled from the ministry. Anathemas against his friends and colleagues were thundered from pulpits.

Help was at hand for the beleaguered dramatist; and the help, logically enough, consisted of hoisting him out of the Scottish scene altogether and into the easygoing climate of London. The Earl of Bute, who became a Douglas fan, persuaded the Prince of Wales to extend his protection to Home, settle a pension on him and find him a government sinecure in the south. Safely away from Scotland, he wrote several further dramatic pieces and prospered. None of his work after *Douglas* is remembered, but he enjoyed a happy exile.

Douglas itself is fairly terrible to a modern eye. The plot is crudely hand-knitted, the dialogue is overblown and unleavened at the same time, the characters are ludicrous cut-outs. The whole thing is nearly bad enough to be good. It opens with a long conversation between Matilda, Lady Randolph, and her maid Anna, in which the heroine relates The Story So Far and the girl responds with gasps of horror. The Story So Far is that many years ago, Douglas secretly courted Matilda (her father Sir Malcolm would have had him slain as a member of the hated Douglas clan), secretly married her and then went to the wars with her brother, Malcolm; both young men to be killed on the same day. On hearing of his son's death, it seems, the callous Sir Malcolm smiled, because the detested Douglas had died simultaneously.

Concealing her pregnancy, by means never explained, Matilda had her boy-child in secret and sent it away at once with a nurse. Knowing nothing of this, Sir Malcolm eventually forced her into a loveless marriage with Lord Randolph.

After this taradiddle, the play proper begins. Lord Randolph is pretty bored (as well he might be) by his wife's insistence on going about in mourning all the time, and moping about the castle making cryptic speeches. In the meantime he gives hospitality to his kinsman Glenalvon, who has previously tried to murder him, but without being identified. Into this glum mess comes Norval, a strapping young peasant who saves Randolph from a strolling band of assassins and bears a curious resemblance to the long-dead Douglas. Aha!

He is indeed the missing son. But the entire business is kept obscure. The evil Glenalvon seduces Matilda, murders the youth and is himself killed. Matilda hurls herself from a precipice. We are irresistibly reminded of those ringing lines from *That's Entertainment*—

> A great Shakespearean scene
> Where a ghost and a prince meet
> And everyone ends in mincemeat . . .

At the world *première* of *Douglas* in Edinburgh, a voice rose clearly above the tumultuous applause with the historic cry,

'Where's your Willie Shakespeare noo!'

Shakespeare, according to recent reports, is just fine. But whatever his limitations, and they are vast, Home did throw a considerable brick into the stagnant pool of Scottish drama. It sank without trace.

Robert Burns turned his hand to dramatic extravaganza. It is full of fire and humour, but it is not remembered. The drama was a sickly growth. In spite of a few interesting sputters here and there, it is not really a very Scottish thing.

The sputters are fascinating, all the same. Where would the English-speaking world be without Peter Pan? Now there's a curious thing. It is hard to think of any play more overpoweringly English than *Peter Pan*. Nevertheless, it is the creation of a strange, lost Scotsman from Kirriemuir.

James Matthew Barrie was born in the heart of Scotland, in a comfortable little village, in comfortable circumstances. He was well educated in schools all over the country. He had a bright mind, a sharp eye and terrifying energy.

One of his stage characters is required to say, 'There are few more impressive sights in the world than a Scotsman on the make.' He is talking about his creator. J. M. Barrie hurled himself into freelance journalism, sketches, novels. He invaded London like a carpetbagger and made it his own. His personality was a fruitful blend of ruthlessness and vulnerability. He was just over five feet tall, with bow legs and a huge head. In psychological jargon, he had a mother fixation. Amateur Freudians adore *Peter Pan*. George Blake, a successful Scottish 'documentary' novelist and near-contemporary, has described his obsession as less maternal than foetal. He was also a dramatic craftsman of something like genius. His plays remain witty, moving and absolutely efficient, and they are still worth performing.

But like many another Scotsman, he found his success on the broader stage outside his native country. *Peter Pan*, of course, never dies. The reason why Barrie is not adored by all his fellow countrymen has little to do with his sparkling success in world theatre, and a lot to do with his earlier writings, particularly his book of little sketches, *Auld Licht Idylls*, and later *A Window in Thrums*. With these, he gave a great boost to the debased area of Scottish literature known as the Kailyard School, and did no service to Scotland.

The kailyard writers—a goodly body of them, and best forgotten—wrote cute little tales, or vignettes, of a folksy rustic life, and folksy rustic characters totally removed from the real character of Scotland and the Scots at the time. In Barrie's case particularly, the sketches were malicious and derisive. They were a huge success, both in Britain and America. (The American equivalent of 'kailyard' would probably be 'cabbage-patch'). Their effect was to hold up the Scot as a primitive source of amusement for more sophisticated peoples, and to create an enduring caricature of the Scot which has distorted him in the eyes of the world—and sometimes even in his own eyes. The canny Scot, the pawky Scot, the tartan, the haggis and the heather were woven from whole cloth by Barrie and his Schoolmates.

It is not insignificant that the eminent mourners at his funeral in Kirriemuir in 1937 included Sir Harry Lauder, who had followed

faithfully and profitably in the kailyard tradition. It is also interesting, and sad, that the funeral was virtually ignored by the local
people, who never forgave him for holding them up to ridicule. 'He
wasn't a hundred per cent, wasn't a hundred per cent,' one bystander
said; and another, who had to ask a visitor whose cortege he was
watching, then muttered, 'Ach, we never thought much o' him here.'

At the time when Barrie was tasting his first success, another Scot
was being born who would make a quite different mark on his
country's consciousness. Osborne Henry Mavor was the product of a
prosperous industrial family, a sickly child who discovered drama in
his infancy through his own dreams and nightmares and imaginary
terrors. Like the routine lad o' parts, he was already reading greedily
by the time he was four—exciting passages in *Pilgrim's Progress*,
snatches of Shakespeare, and Victorian fairy stories. One of these
which particularly took his fancy, he remembered as an adult, was
all about huge tubs of human gore.

This would have surprised many people who encountered him in
maturity, because he developed into the most urbane, balanced and
kindly of men, and a visible tower of Scottish intellectual society. He
graduated in medicine in 1913, but even before then he had dabbled
in writing and drawing, with skill and originality. He came to some
eminence as a physician, but he was writing all the time, and in time
he had to give himself entirely to the drama.

As James Bridie, he wrote Scottish plays, in Scots. But he wrote in
any area, and he wrote with a volcanic humour and jewel-hard
intellectual power. A friendly critic called his *Baikie Charivari* the
Peer Gynt of Scotland. It was one of more than forty pieces Bridie
produced for the theatre in his fairly short life (he died at sixty-
three). Some of his important work found more acceptance in
London and elsewhere than in his own country. But unlike Barrie,
he remained well rooted in Scotland, and pioneered the creation of
a permanent live theatre in his native Glasgow.

Bridie was a man of great, even excessive generosity to other
writers. When he was an important figure in world theatre, he was
reading several plays a week by struggling unknown dramatists
because he couldn't refuse a kindly service, and his own work was
continually interrupted by people who tracked him down to sit at his
feet or pick his brains.

Many of his works live and revive. Maybe his uniqueness is that
he himself lived surrounded by the respect and affection of brother
Scots. That achievement calls for a big man; and maybe a lot of luck.

14

A
DRAMATIC DOCTOR

(*Criminal Compendium 3*)

ALL THE world was a stage to Doctor Pritchard. The most casual reading of his history evokes the picture of a great ham actor-manager of Victorian times. I have failed to discover whether he wore an astrakhan collar or brandished a silver-knobbed cane, but I would take bets on it. Every room he came into, every pavement he strode, became a fit-up theatre.

Let us pick up his histrionic career in the small hours of a May morning in 1863. The curtain rises on a deserted street in the West End of Glasgow, and out of a dank swirl of Hollywood fog we hear the measured tread of a police constable. As he comes into full view, centre stage, he stops, as if by some sixth sense, and his movements are so unconvincing that we know something real has happened.

Late arrivals begin here.

Something real had happened. Flames were roaring at the attic window of a terrace house, and the officer almost instantly deduced that something was amiss. He rang the bell, and the door was opened at once by Doctor Pritchard, a medical practitioner of eminence and respectability. The doctor didn't wait for a question. He said he could smell smoke from somewhere. The fire brigade was called out, and the fire was extinguished. Unfortunately, the servant girl who occupied the attic room was already dead.

It was just one of those things. The cause of the fire was never discovered. It may well have been an accident. All the same, little accidents did seem to dog the doctor's household; a pity, because he was such a cheerful, outgoing man. Outside of his medical practice, he enjoyed giving lectures about his travels, full of rich local colour and inaccurate biology. He had pictures of himself printed, and persuaded local stationery shops to stock them for sale. He was a genuine character and an ornament to the city.

His wife, Mary Jane Pritchard, did not enjoy Glasgow. She kept being ill, suffering recurrent headaches and sickness. Her mother, who lived in Edinburgh, was so concerned that she wanted Mrs

When James Watt was growing up in the middle eighteenth century the steam engine already existed. It just didn't work very well (*Mansell Collection*)

Today we may question the arrogance of the western races in 'discovering' areas of the world already well known to the local people, but Mungo Park's explorations and writings did open up Africa, for good or ill (*Mansell Collection*)

(*above*) The meeting of Burns and Scott
(*left and right standing*) as imagined by C. M.
Hardie: Scott made his real mark with the
invention of a romantic Scotland nobody had
noticed before – perhaps because it was not
entirely there. In proposing the Immortal
Memory (of Burns) orators speak more sense
and nonsense than has been spoken of any
other man in history except Jesus Christ
(*Mansell Collection*)

(*left*) Robert Louis Stevenson: few novels have
inspired more imitators than his *Treasure Island*
(*Mansell Collection*)

Pritchard to come home for a rest, but the doctor pleaded that he couldn't spare his wife unless grandmother came to Glasgow in her place.

Mrs Taylor, the grandmother, was willing to agree to anything that might help her daughter, and she arrived to manage the Doctor's household while Mrs Pritchard travelled east. The effects were immediate. Mrs Pritchard in Edinburgh recovered her health. Mrs Taylor in Glasgow began to feel awful.

Now the daughter was concerned for the mother. She came back to Glasgow to be by Mrs Taylor's side. Her presence didn't help much. She was soon ill again herself. Dr Pritchard was so perplexed that he called another medico, Dr James Paterson, who lived nearby, to examine both women. When Dr Paterson arrived, Pritchard took him aside for a private chat and warned him that the older woman was drunk, and that she had been secretly swigging Battley's, a patent medicine heavily laced with opium.

Mrs Taylor was certainly not herself. In fact, she was very shortly dead. When her horrified husband rushed from Edinburgh at the news, Dr Pritchard offered his sympathy and promptly sent Mr Taylor to Dr Paterson's house to ask for a death certificate. When Dr Paterson refused to be connected with the business, Pritchard made out the certificate himself, ascribing the death to 'Paralysis, 2 hours. Apoplexy, 1 hour.'

Dr Pritchard then took a little holiday in Edinburgh, and asked Dr Paterson to call on his wife during his absence. Dr Paterson didn't like the look of the patient, and apart from the look, he smelled something suspicious; but not soon enough to avert the death of Mrs Pritchard.

Returning to Glasgow, the bereaved husband bore his grief bravely, and found comfort in the arms of a sixteen-year-old housemaid, Mary McLeod. He was a man of such energy and self-confidence that his career might have gone in almost any direction, but for an anonymous letter to the authorities which resulted in his arrest and conviction for murder.

Pritchard is one of the puzzles in the murder annals. He undoubtedly, and callously, and arrogantly, did away with both women, but he had very little to gain from either death. Perhaps he started the fire that killed the other servant girl. The simplest analysis is that he lived in his own little dream, and that when people became slightly inconvenient, or boring, he pushed them out of his dream.

His other claim to fame is that he was the last person to be hanged publicly in Scotland. The event took place on Glasgow Green, opposite the High Court buildings, on a pleasant July day in 1865.

There was a most satisfactory turn-out of spectators, and although he was not allowed to deliver a lecture to them, he seemed on the whole to be quite pleased with the arrangements.

15

DE HAUT
EN BAS

WE HAVE to deny that Doctor Pritchard was a true Scot; and the reason is, not that he was a murderer (murder is a respectable Scottish institution) but that he was a snob. Snobbery does not exist in Scotland, as any superior person will tell you.

It is peculiarly an English disease. In that country below the border, people are still happy to tug their forelocks to the gentry, the working classes are essentially comic relief characters, and the class structure was created unshakable by God. Why, an English hymn flatly asserts it.

> The rich man in his castle,
> The poor man at his gate,
> God made them, high or lowly,
> And ordered their estate . . .

North of the border, on the other hand, is a race of rugged egalitarians who have no truck with such servile nonsense. The national Bard made it quite clear in *his* lines.

> The rank is but the guinea's stamp
> The man's the gold for a' that . . .

The Scot holds firm to the Burnsian principle, and knows that we are all Jock Tamson's bairns. In the meantime, he goes right ahead keeping up with the McGregors, or ahead of them if possible. In fact, we are as other men, and if snobbery is kept in check by the national habit of disrespect, it bubbles away quite merrily while denying that it's there at all. Small snobbery is a popular pastime. My own view is that small snobbery is a lot of fun, and should be encouraged if possible.

The place where people live is a fruitful source of pride or shame, even here. The major conflict is between the capital city of Edinburgh and the principal city of Glasgow forty miles distant. Each accepts its own superiority. The Edinburgher claims that the only decent thing in Glasgow is the fast railway service to Edinburgh. The Glaswegian dismisses the Edinburgher as cold and thin-blooded. The Edinburgher regards the Glaswegian as foul-mouthed and scruffy.

One analysis is that in Edinburgh, breeding is equated with good form, while in Glasgow it is accepted as good fun. Glasgow's description of Edinburgh hospitality is a householder opening his door to a visitor and crying, 'Come in, come in—you'll have had your tea.'

A variant on the theme is the Edinburgh boarding-house landlady who greets an arriving guest, 'Come in, you'll be hungry!' And she is not making a statement, but a promise.

Even inside Edinburgh, there are clear divisions. Morningside is the district of *la haute snobisme*, which refuses to rub shoulders with Craigmillar. A Morningside lady, window-shopping in Princes Street, found herself being examined by a female person who finally said, 'You're Mrs Mackay from Craigmillar!'

'Quite the contrary!' was the crushing retort.

'I was born in Edinburgh,' said a complacent citizen, 'I live in Edinburgh and I will die in Edinburgh.'

'Man,' said the fellow from Glasgow, 'have you no ambition at all?'

But Glasgow has its own graduations of geographical status. The Kelvinside district is nothing very special, but it is a legendary state of mind to lowlier residents, an area where people speak in genteel or 'pan-loaf' accents and demonstrate their impoverished gentility by having lace curtains on the windows and no sheets on the beds.

The urge to assert one's natural superiority, luckily, permeates all the way down and up. There is a working-class housing project in the East End of Glasgow called Sandyhills built between the wars by the local authority. It is bisected east to west by a little burn, separating one group of houses from another group of identical houses. The first tenants were hardly in before some of them decided that the prestigious name Sandyhills referred exclusively to their side of the burn, and that the other side was properly called Shettleston. Strangers may wonder how one name can be inherently superior to the other. Such strangers do not understand the joys of snobbery. Anything can be superior to anything, if people keep assuring themselves it is.

The town of Greenock on the river Clyde is almost unknown to outsiders, except as a place to hurry through on the way to somewhere else. Its aspect is grey and humble, and travellers see it as a homogeneous sprawl. From the inside, it is quite different. Greenock has a West End and an East End, and ne'er the twain shall meet. A boy from the East End enrolling in Greenock Academy felt compelled to claim that he lived in the West End. When his schoolmates caught him out in the lie, he said, 'Well, I don't live in the East End, I live in central Greenock!' Facing the shameful fact that his home was a tenement apartment, and not a villa, he blustered that it was a very high-class tenement, full of university professors and million-aire industrialists.

The same boy—I knew him well—sometimes spent holidays with an aunt in the unprepossessing town of Kirkcaldy in Fife. He stood in deep awe of this lady because, as he discovered, she was the acknowledged leader of the social set of Kirkcaldy.

Family snobbery does quite well. To some people, Highland names are good, Irish names bad. Many Highland names are also Irish names, as it happens, but such a triviality will not deter the enthusiast. Matrons of inflexible moral rectitude will nevertheless let it slip into conversation that an ancestor was born on the wrong side of the blanket to a viscount or a duke.

An elegant variation of this harmless ploy is the experience of a laird of ancient title who had it pointed out to him that his game-keeper resembled him so closely they might almost be brothers. Intrigued, he summoned the man and asked him if his mother had ever been in service at the Big House.

'No, my lord,' said the gamekeeper, 'but my father was your mother's butler for a while.'

There is a Scottish aristocracy, some of it with quite ancient titles and some of it still quite rich in land and other things. Since it is mostly rural, it does not impinge much on the mass of urban Scots, and can be ignored for most of the time. Apart from its habit of sporting Highland dress on suitable occasions, it is not recognisably Scottish at all, since the landed gentry is nearly always educated in English schools. One of the best received lines in a Glasgow play was, 'Him? He can't be a Scottish laird—he hasn't got an English accent!'

Accent and language are hotbeds of snobbery in Scotland, as they are in some other places. This is a vigorous sport throughout Britain, but the Scots have given it their own peculiar flavour. One reason is that England has for centuries been the dominant partner in the alliance, the seat of government and power and wealth, the metro-politan society. Like the Scottish aristocrat, the Scottish snob thinks of English speech as the speech of good-class people in the south of England, and suspects that local variations in his native country must be corrupt and *déclassé*.

There is always Inverness. The myth is that the Inverness accent is the purest English of all. But as a Glaswegian has pointed out, the Invernesians speak perfect English and nobody can understand them.

Among snobs elsewhere, the battle for social perfection consists in ironing out anything that might be recognised as Scottish and scruffy, whether it's vocabulary or simple pronunciation. The common language is still rich in words of its own, but it is social death to let one of them out by accident, and call an armpit an oxter, or a snib a sneck. A few of us, if keen enough and daft enough, recall that we were told 'me and you' was an impolite usage, and we suspect that the very word 'me' is dangerous; so we say 'a person like I', and 'between you and I', and feel superior.

Sometimes we work by false analogy. If 'swimmin'' is improper, we take the hint and talk about oranges and lemmings, or huming beings. But by that time it's hard to say whether we are taking it seriously or taking the micky. Snob hunters should take care.

But then, snob hunting is a form of snobbery.

16

BACK
AT THE
DRAWING BOARD

FOR INSTANCE, who was William Smith of Aberdeen? The answer is not too important. He was only one of a seething mob of Scottish architects who tried to do something bigger and better, and what he did, principally, was Balmoral Castle, which later became the Scottish home of Queen Victoria. It is a nice, kitsch conception, a fantasy inspired by the fantasies of Walter Scott's writings, suggesting battles long ago and putting them firmly behind it in favour of peace and complacency.

The royal connection gave it enormous respectability, and cheerfully bad architects have imitated its Victorian grandeur in big houses scattered all over the Scottish countryside and even tiny bungalows with ideas above their station. The house even created a word: Balmorality. Balmorality embraces the solid building style and the prim middle-class ethos that went with its time.

No architect laid his hand on the other Scottish style, the Vernacular, which has happily endured in humbler homes for centuries. It is a simple rectangle of local stone, with four windows at the front and four at the back, it makes no pretensions, and it works. Modern architects, who design stark bold *machines-à-habiter*, tend to buy Scottish Vernacular cottages for themselves, put in new wiring and central heating, and feel enormously smug.

But before Smith saw Balmoral completed in 1855, a genuinely creative tribe of Scottish architects had already sprung up and given a lead to anybody who cared to follow it. The lead was followed in places as far removed as Imperial Russia and republican America, and fairly thoroughly ignored in Scotland.

Robert Adam was the kingpin of this feverish family, the second of four brothers who formed a family company and put their stamp on an age. They were born to the profession, sons of William Adam, himself a successful architect with an estate in Kinross-shire. The boys grew up in a time of fairly heavy-handed design. High-class people were thirled to the Palladian style, which was fine but fairly thick.

Robert graduated at Edinburgh and then buried himself in a postgraduate study of Italy, absorbed antique styles at Herculaneum and Pompeii and drank in the Renaissance artists while he formed his own style. He created a neoclassical mode, in building and furniture and decoration, and became the most popular and successful architect in London while he was still in his thirties. He was the foraging Scot, telling the rest of the world how things should be; and the rest of the world had the good sense to believe him.

He encountered the routine financial disaster with the massive speculative building scheme of the Adelphi on the north bank of the Thames. In the life of a man like Adam, these experiences are almost trivial. He went on to fine down his style, create fine town houses in London and Edinburgh, and went on from there to enormous educational and civic buildings. They are still with us, and the name Adam is still a totem.

Meanwhile, back in Edinburgh, something really big was happening in world architecture. The city council was planning an ideal town. City councils all over the world have been doing this ever since. The difference is that Edinburgh got away with it.

The council, in an age when democracy was a fairly rude word, was authoritarian and marvellously corrupt. The members elected themselves. They tended to come from the building and ancillary industries, and they didn't go in for any moralistic nonsense like disqualifying themselves from making a profit out of their civic power. If the city had building jobs to hand out, the councillors handed the jobs to themselves as a matter of duty. Nobody complained very loudly.

Old Edinburgh was a fairly messy place in general. In its time it had known rickety tenements rising to a dozen sordid storeys. There is an exhilarating Scottish dance tune called 'The Flowers of Edinburgh'. It is a beautifully cynical title. The Flowers of Edinburgh was a euphemism for the stinks of Edinburgh. Lacking indoor plumbing, the douce burghers were once in the habit of emptying chamberpots and other domestic utensils from their high windows, with the grudging warning, 'Gardey-loo!' (*Prenez-garde de l'eau*—watch out for the water.) Strolling the streets of the capital was an adventurous undertaking.

By the middle of the eighteenth century, some of the old tenements were showing a tendency to fall down spontaneously, and the far-sighted, calculating city council decided to create a new town beside the old town, and accommodate a better class of people.

Adam brothers were deeply involved in it. And it is a fine achievement. It has made Edinburgh one of the most beautiful cities in

Europe, as far as it goes. What happened in modern times is another story. The New Town is still there, although Edinburgh councils in recent times have considered running motorways through it in order to prepare for the day when the world's supply of oil runs out.

Christopher Wren had hoped for something of the kind in London, but he didn't get much farther than St Paul's Cathedral before his fellow Londoners whisked him into an honourable grave in Westminster and proceeded to make a total mess of their city. The Scots were, briefly, made of more visionary stuff. They planned the New Town, and in the space of seventy-five years they built the New Town.

Town planners today, for the best of reasons, have a bad image. The odium that attaches to them probably more justly belongs to the people who employ them. Anyway, nobody likes them very much. It is interesting to see how that money-grubbing crowd of Edinburgh councillors laid down the simple rules of town planning in 1766.

> The Magistrates and Council are desirous to give all encouragement to such persons as incline to build upon the grounds belonging to the Town upon the north, and propose to feu them with all expedition, according to a scheme to be hereafter made public, for preventing the inconvenience and disadvantages which arise from carrying on building, without regard to order or regularity. This notice is therefore made inviting architects and others to give any plans of a new town, marking out its streets of a proper breadth, and by-lanes, and the best situation for a reservoir, and any other public buildings which may be thought necessary.

No nitpicking there. No pettifogging regulations. All the notice means is: come on, clever fellows, show us a design for a splendid town and you're in business.

The designer they finally chose was James Craig; and there was an Adam brother right in there helping to choose him.

There were arguments about this and that, of course. We are speaking of Scotland. There are always arguments about this and that. According to modern architectural writers, the New Town contained, and contains, serious imperfections. The writers are wrong. The minor inconsistencies of the area make it itself.

John Adam (you can't keep the family out) designed the Exchange Building, to get the squalid noise of commerce off the streets. The merchants stubbornly went on haggling in the open air. It doesn't matter. The Exchange Building is there. So is Register House, designed, oddly enough, by Robert and James Adam.

Other architects managed to push themselves into the New Town boom, jostling between the elbows of the Adam family. The easiest example for a visitor to see plain is now the Royal Bank of Scotland, off St Andrew Square, which was created by Sir William Chambers as a town house for the aristocratic tycoon Sir Laurence Dundas. Sir Laurence was as arrogant and conniving as any of the city councillors. He quietly bought control of the ground where the city had planned to put up a church, and got himself one of the most delightful sites in any city in the world.

Robert Adam himself is seen at his best in his Charlotte Square. Unlike many of the other Edinburgh squares going up nearby, this was designed as a unity, and it would be hard to find any residential corner in Europe to beat it for grace and elegance.

After the New Town came the exuberance of the Victorians, which tasteful Edinburghers today absolutely detest. It is interesting to compare that Royal Bank of Scotland building with its commercial rival the Bank of Scotland, only a hundred yards away. This money palace has all the massive vulgarity that offends the modern aesthete. It is perfectly gorgeous.

What does taste mean, anyway? When Gilbert Scott produced drawings for the new Glasgow University, which was completed in 1870, shudders of horror ran through the critics. He intended to do something odd and exuberant with the main tower, and even put a clock in it. The clock itself offended right-thinking people, and was left out. Even so, in the words of a modern observer, the final design was 'not free of Victorian embellishment'. A grave crime. And, as the same writer added, 'No doubt a modern architect would have made better use of the magnificent site.'

These criticisms were made perhaps thirty or forty years ago. The criticisms are now curiously old fashioned. We have seen what modern architects can do with university designs, and suddenly Scott's extravagant wedding-cake university looks rather good.

But a new Scottish giant was about to emerge and ring his name round the architectural world. Charles Rennie Mackintosh was born in 1868, the same year that the foundation was laid for Glasgow University. Within forty years his genius had flowered and withered.

The great builder in Mackintosh's youth was Alexander ('Greek') Thomson, who discarded the greater excesses of his time and made plain, graceful churches and splendid terraces in Glasgow, some of which have survived that city's passion for bulldozing anything that looks uppity or attracts international attention. The link with Greek Thomson is that the young Mackintosh won the Thomson travelling scholarship, travelled to Italy and began to see his native country clearly from that distance.

What he saw was the Scottish Baronial tradition which he favoured because it was natural and indigenous. He dismissed the great Victorian booms in Greek and Roman imitation because they were uncomfortable imports. It is hard for an ordinary observer to see the connection between Scottish Baronial and what Mackintosh actually produced, but that was the root he recognised.

His best known product is the Glasgow School of Art. It works. After seventy years it still pleases the students. It is a picture as well as a building. It is solid, and light, and the marriage of stone and glass and spidery wrought-iron is as imposing a demonstration of Art Nouveau as the world contains. It was built between 1898 and 1909 and made a profound impression on the Continent at the time.

But in the ten short years of his flowering, he was wildly prolific and wildly versatile. His inventive passion ranged from great buildings down to their furniture and even their door knobs. His chairs have a curious stark elegance. His interior designs are airy and solid at the same time. Everything he did is recognisably Mackintosh, and one reason, sadly, is that he didn't launch a new school of design. It stopped with him. He was an isolated genius, a likeable but broody man, who crammed a lifetime of splendour into ten years and then lost his way. He lived into his fifties, but almost forgotten, and died poor and virtually unnoticed.

But his monuments, or most of them, remain and half a century later his reputation has revived. An Italian company today is making reproductions of Mackintosh furniture, and even his native city has discovered that he was one of its great men.

Compared with this sublimity, the Glasgow tenement is fairly ridiculous, but it would be wrong to look at Scottish architecture and overlook this humble and inescapable phenomenon. We may take it seriously, but without solemnity.

It seems doubtful that any architect ever laid his lordly hands on the design of the Glasgow tenement. To generations of Scots, it is not so much an artifact as a fact of nature, an immemorial landscape. The natives sometimes imagine it was always there, that Picts and Scots fought out their territorial brawls across its back courts and over its wash houses, that the Roman legions marched, apprehensively, in the dangerous shadows of its grimy grey stone.

It is like other tenements: a collection of small houses stuck together horizontally and vertically with stairs leading to its upper apartments. It is also particular.

The main particularity is the Glasgow close. The close is a rectangular hole, or passageway, punched through a tenement building from back to front at intervals. It gives access from the street outside to the open quadrangle inside, and it kinks slightly in the middle to prevent the south-westerlies from whistling straight through, and to provide space for the stairway leading up. It is a simple, functional notion, and no doubt that was how the original designer saw it, if there ever was an original designer. To the tenement denizens of Glasgow, it is something else. It is a way of life.

For some, it was an art gallery. Till recent times, housewives would wash its stone flags—each housewife living up a close does this in strict and legally enforceable rotation—and then take a block of pipeclay, a strange chalky substance of unknown origin, soak it, and use it to draw intricate designs along the edges of its floors. Nobody ever taught anybody those designs. They filtered into the female mind by osmosis, or folk memory, or some other intangible magic. They were pride, they were assertion, they were self-expression, they were impermanent and delightful.

The close was also a survival mechanism for small children faced with the perils of childhood, which mostly consist of other small children. An urchin in flight knew that closes had been built for jouking (dodging) through to avoid mortal combat.

The same urchin probably got his first introduction to legitimate crime by means of the close. Crime is probably the wrong word. I really mean honourable warfare, the permanent hostilities between adult and child that my own tenement generation certainly took for granted. Before the sub-Freudian quacks started poking their clichés into this, there was no such thing as a communication gap between the generations. Adults in the mass, and children in the mass, understood each other perfectly well, and were enemies. It was a completely satisfactory arrangement.

And the close was, among other things, the field of combat. On the simplest level, the child could make a lightning strike by ringing doorbells up a close and running away. This caused no bodily harm to anybody, unless he was caught in the act. It was only a basic ploy in the war of nerves.

More ambitious infants found a piece of stout cord, took it to two doors facing each other across a close, tied the door knockers together, and then kicked one of the doors. Adults could be driven to the edge of madness by this tactic.

Closes—and if there was a designer, he never thought of this— were also efficient echo chambers. With no physical effort, a small child could stand at the entrance, or close-mouth, and just scream; and with any luck, some woman in a flat upstairs would drop a valuable dish.

The back courts enclosed by tenement squares were usually divided into sections by brick walls, marking off each close's territory. These walls themselves provided rudimentary training in mountain climbing, and occasional experience of greenstick fractures, and they nurtured the capacity of survival so essential to the urban Scot. In the days before washing machines, each section also had a brick wash house with a lean-to roof, a chimney and a ventilator.

The intention of the wash house was perfectly practical, if primitive. The whole point of tenement life is that every practical intention was transformed into some odd adventure by the incorrigible human beings who lived in the things. Inside the wash house was an iron boiler. The housewives, again by rotation, took over the place, lit a coal fire under the boiler and boiled their laundry. They poked at it with a stick, were swirled in smoke and steam and usually in a foul temper.

The young generation could then climb furtively on to the wash-house roof and stuff things, or stuff other children, into the chimney or the ventilator.

There was another, sophisticated form of warfare known as clockwork, and it assuredly still happens here and there. It is a nocturnal pursuit, and requires a long length of dark cotton thread, a pin, and a small hard object such as a heavy button or an iron bolt. One end of the thread is tied to the pin. The hard object is fitted to the thread a few inches from the end.

The child then finds a ground-floor window in the back court, sticks the pin into one of the wooden glazing bars and retreats into the darkness with the other end of the thread. A gentle pulling motion taps the button insistently against the window. The housewife, if she has the courage, puts up the window to see who is there. There is nobody there. She closes the window. The tapping starts again.

If she doesn't have the courage to open the window, even better. And if she lives alone and has a nervous disposition, or a weak heart, better still.

Thus the Glasgow tenement, without the *imprimatur* of an eminent architect, has created a social ambience both rich and educational. But there is more to it.

The tenements, and their closes, create a loose but firm community in which people have identities. Since they rise to only three or four storeys, and don't need lifts, the closes and their stairways become like tilted village streets. Neighbours pass one another day by day and pass the time of day. Even if they don't particularly like one another (and they usually do) they know one another. They know, slightly more distantly, the neighbours in nearby closes. They share the same back court. They are together. This creates the same social benefits as the extended tribal family.

A small child, for instance, can be safely let out to play in his own back court, because he is visible there. If a lout from some distant close should stroll into the back court and try, for instance, to damage the infant's gollywog, or his teeth, and the child's mother doesn't happen to be watching, the law of averages enacts that at least two other housewives will be at their windows at that moment, and that they will know the child and recognise the lout as a stranger in the territory.

One of them will open her window and call out, 'I say, young man, kindly unhand that child's gollywog/pram/teeth and return to your own back court.' That at least is the gist of the monologue. And in the experience of generations of Glaswegians, an exhortation from a Glasgow housewife is instantly effective. In this way, the tenement promotes law and order and protects the teeth and gollywogs of small children.

As some of the tenements grow old and feeble, they have been replaced by trendier and bolder architectural systems imported from abroad; great sprawls of suburb and dramatic skyscrapers. In social terms, these are catastrophic, and the sub-Freudians have leapt in, quite properly this time, with such clichés as 'alienation' and 'loss of identity.'

The Scottish tenement, and particularly the Glasgow tenement, is a unique contribution to social architecture. Built by hardnosed entrepreneurs for the purpose of squeezing a lot of people into a small space and making money out of them, it became by chance, and by the adaptation of the tenement dwellers themselves, a form of community-living containing almost everything that a community really needs. While the Scots, who created them, are pulling the tenements down, farsighted foreigners will probably catch on and return to a form of urban planning that makes inner cities worth living in.

17

DEAR MADELEINE

(Criminal Compendium 4)

FOR THE moment, let us leave the earthy ambience of the tenement, and relax in more cultivated company; the *grand bourgeois* purlieus of Glasgow's Victorian West End, and the educated pastime of death by poisoning.

Some people still argue about Madeleine Smith. Men of strong sentiment, and men of strong susceptibility, find it hard to believe that a beautiful young woman can be capable of cold-blooded murder; or maybe they are drawn to one who is capable of it. When Madeleine was standing trial in the High Court in Edinburgh, she had dozens of proposals of marriage from strangers. There is something about a girl who will dare all for love, or hate.

It was a Victorian romance, straight from a bad novel. Madeleine was the daughter of a wealthy Glasgow architect. One of his works, the McLellan Galleries, survives as a monument to his solid skill in the magic thoroughfare of Sauchiehall Street. Madeleine met a penniless Channel Islander, Pierre Emil l'Angelier, in 1855, and they fell pasionately in love. Their prospects were nil. L'Angelier was earning only ten shillings a week. But love dares all, and they met, often and passionately; sometimes with the help of Mary Perry, Madeleine's middle-aged friend and confidante.

The Smiths lived at number 7 Blythswood Square (the house is still standing, and in good condition), and on occasion, Madeleine would slip down to the kitchen in the semi-basement, and Pierre would come to the barred window by appointment and crouch to exchange romantic words with her. They were in a stupor of young desire.

The liaison had been running for over a year when Madeleine encountered William Minnoch, an immensely respectable and eligible young man who lived in the apartment above the Smiths'. Minnoch was greatly drawn to her, as was everybody else. He courted her. She liked it. Her family approved, too. No doubt (I must try not to be too partisan towards a murderess, but it is difficult) it was a relief, it was a comfort to Madeleine, to be admired by a wealthy young merchant, with the approval of the family, in contrast to the febrile delights of muttering through a barred window to a passionate pauper. Star-crossed love is dramatic, conspiracy is exciting. After a time, and I know whereof I speak, both are exhausting.

In January of 1857 she accepted Minnoch's proposal of marriage, and they were formally engaged.

About six weeks later, young l'Angelier had an agonising fit of sickness, after a visit to the romantic window during which Madeleine handed him out a cup of cocoa. Nobody knows how the sickness came about. It is known that Miss Smith had previously tried to buy prussic acid, to make up some curious lotion for her hands; but she failed to get any.

However, three days after Pierre's distressing attack, she did buy an ounce of arsenic from a local chemist—on behalf, she said, of the gardener at the family's country house at Rhu. On the evening after this purchase, her lover had another violent attack of sickness and pain. Madeleine bought a second ounce of arsenic from another shop, this time, she explained, to kill rats in the house at Blythswood Square; and went back for yet another ounce, since the first had been so effective.

In less than a week, l'Angelier turned up at his lodgings one night after twelve, and his landlady answered the bell to find him writhing on the doorstep. She helped him to bed and summoned Mary Perry, his and Madeleine's friend. When Miss Perry arrived, he was dead.

In his pocket was a letter signed 'Mimi'—Madeleine's pseudonym in their torrid correspondence. It was written in terms of wild desire to see him. Miss Perry had no doubt he had responded to the invitation.

Madeleine's deportment during the High Court trial was impeccable. In fact, she was perfectly ravishing. Her family had turned from her in disgust. She bore this rejection with dignity. She was not obliged to speak in her own defence, and in fact was not allowed, because Scottish law at the time compelled the accused in a murder trial to sit silent in the dock. But she made a fine impression.

There were two charges of attempted murder and one of murder. On the first charge the jury acquitted her. The two other counts were found 'Not proven', that odd Scottish verdict that frees the prisoner but can mean nearly anything. According to one commentator, in this case the jury meant, 'Well, if she did it he deserved it.'

It was, in part, a class-conscious trial. The victim was a working-class nobody. The accused was a gently born lady of good family.

Anything that had happened between them was doubtless the man's fault, and guttersnipe seducers are better out of the way. Or maybe the jury was just taken by the beautiful girl in the dock, like all the strangers who were writing those proposals of marriage.

The 'Not proven' verdict has allowed writers in this century to speculate their heads off. There is no doubt l'Angelier was murdered. But since Madeleine was not convicted, is it possible that Mary Perry was the assassin? A spinster, a suppressed Victorian, not equipped to inspire passion but capable of feeling it . . . a woman trying to contain a volcano of sinful lust, and driven to kill the object of her desire in order to save herself? Was it a murder of jealousy?

Not very likely. But the speculation will go on because Madeleine goes on fascinating people, just as people go on being fascinated by Mary Stuart (who is also suspected of complicity in murder).

Rumour and speculation pursued her after her release. She accepted the ostracism of her family with aplomb and moved to London. Her death was reported several times, and various marriages were hinted at. She certainly married once, a Mr Wardle, who was progressive and intellectual, and for a while she presided over a salon in the old style, attended by enthusiasts for socialism and literature. She emigrated to America, and lived into the early days of the movies. Somebody dreamed up a Madeleine Smith film in which the ageing lady would play her young self, but she discreetly refused. She died in her nineties.

Her memory lingers vividly on because she has glamour; which is incidentally an old Scottish word.

THE
JESTERS

Y ES, GLAMOUR explains Madeleine. Terror, yes, callousness, maybe,
foolhardiness for certain. But glamour is what lifts her predica-
ment out of the rut.

We can name it. We cannot define it. No more can we define the
thing, the force, that has given the Scots their comic force, and the
only really indigenous Scottish theatre—vaudeville comedy. For
Scotland's first world figure in theatre came from the music-hall
stage, and it is still impossible to explain what made the master a
master. If you mention the name Harry Lauder in Scotland, in fact,
you will provoke some Scots to spluttering rage and hate. But his
achievement is still there, and it is prodigious.

Lauder was born poor, in a village outside Edinburgh, in 1870.
In his early teens he won a talent competition as a singer, and almost
literally went on to bigger and better things without a setback. He
had the musical equivalent of a better mousetrap, and if the world
didn't beat a path to his door, he was ready to get out on the road
with his wares.

There is no sense in analysing the appeal of a live performer long
dead. If we listen to recordings of Lauder today, all we get is a thin
mechanical shorthand note. We can't transport ourselves back to
the habits and tastes and expectations of another time. Some of
Shakespeare's comedy sequences, after all, read like rubbish today,
because he wasn't writing them for the audience of today. We are
forced to make assumptions from the reports of Lauder's own time,
and the reports are startling.

He was not primarily a comedian. He was a gifted singer, with a
repertoire of songs deliberately limited to what would grip a broad
audience and offend nobody. Love songs were fine—but not melancholy love, or blind passion or desperation. Nice cheerful love songs
were guaranteed. Consider these lines: 'Roamin' in the gloamin',
on the bonny banks o' Clyde;/roamin' in the gloamin' wi' a lassie by
my side;/when the sun has gone to rest, that's the time that I love

best;/oh it's lovely roamin' in the gloamin'.' They are about the ancient mystery of what a man says to a maid, about the most explosive impulse in human experience, they are even about sex. But all the dark undertones are laundered out, and the thing is then wrapped in nice Scottish scenery. The Lauder love lyrics are innocent and pure and, where possible, mildly funny too. His humorous songs, equally, are not going to damage anybody. They are about the small familiar oddities of life.

But this is really a heavy-handed assessment. If we get too high-falutin about the art of Lauder we are in danger of falling into another Scottish trap: the temptation to analyse simple things out of existence. A light entertainer has no obligation to explore the deeps of the spirit. He is entitled to be light. My solemn comments on this international success are merely to indicate the reaction of the anti-Lauder lobby, which blames him for limiting his view of the Scottish thing so closely that it tended to convince the world that everything Scottish was a pawky wee joke.

And he did deliver his wares to the world, and superbly. Some modern Scottish performers find that their very accents make them unacceptable outside the country's borders. Lauder had no such problem. He even exaggerated his accent, he stuck to his rolling r's and couthy Scots phrases, and transcended them. He imposed his Scotland on the English with arrogant aplomb. As a young man, he was already in the star situation where a fast cab waited at the stage door to whisk him round several London theatres each evening; the nearest thing in the pre-broadcasting age to being in several places at the same time. He made a score of American tours, every one a triumph.

He worked hard at the legend of the canny, even the stingy, Scot. Admirers insist that after giving a tiny tip or no tip at all to a menial, in order to maintain the posture publicly, he would seek the man out later and tip him heavily in stealth. Detractors claim that he made a public show of being a skinflint in order to disguise the fact that he was a skinflint.

None of that matters. Lauder, the first popular artiste in Scotland to be knighted, was an electrifying performer with that magic ingredient, the effortless power over audiences, that squashes all intellectual criticism. He was elected to international stardom by the only vote that counts, the voice of the customer. He invented himself, he invented his own style. It has been emulated and imitated by hundreds of others. It still works, even in pale imitations. Masses of Scots, and others, have an unquenchable craving for pawky wee songs and facile tear-jerkers. In this, they don't differ too much from ordinary, non-Scottish human beings.

Will Fyffe is sometimes confused with Sir Harry Lauder. The contrasts are more interesting than the resemblances. Lauder was a singer who told jokes. Fyffe was a comic actor who sang. He did a great deal, but his monument, even in his lifetime, became one song, 'I belong to Glasgow'. It has become the drunk man's international anthem. For anyone who, incredibly, doesn't know the song, it should be explained that it is sung in the character of a mellow-drunk Glaswegian prole who belongs to Glasgow; but after a few drinks on a Saturday, Glasgow belongs to him. It embodies, in fact, one of the prime elements of Scots humour, the underdog's stubborn assertion of the Rights of Man. When Fyffe added a long preamble to it, the song became a complete entertainment. Early recordings of this are still alive after forty years:

> I have been deputed. Deputed! An' not only deputed, but *asked*. To speak on behalf of the working man . . . The rich, driving past in their limousines, point the skinger of forn . . . the skinger of forn . . . at a poor working chap crawling in the gutter. That man is under the affluence of incohol, they say. The affluence of incohol. What about them? They go by so fast nobody knows whether they're drunk or sober. Anyway, what's the poor man to do? He's got to get home, hasn' the . . . You see, when you've had a drink, everybody's your friend. When you're sober . . . you get the terrible feeling everybody's your boss . . .

Scottish humour, even more than Jewish humour, is the humour of the proletariat, the humble working man who is not humble at all. And the real Scottish theatre, the theatre of the people, is the theatre of the comics.

Unlike Lauder, most of the native jesters, like some exotic wines, didn't travel. They didn't need to; their own country could richly support them. But it is nearly impossible to explain or analyse their individual achievements, in an art that leaves no trace except happy memories. When Tommy Lorne died, there was no way of repro-ducing whatever it was that made him magic. Lorne was regarded by many other professionals as the daddy of them all, and his Glasgow public classed him as not short of divine. But the things he said, if written down or spoken by somebody else, are bewilderingly unfunny. His genius was in his presence.

He was long, thin and angular. His body, his face, his voice, comprised an instrument so irresistible that it made any trumpery tune fantastic. With the instrument gone, the music was irrelevant. It is credibly reported that people who saw him simply crossing the street were convulsed with merriment. It would be a waste of time to try to dissect that vanished wonder.

Some of the same power resided in Dave Willis. Willis was short and stocky, with heavy bones. He affected a Chaplin moustache, which doubled usefully as a Hitler moustache during World War II. During his long runs in revues in Glasgow and Edinburgh, immature newspaper critics would sometimes complain that Mr Willis was badly in need of new material. They missed the point that the material was of no importance. He could roll an audience in the aisles by rolling his eyes, and the faithful worked themselves into a giggling frenzy of anticipation when they recognised the trick he was about to perform for the hundredth time.

Willis transformed the walk-down, for instance. The walk-down is the coda to a revue, or a pantomime, when the entire company enters the stage *seriatim*, beginning with the most lowly and cul-minating with the star's triumphal appearance. As Willis did it, the star's triumph collapsed as he dodged about, masked, dwarfed and buffeted by unseeing lines of dancers. At the hundredth repetition it still brought the house down.

His contemporary and admirer Tommy Morgan was another self entire in itself. Morgan was one of many children born to a poor tannery worker in Bridgeton, Glasgow, with an effortless capacity for survival. He once told me he had never been short of a shilling in his life. He grew up burly, sentimental and aggressive, and he hypnotised a generation of Scots by being candidly, arrogantly working class and not giving a damn for any power or principality. On meeting Morgan, one got the impression that if life got tough, he would take it by the throat and shake sense into it.

It did get tough. In the thirties, vaudeville took a nose dive, in Scotland as elsewhere. Little hordes of pros would congregate aim-lessly on fine days at the corner of Sauchiehall Street and Renfield Street, hoping to catch the eye of a midget who had established himself as the Mr Fixit for scarce and underpaid engagements. He offered jobs by a furtive and cryptic system of tictac and permitted nobody actually to speak to him. The Sauchiehall Street talent market would have been one of the funniest sketches in variety if it had not been deadly serious.

Morgan forced his way to the top of the trade, taking his partner Tommy Yorke with him. He invented summer revue in Glasgow. In his time, variety theatres in the city went dark throughout the sum-mer, on the basis that the customers would be on holiday elsewhere. Morgan took the Pavilion Theatre at his own expense, in defiance of gloomy warnings in the profession. The year he chose was 1940, which had a spectacular un-British record of continuous sunshine that virtually bankrupted him. But from 1941, when he bounced back, he was able to fill the house for twenty-six weeks every year and make a fortune.

He played himself, and a terrifying female *alter ego* Big Beenie, whose personality is still recalled with tearful joy by Glaswegians. Other comedians, like the likeable Aberdonian Harry Gordon, richly exploited the traditions of appearing in Dame. Many of them, like Gordon, made their dames works of high art, with spectacular costumes and meticulous make-up. Morgan's Big Beenie was horrible. There was never any doubt that she was a gravel-voiced man, with droopy woollen stockings and elastic-sided carpet slippers. As a prospective GI bride, she ate men. If one of them looked like going too far in amorous dalliance she stopped him short with a brutal gesture and the hoarse catch phrase, 'The ring on the finger first!'

The star who dominated the Glasgow scene throughout the last war and beyond enjoyed his humble origins and the memory of his dismal struggles. During the depression, he and his partner picked up a one-night stand at a cinema in a grim little industrial town. The cinema itself was struggling for survival, and some houses threw in a live act occasionally to lure the trade.

When the lads arrived and asked for their dressing room, the manager showed them to a tin hut behind the theatre. There was no actual stage. A number of bricks had been pulled out of the back wall just under the screen, and the floor was the performance area. There was a cloudburst. On their cue, Morgan and Yorke had to dash from the tin hut across a knee-deep quagmire and make their dramatic entrance by crawling through the hole in the wall. At the end of the act they knelt on the floor and took a bow while crawling out backwards into the cloudburst. From scenes like these old Scotia's grandeur springs. The man who means to triumph in Scotland has to take the rough with the rough.

The era after Morgan saw the theatrical scene in Scotland steadily shrinking. It remained rich in comic talent of the middle-upper level. A good funny man will always make a living in Scotland. It was, however, a generation more before the arrival of another phenomenon as large as . . . no, even larger than Morgan. We are well supplied with good jesters. An entire original is another matter, and Billy Connolly is an entire original.

Again, as with Morgan, the brash aggressive assertion of working-class manners and working-class patois. One additional triumph of Connolly is that although he speaks a natural, coarse Glasgow dialect—a thing that traditionally kills a comedian's chances of winning audiences outside Scotland—he has imposed himself on the English and even the Americans, and he has done it by refusing to compromise or abandon his roots. He began as a folk singer and member of a folk group, strumming stringed instruments and singing demotic ditties; then discovered that there was more mileage in what he said between the songs.

His stage appearance is also uncompromising, and outrageous. He is tall and thin, and compounds this by wearing built-up boots, yellow Wellingtons, suits of lights and a tangled Jesus hair style. It all helps, but what matters is what he says. Connolly does tell jokes; but if he uses a standard joke he converts it into a long short story which is a completely different thing, *sui generis*. He has said, privately, that the idea of analysing humour horrifies him, and will kill humour stone dead. He is wrong, and a brief simple analysis of the Connolly phenomenon will not lose him a single laugh.

At his most characteristic, Billy is cathartic. He has a childlike fascination with the simple facts of nature that most respectable people hesitate to mention even to a psychiatrist. His early idolaters, when he was fairly unknown, were students at Glasgow Art School, who made him their cult figure. Art students have an obligation to be unshockable. When he emerged to face middle-aged and, even more dangerously, middle-class audiences, there must have been tightening of the lips, whitening of the nostrils and clenching of the jaws when he plunged with innocent joy into tales that brandished and celebrated the bowel functions, the desperate need of small boys to have a pee in the middle of the night, and the subtleties of drunk men's vomit. Even putting these things in black and white suggest a crude and nauseating performance.

In the event, it is not. It is more like group therapy. Respectable, carefully inhibited people, jolted against their will into laughter, realise that their secret little shames are not private but universal and therefore okay, so what was all the fuss about?

The analysis is inadequate. Connolly talks about other things. He talks about everything. Everything in human nature astonishes and delights him. In the end, all the same, the man himself is not wholly wrong in being suspicious of people who analyse humour. All of these things are elements in the Connolly performance. By themselves, they would not add up to a phenomenon, without the underlying, the indefinable element. The thing that defies analysis is the individual human being who is doing all this. Connolly is funny.

Another phenomenon has slipped out of this short catalogue because he is a sociological 'sport'. Jack Buchanan's public person had no trace of Scottishness. Like David Niven, Buchanan has charmed his millions by being the archetypal suave, self-deprecating Englishman. This statement implies not the faintest whiff of criticism. His life demonstrates another native talent—versatility and the knack of assimilating.

He was born and raised in the pleasant, affluent little coastal town of Helensburgh, dabbled in amateur theatricals, and as soon as he could, shot to London, where the urbane cosmopolitan butterfly popped out of the Scots chrysalis. Now, the average Scot has a louring hostility to those of his number who get uppity and posh and 'Englified'. Occasionally, somebody gets away with it, and Buchanan did because it was impossible to dislike him or disapprove of him in public or in private. In his one film with Fred Astaire, he absent-mindedly out-acted and out-danced the master. There is no answer to that.

He made another adventitious contribution to entertainment when he found his fellow townsman Logie Baird destitute in London while he wrestled with the improbable invention of television. Buchanan gave him financial comfort and encouragement. We got television.

The performer, however, is the man, and here is one small measure of his achievement. Just as it is nearly impossible to sing 'Mammy' without imitating Al Jolson, it is difficult to sing 'Goodnight Vienna' without echoing Buchanan; the lazy movement, the half-choked nasal twang; ludicrously inadequate equipment for a big song. Nobody worried about that. J. M. Barrie could have been thinking of Jack Buchanan when he wrote this about charm: 'If you have it, you don't need to have anything else; and if you don't have it, it doesn't much matter what else you have.'

19

A
WEE DISASTER

COMEDY is basically a subversion, an act of violence on what we think are established values and universal truths. When it happens in real life, it is quite irresistible. There is always a deep pleasure in the spectacle of somebody high and mighty coming a cropper, and nineteenth-century history provides a specimen of the purest vintage in the 13th Earl of Eglinton. It is equally pleasant to note that the present young earl is alive and well, living in Hampshire and maintaining a family seat near the ancient home area of his ancestors.

The story should briefly sketch in the notable characteristic of the Eglintons, who held one of the most venerable titles in the Scottish aristocracy, and lived up to it like emperors. They had a habit of dying with prodigious loads of debt. One of them had enjoyably run up a bill equal to £125,000 at twentieth-century values. The eleventh of the line pushed his contribution of unpaid bills up to £160,000. The twelfth inherited this lot at the age of fifty-seven after a lifetime of pennypinching, and promptly went on a hectic spree with other people's money.

He demolished the family seat entirely and built another, bigger and better. He was addicted to extravagant civil engineering projects, and poured a fortune into making a new harbour on the Firth of Clyde for the benefit of sailing ships which found difficulty in navigating the upper reaches. It was still in the making when sailing ships became obsolete. A canal which was to link the harbour with the city of Glasgow was never finished.

The old man's sons died while the grandsons were infants. The elder grandson died in childhood. The younger, Archibald William Montgomerie, was brought up by the grandfather, and came to the title in 1819, at the age of seven. He had been outrageously spoiled. After his grandfather's death he renewed contact with his mother, who was remarried to an English baronet. In the care of this couple, the lad went on being spoiled. His stepfather, Sir Charles Lamb, took to the boy, detecting a kindred spirit. Lamb himself was a dedicated drinker and womaniser. He introduced the boy, in his teens, to the pleasures of the flesh, and even passed on some of his own mistresses to extend the young man's education. At fifteen, the young earl found this agreeable and instructive. When he went to Eton, he swiftly enrolled his landlord's daughter as doxy and put back quantities of gin to keep his mind occupied. He became an expert billiards player, and wheedled money out of the estate trustees to run a stud of racehorses.

For his twenty-first birthday he organised an enormous entertainment at Eglinton, in Ayrshire, and sharpened his taste for grandiose shows. His biggest show of all was to be the Eglinton Tournament.

It was a time when practicality and sound business practice were becoming the basic faiths of the new Britain, the rising industrial class was getting into steel and steam and Gradgrindery. The earl was hardly even conscious of any of this. He had a medieval mania, and he decided to electrify society by reviving the great days of jousting. The young bloods of his acquaintance were all for it. Many of them had caught the same infection, and scores of people were digging up ancient titles and laying claim to them. There was a whole industry of experts producing fake evidence to prove these claims. In spite of the black satanic mills making machinery for the modern world, the time was right for a return to the panoply of the lists.

When the earl summoned a meeting to discuss his plan, 150 bold chevaliers attended. Enthusiasm infected the newspapers. It seemed everybody was talking about the tournament. One William Pratt was hired to stage-manage the event, and he went to work with a lot of enthusiasm and not quite so much efficiency. Sprigs of the nobility had themselves fitted for suits of mail and practised getting on and off horses with a couple of hundred pounds of metal on.

Crowds jammed the streets of London to get to the final dress rehearsal in a field of honour near Regents Park. The Metropolitan Police were not amused. The Sheriff of Ayrshire was also unhappy at the prospect of young men poking one another with lances inside his jurisdiction, but the earl managed to convince him that the sport was safer than hunting, and he withdrew his objections.

The great day was fixed for 29 August 1839. Admission to the grounds of Eglinton Castle was to be free, but there was a special enclosure for ticket holders. Hundreds of applications arrived at once, from all over Britain and even outside. They were still pouring in after every seat had been allocated. Special trains were arranged on a newly completed line between Ayr and Irvine. Two steamships brought crowds from Liverpool. Romantically inclined fans set out for Eglinton in every kind of fancy dress to match the occasion. It was a smash.

The original 150 warriors had unfortunately dwindled to thirteen, but it was still enough for a show, with all the trimmings, a Queen of Beauty, gorgeously decorated grandstand, a glittering assembly of high-class people and superb bloodstock. People streamed in by coach and train, on horseback, on foot. The organisers started to get nervous at the sheer success of it all.

The day broke fine and clear. Then a very Scottish thing happened.

There is an old saying in Ayrshire that if you look across the Firth of Clyde and can see the Isle of Arran clearly, it's going to rain; if you can't see it clearly, it's raining.

It rained. A deluge swept across Ayrshire. In genuine medieval times, the doughty knights would probably have called off the nonsense in such weather. But at Eglinton the show had to go on.

Some of the show, at any rate. The preliminary spectacle, with high-born ladies processing splendidly into the lists, was hastily cancelled. Then there was a routine confusion when the knights, and their troops of hired men-at-arms, discovered that when they marched to the castle to assemble, and then marched back to the lists, they were meeting each other on the way. Instead of one gate for inward traffic and another for outward, there was only one gate. Performers in magnificent outfits found themselves scrambling and jostling at the gate like crazed shoppers in a bargain basement. Everything got later and later.

The spectators, having nowhere else to go, stood miserably getting wetter and colder. By now the rain had been joined by a savagely cold Caledonian wind of near gale force.

In the grandstand it became clear that the roof had not been designed with rain in mind. Cascades of water fell on the important people, on the ladies' spectacular *coiffures*, on their beautiful dresses. A court jester hired for the show tried to be funny. Nobody laughed. He stamped off in a rage.

Hours after starting time, the gallant knights finally got round to charging at one another. Nobody knew who they were. Somebody should have been announcing the heroes' names as they appeared, but nobody got round to it, and although they bore their coats of arms, these meant nothing to the spectators.

Watching the champions thundering back and forth, they greeted them first with the sullen boredom guaranteed by a Scottish downpour. Then, too wet and cold to care any more, they started to laugh. The sight of grown men on horseback prancing about in a foot of mud became irresistibly daft.

The catastrophe wasn't over. When the tournament had reached its sodden end, the roads were jammed again with spectators trying to get away. The special train filled and overfilled in a few minutes. Frantic passengers travelled clinging to the outside. Others who hadn't even reached the station looked for shelter behind walls and haystacks and spent the night in the open in their drenched finery.

Since the expenses of an individual knight could run into four figures for the afternoon romp, the total cost of the tournament was stupefying. Lord Eglinton himself jousted well, displayed much dignity and forbearance, and never attempted to blame anybody else for the disaster.

Oh well. That's show business.

20

HANDY CHAPS

A FTER THE chivalric fantasies of Eglinton, it seems cruel to come down to practical Scotsmen who performed the grimy routine of mastering metal and mathematics and machinery. Fear not. The practical fantasies of the Scottish realists are more exciting than the spectacle of wet aristocrats falling off horses.

We do grow up, in this country, in the comfortable knowledge that everything worth a button was invented by brother Scots. We don't know the name of the fellow who built the first wheel, but we are fairly sure he lived in Clydebank. Every great innovation has a recognisably Scottish name attached to it. Radio, of course—Mac-Roni; Russian music—MacOwski; even diplomacy—MacHiavelli.

Even if we push it too far, we have room for complacency. The Scots have indeed shown a meddlesome curiosity about how things work, and a stubborn resolution to make them work better, or at least differently. For such a wee place, we have a good list of inventors.

Teachers in Scottish schools in my own day told, in dead earnest, the story of how young James Watt was sitting at the fire in his humble Greenock home, idly watching steam hissing from a kettle, when a dazzling revelation came to him. He held a teaspoon in the steam, and it was pushed away by the force. In one flash of genius, he had invented steam power.

It's a good story. Readers with access to a kettle and a teaspoon may like to repeat the experiment and they will get nowhere. Steam coming from a kettle doesn't have enough kick in it to move a spider's web.

The truth is a longer story, and all the better for it. When Watt was growing up in the middle of the eighteenth century, the steam engine already existed. It just didn't work very well. The boy had a passion for mechanical things, and got a job at Glasgow University as an instrument maker. With time to spare, and a workshop of his own, he was able to poke into the complexities of steam, and what he did invent was a model with a separate condenser which trebled the efficiency of the thing.

He was nearly forty when his tinkerings came to the attention of Matthew Boulton, an English industrialist, who took him to Birmingham and gave him his head.

Other men with the essential knack were involved in the painstaking business of producing a commercially useful engine. The Englishman John Wilkinson perfected a system of drilling out metal to accurate dimensions and made it possible to produce cylinders that would hold the steam in. The partnership of Boulton and Watt was in business, and very good business.

The early machines were used as stationary engines in the tin mines of Cornwall, and their important limitation was that they could produce only up-and-down movement. The obvious answer to this, as any motorcar engine demonstrates, is to put a crank at the end of the piston and convert up-and-down into circular motion; and the crank was already available. But it was covered by patent, and Watt looked for some other gadget to sidestep the patent complications. It came out in the form of an epicyclic gear train, which may have been suggested by his resourceful assistant William Murdock from Ayrshire.

Watt had suffered from poor health in boyhood, and remained introverted and unsure of himself as a man. His talents might have withered away unfulfilled if he hadn't been liked, and pushed, by vigorous go-getters like Boulton, who was greatly fond of the shy Scot and had more faith in his genius than he had himself. If genius is a function of mental energy, genius is what Watt had. He kept beavering away at new problems and coming up with the right answers; parallel linkages for power transmission, the two-cylinder engine, the centrifugal governor, the pressure gauge. His completely practical, well-trained toil, illuminated by imagination, is a lot more exciting than kettles and teaspoons.

Before typewriters and carbon paper were thought of, he saw that handwritten letters could be duplicated by using a suitable ink and transferring the image under pressure to blank sheets. Well into this century, business offices had elegant cast-iron machines in an odd corner, with a bar bell at the top working a vertical screw to generate the pressure for letter copying and save laborious toil. Not one clerk in ten thousand ever suspected that this ingenious gadget came from the Greenock man who gave the world steam power and the prime mover that launched the first industrial revolution.

William Murdock, that bright assistant who helped Watt with the sun-and-planet gear system, was a notable discoverer in his own right. He was born in Ayrshire and worked as a millwright before he decided that Scotland was too small for his energies. Like his boss, he was interested in every mechanical challenge. There is a story that when he set out for England to seek his fortune, he wore a kind of bowler hat which he had produced on a lathe from a solid block of wood. It must be true.

As well as his work on steam—he spent twenty years in Cornwall putting up the Boulton–Watt engines he had helped to create—he turned his mind to anything he saw. He played with coal at the Birmingham factory and succeeded in extracting gas for lighting, and in 1800 the works themselves installed the first gas-lighting system, and diversified into the gas business. It needed all Murdock's confidence and all Boulton's salesmanship to impose this boon on society. When the process was demonstrated for Members of Parliament, some of them had the horrors because they were convinced that the pipes leading to the gas lamps were themselves full of roaring flame and that a holocaust was only minutes away.

Murdock never stopped inventing. His house was filled with experimental gadgets now forgotten or superseded. But he and his fellow Scot transformed the world they lived in. The Lord said, Let there be light; and Murdock turned on the tap.

Macadam means roads. Tarmac is short for tar-Macadam. Airfields today are surfaced with concrete, but it is still called the tarmac. The original discovery of John Loudoun Macadam, however, did not involve tar. It was simply the realisation that if roads were covered with precisely the right sizes of stones, the weight of vehicles bearing down on them would force the stones together, rather than scattering them. It was a blaze of insight akin to the discovery of cooking.

Macadam did not have to concern himself with inventions. He had left his Ayrshire home at the age of fourteen to work with a relative in New York, and when he returned to Britain a mere thirteen years later, he was a retired merchant with a comfortable fortune. In fact, he enjoyed his retirement for a couple of decades before his obsession with roads took hold of him, and from then on nothing could stand in the way of Macadam's roads. He first took charge of roadworks in Bristol and was later appointed Surveyor-General of Metropolitan Roads, and awarded £10,000, a gigantic sum for the times.

His contemporary Thomas Telford was even more spectacular. The poet Southey christened him the Colossus of Roads, and alternatively the Pontifex Maximus. Telford was the son of a Dumfries-shire shepherd, and served an apprenticeship as a stonemason, which is mildly interesting since he made his name in metal. What dazzled his generation was that he was able to take massive quantities of iron and weave them into spidery fabrics consisting mostly of air. He fairly plastered the British Isles with bridges, over 1,200 of them, and laid down a thousand miles of road. In the intervals he built churches, harbours and canals. Telford was one of those nineteenth-century beavers who knew that his destiny was more important than anything else. His most grandiose undertaking, the linking of the string of inland lochs across Scotland to form the Caledonian Canal, ran millions of pounds over budget, but he blandly demanded the rest of the money, and got it.

Charles Macintosh was of the same generation. It must have been a frenzied time all round. He left school to work as a clerk, but he was swept up in the great self-improvement passion of his age, attended scientific lectures and was in business for himself by the age of twenty, manufacturing sal-ammoniac. He took out several patents in the use of dyestuffs, pioneered a new system for manufacturing chloride of lime, and another for converting iron into steel. In 1823 he was studying the waste products from gasworks in the hope that they might be commercial, when he noticed, by chance, that rubber dissolved on contact with coal-tar naphtha. He immediately went into the clothing business.

The coat that took his name was made from two layers of woollen cloth, sandwiching a sheet of rubber that melted into the fabric. There were little problems. When the tailor's needle bit into the stuff it created perforated seams that let the rain in. The rubber itself in the early macs tended to perish. The coats were as stiff as boards in cold weather, and sticky and horrible in hot weather. People bought them, all the same, and before he died he was able to switch to the newly invented vulcanised rubber. He left a gadget that kept the rain off the just and the unjust.

The Americans are probably entitled to claim Alexander Graham Bell as their own. Movie fans are sometimes uncertain whether it was Bell or Don Ameche who invented the telephone. The Scottish connection is firmly established, all the same. His father, Alexander Melville Bell, was born in Edinburgh, although he did much of his creative work in the United States.

The father's life predicted the son's eventual triumph. He was an educationalist and phonetician who brought scientific analysis to the sounds of human speech, and devised a machine to produce 'visible sound', an optical analogue of speech. Graham Bell too was a native

Thomas Carlyle, 'the prophet of Ecclefechan', author of *The French Revolution* and other works. It is astonishing that anything worth a button came out of this carnaptious egocentric (*Mansell Collection*)

Like R. L. Stevenson, John Buchan is a great spinner of tales and in Richard Hannay he gave us what we wanted – an aristocrat who is elegant, humorous, brave and resourceful (*cartoon by Spy, Mansell Collection*)

of Edinburgh, and he took up where his father had left off. He was a gentle and passionate humanitarian, absorbed in the plight of the deaf, and he worked stubbornly, sometimes in a hostile educational climate, to teach them to communicate. He was tubercular, moved to Canada for his health, and later settled in Boston. It was there that the patient work of two lives produced the machine that mankind has blessed and cursed ever since. The first magnetic telephone of 1876 has changed science irreversibly.

Like Bell, James Young Simpson put his energies into the search for a more humane society. Like many other Scots, he was precocious, an ordinary boy from the village of Bathgate who started his university studies in Edinburgh at the age of fourteen, in 1825. By the time he was twenty-eight he was already Professor of Midwifery.

Scotland cannot claim the discovery of anaesthesia. The human race has had methods of knocking itself out since history began, starting with the caveman's club and running through natural herbs to alcohol, which many people still favour as the easy road to oblivion. Simpson did have the reckless courage to use the newly discovered properties of ether on women in childbirth, and in the climate of his time, it did take courage. The medical establishment just hated anything new. The religious establishment looked up the Book of Genesis and shouted, 'In sorrow thou shalt bring forth children!' Relieving a woman's physical sorrow was clearly a blasphemy. God meant women to suffer, as a punishment for that business with the serpent and the fruit of the tree of the knowledge of good and evil.

Simpson went right ahead.

He did not in truth discover chloroform either. That was done, virtually simultaneously, by two chemists working quite separately in France and Germany. Simpson's contribution was to apply this new palliative to childbirth, and to cause a fresh frenetic outcry by doctors and divines. The hysterical naggers were silenced only when the new drug was used on Queen Victoria at the birth of Prince Leopold in 1853. All the modern advances in anaesthesia stem from Simpson. He didn't invent drugs. He invented compassion.

The lifelong struggle of John Logie Baird is more pathetic, because he spent it patiently exploring a blind alley. But his place in the history of invention is still secure. He did originate television.

As with many other mechanical discoveries, he was but one of many explorers after the same goal. The Russian Nipkov had already produced a little machine, hardly more than a crude toy, that held the secret of transmitting images. It was a disc, with a line of little holes spiralling out from the centre. The disc was on a spindle and could be rotated against another, stationary disc with a square aperture. As the little holes slid past the square aperture, an observer could see that they made up a kind of mosaic of the varying light and shade reflected by an object on the far side. If this variation could be reproduced through another Nipkov scanner turning in synchrony with the first one, television was a fact.

Baird moved from his home in Helensburgh to London, and worked in miserable poverty to transform the crudity of Nipkov's principle into a sophisticated process that would make television a commercial fact; and he succeeded. He was able to return in modest triumph to Scotland and be welcomed at Glasgow University to demonstrate his machine. Local journalists were somewhat baffled and certainly not overwhelmed; but one of them, Jack House, a cub reporter who couldn't understand Logie Baird's explanation and had no shorthand, waited behind to beg for a fuller description. He had just seen the miracle of a doll in one room appearing on a little screen in another room. Being younger and therefore impressionable and conscientious, he skipped lunch and went straight to his office to tell the world. So he had a scoop on another Scottish brainwave that was to change everything.

Mechanical scanning was superseded almost at once by electronic scanning, which was finer, faster, more controllable and capable of limitless improvement and refinement. When the British Broadcasting Corporation tested the two methods, it was forced to choose the rival system.

But Baird had not worked in vain. His painstaking research along the wrong line stimulated all other research into the new medium. With Galileo, he could say *E pur si muove*. And yet it moves.

Alexander Fleming's place in history begins with a scene worthy of a fairly corny movie. The time is 1928. The place is Professor Fleming's laboratory in St Mary's Hospital, London. The hero, a handsome man in his forties with the fine-boned face of the Hollywood intellectual, is busying himself with some routine task when he happens to glance at a culture plate. The camera cuts to a close-up of the plate, and we see that a patch of everyday green mould is steadily growing among the colony of bacteria there. Its presence is pure accident. Doubtless a spore of the mould drifted on the air and settled among the culture.

We now go into a speeded-up film sequence, with sonorous background music and, before our very eyes, the mould expands and kills the villainous staphylococci. Change to close-up of the professor as his eyes widen slightly. He does not actually shout 'Eureka', unless it is a very corny film indeed, but he is thinking something very like Eureka.

In the film, the next scene would be a hospital ward, a patient in a high fever, the hero visibly coming to a firm decision, applying a hypodermic needle, and an incredulous young colleague whispering, 'The fever's down, Professor! It's a miracle!'

It isn't really too bad a script, except that there should be a time lapse of many years between the two scenes. Fleming did see, instantly, the possibilities of *Penicillium notatum* in his laboratory that day in 1928, and instead of being irritated by the interruption of his routine experiment, he pursued the chemical effect by trying penicillin on a variety of bacteria. Some were susceptible to it, others were not, and this in itself was a useful discovery, since the substance could be used to separate some species from others. Fleming did try the stuff as an antiseptic, but it was unreliable and short-lived, and he was unable to isolate the essential element.

As with most advances in science, many other people joined in, notably Florey and Chain at Oxford, and they managed to extract an impure, but enormously concentrated form of the magic ingredient that killed off bacteria. It was found to be an almost perfect antiseptic, doing its work without harming the patient. The later discovery that some individuals have a hostile reaction to penicillin has not reduced its general value.

The large-scale production was left to the superior resources of the United States, and it saved lives on a prodigious scale during World War II. In 1945, Florey and Chain shared with Fleming in the Nobel Prize for medicine; and quite right, too.

A fair number of lives have also been saved by Robert Watson Watt.

On 6 February 1935, a report was submitted to the British Air Ministry, regretting that there was no practical possibility of devising any kind of radiation beam in air defence. Three weeks later, Watson Watt, without being asked, gave the ministry a detailed plan of a large-scale defence system based on radiolocation, later renamed radar.

In a reminiscent article many years later, Watson Watt has given generous credit to other experimenters in the field. Marconi in 1922 had a rudimentary idea of using short-wave reflections from solid objects as a way of avoiding collisions in the dark. Something of the kind had been tried by a German scientist as early as 1903, but his equipment was too primitive to get practical results. Pioneering work started in Germany in 1933, and developed into the Freya system, which produced a few isolated tactical triumphs at the beginning of

World War II. Unfortunately, the German authorities thought it was newfangled and unnecessary nonsense, and its future was stunted.

The British authorities, with a foresight not too common, gave their pioneers a free hand, and when America put her weight behind the new technique, radar was a reality.

Ordinary citizens knew nothing about this. When radar was introduced to the aircraft of the Allies during the war, and produced immediate and dramatic results, the official story was put out that pilots improved their night vision by eating carrots. Apart from his solid achievement in giving radio vision to wartime navigators, and an essential tool to civil navigation in peacetime, Robert Watson Watt was a blessing to market gardeners.

If we drag in Joseph Black at this point, when according to chronology he should be leading the pack, it's partly because his notability is almost a secret known only to people in the scientific trade. But in his way, he may have been the handiest chap of all. Some modern students give him the credit for inventing chemistry. He happened to be born in Bordeaux, but this was merely to be near his mother, who was there at the time. His father spent much of his adult life in France, in the wine trade.

Young Black enrolled at Glasgow University in 1746, and he was still a student when he had his Eureka moment, an event which he treated with traditional Scottish composure. He had been playing about in a purposeful manner with magnesium carbonate. What he did, in fact, was weigh some of the stuff and then heat it, and weigh what was left. The magnesium residue was lighter, and being a logical chap he decided that something had been removed from the compound by heat. This simple observation, since it was made by a genius, provided the very beginnings of chemistry throughout the world.

He reported his findings in his degree thesis. (He got his degree, of course, and promptly acquired another, in medicine, at Edinburgh.) Later, he wrote an extended version on which he called the elusive ingredient 'fixed air'. The Frenchman Lavoisier later renamed it carbonic acid. But this experiment was mainly important as a model of procedure which was taken up by scientists everywhere.

The man himself continued his life in a flurry of busy-ness, as a professor of anatomy and a university lecturer in chemistry and medicine, running a successful medical practice on the side and tinkering with original ideas almost automatically. He was still in his thirties when he discovered latent heat, almost as a casual afterthought. It is an achievement that brings this chapter full circle. It was Black's explanation of latent heat that gave James Watt the basis for making his steam engine and launching the Industrial Revolution.

21

THE
LIFE MAN

JAMES BOSWELL, on the other hand, was a sycophant who created nothing and invented nothing; a parasitic growth on the great Samuel Johnson, an oafish camp-follower scraping his way into history by preserving the crumbs that fell from Johnson's overripe lips.

No! Boswell was a great inventor in his own strange Scots way. If he had been nothing more than an appendage to the Grand Cham, he would still be remarkable. His *Life of Johnson*, to a schoolboy's eyes, is a formless rambling account of trivial incidents involving forgotten people; in which the writer is seen as a blundering adolescent with a genius for saying the wrong thing, and the hero, Doctor Johnson, comes out as an overbearing curmudgeon spouting obsolete prejudices.

That is, of course, exactly the value of the *Life*. The schoolboy's irritation with both characters is the measure of Boswell's achievement in creating character while he seems to do nothing more than scribble unimportant encounters. It is a work of art.

> I told Mr Johnson [Boswell wrote] that I put all sorts of little incidents in it. 'Sir,' said he, 'there is nothing too little for so little a creature as man. It is by studying little things that we attain the great knowledge of having as little misery and as much happiness as possible.'

What the schoolboy doesn't realise is that the *Life* is no more than the iceberg tip of an enormous pile of writing, every piece of which adds to our understanding of a man who told the truth and told it plain. In reading Boswell we get closer to knowing this daft, brilliant, complicated creature than most men get to knowing their own wives.

Although he died in 1795, it is only in this century that the mass of his papers have been unearthed. Earlier scholars had to assume that if they existed at all, they had been destroyed by his family to avoid disgrace.

They had merely been hidden. They survived and in modern times the boy from Auchinleck in Ayrshire has become a growth industry.

Boswell was born in Edinburgh in 1740, with antecedents of terrifying respectability. Even Robert the Bruce appeared on his family tree. His father was an eminent Edinburgh advocate and laird of the large Auchinleck estate in Ayrshire, and was elevated to the High Court bench as Lord Auchinleck when the boy was in his teens. He was an old-school Scotsman of rigid Presbyterian principles, including the divine right of fathers. The boy grew up a nervous creature, shy and tongue-tied, terrified of ghosts, and deeply puritanical.

After an illness in his late teens, he appears to have drunk a Doctor Jekyll potion. He fell in love with the theatre, a shameful thing in the Edinburgh of his time, and fell in love with actresses. Before he was twenty he even wanted to marry one. It was a shocking fall for the son of a judge. He even wrote verses and drank.

He was frantic to escape from the unco-guid atmosphere of his family, and ran away to London when he was twenty, riding hell-for-leather for two and a half days. In London, he joyfully fell into bad company.

Lord Auchinleck was deeply worried when James wrote from the capital, and asked a friend in London to keep an eye on him. The choice of friend was richly ironic. He was the Earl of Eglinton, one of a long line who spent their all in raising decadence to a high art. Boswell found himself in the dizzy whirl of high society and surrounded by easygoing women, and realised that London was for him. His first idea was to get a commission in the Guards. He didn't go the length of wanting to fight. The Guards were permanently stationed in London, handy for all its delights, while other regiments were sent abroad for the inconvenient chore of shooting at people and being shot at.

His father hated the idea. His father probably had a good idea of what James was really after. He persuaded the boy to come home, and played for time. He cannily offered to buy a commission for James in a marching regiment, which wasn't James's idea of fun at all, and persuaded him in the meantime to study law.

The law was all right—James was a facile scholar—but he put more of his energy into collecting literary cronies and writing. He also studied English speech. It was that peculiar time in Scottish history when ambitious natives realised that their tongue was parochial, boorish and un-English. Adam Smith was one of the intellectual darlings of society, and Adam Smith absolutely detested

Scotticisms in speech. Thomas Sheridan, father of the playwright, made a pretty packet from lecturing on proper elocution to the Edinburgh aborigines, and Boswell thought he was great. Like the eminent Adam Smith and many other compatriots, he realised that there was something shameful about not being English. He still lusted for London, of course, and wanted to be able to hold his head up in fashionable society there. Much later, when he first met Samuel Johnson, his first words to the Great Cham were, 'Indeed, I come from Scotland, but I cannot help it.'

Sheridan took to the boy. When we read Boswell's works we are regularly brought up against his contempt for himself, and his conviction of worthlessness. The fact also comes through that people liked him. He was constantly befriended by strangers.

He eventually wore his father down, and was allowed to go to London with a modest allowance. He was spiritually home, and was interminably recording everything that happened to him, in his *London Journal;* and it does read like absolutely everything, as if he were constantly recording a running commentary throughout his waking minutes. He was not, of course. But he left out nothing worth remembering, and the 'little things' range from mellow philosophical chats to roaring passion.

> Lord Eglinton and Sir James disputed about vanity. Sir James said it always made a man disagreeable. My Lord said vanity did not, because a vain man in order to be flattered always pays you great court. But a great man despises you. The vain man piques himself on some qualities which you must know and admire. The proud man piques himself on being quite above you; so the lower he can thrust you, the higher he is himself; and of all things a purse-proud man is the most terrible. Sir James mentioned a disagreeable pride of understanding, which I thought very applicable to myself . . .

A few pages later, James is recounting a meeting with the young actress he calls Louisa.

> I came softly into the room, and in a sweet delirium slipped into bed and was immediately clasped in her snowy arms and pressed to her milk-white bosom. Good heavens, what a loose did we give to amorous dalliance! . . . I was in full glow of health. Sobriety had preserved me from effeminacy and weakness, and my bounding blood beat quick and high alarms. A more voluptuous night I never enjoyed. Five times was I fairly lost in supreme rapture. Louisa was madly fond of me; she declared I

was a prodigy, and asked me if this was not extraordinary for human nature. I said twice as much might be, but this was not, although in my own mind I was somewhat proud of my performance . . . She said it was what we had in common with the beasts. I said no. For we had it highly improved by the pleasures of sentiment. I asked her what she thought enough. She gently chid me for asking such questions, but said two times . . .

The triumph of Boswell is that everything made an impression on him. At the age of twenty-five he visited Corsica, mainly because most people at the time did not visit Corsica. The holiday trip turned him into a fervent pro-Corsican and made his name in London. The islanders were in the throes of a struggle for independence, and Boswell, who had gone through all that himself, became their champion. Back in London he published passionate articles on their plight, raised money to help them, and finally wrote his *Account of Corsica*. It was a success, ran to several editions and was translated into four languages. In a modest way, it influenced the actions of governments; and although Boswell regarded Dr Johnson with something not far short of idolatry, his own name was as well known in Europe as the great man's.

He was certainly servile to Johnson, and when he did occasionally bandy words with the master, he was usually crushed, and faithfully recorded his humiliation. But if Boswell had never lived, hardly anybody today would remember Johnson. Johnson's own writing was interesting enough but less than great. He deserves the fullest credit for his pioneer English dictionary. But his greatest work was his conversation, and every man who has ever cracked an original joke must wish that he had a Boswell at his elbow to preserve it for all time. Since Boswell lived, Samuel Johnson lives.

Why, sir, Sherry [Thomas Sheridan] is dull, naturally dull; but it must have taken a great deal of pains to become what we now see him. Such an excess of stupidity, Sir, is not in Nature.

Sir, a woman's preaching is like a dog's walking on his hind legs. It is not done well; but you are surprised to find it done at all.

Patriotism is the last refuge of a scoundrel.

Depend upon it, Sir, when a man knows he is to be hanged in a fortnight, it concentrates his mind wonderfully.

These are some of the spoken words of Samuel Johnson. With Shakespeare and Chesterton, he is one of the most quotable and quoted men in the language; but Shakespeare and Chesterton put their luminous thoughts on paper. Johnson's were written on the wind, but for Boswell.

There has not been anything quite like Boswell, and there will not be anything quite like Boswell. The eager, randy, ragamuffin intellectual created an art form out of nothing in particular, and the secret died with him.

22

THE
SCOTTISH GOD

A T HIS BEST, or sometimes at his worst, the Scot likes a passionate
creed to live by. It need not always be logical; just so long as it is
passionate. It is still possible to raise a laugh in Glasgow by declaring:
'Two things I abominate—religious intolerance, and Catholics.'

This fervour has a colourful background in which the predominant
hue is the red of human blood. For all its poverty, and lack of
population, the country was usually able to generate as much high-
principled savagery as any wealthy European kingdom.

The causes of the Protestant Reformation were the same in Scotland as elsewhere. The established Roman Catholic Church had
become flabby, mercenary and venal. The priests were fat and rich,
their flocks were poor and neglected. The plums in the Church were
awarded not for piety or conscientious toil, but for knowing the right
people. At the beginning of the sixteenth century, the lush Arch-
bishopric of St Andrews was awarded to one Alexander Stewart for
no reason except that he was a close relative of the king. Stewart was
thirteen years old when he was elevated.

Honest prelates, who still adored the Church and detested the
doctrines of Martin Luther, the Protestant rebel of Germany, still
recognised that radical reforms were needed, without changing
structure or dogma. But the Lutheran heresies appealed to reckless
outsiders like Patrick Hamilton, who preached a return to the Bible
itself, and a dismissal of the customs and canons of Rome. In 1528
he was arrested on the orders of Cardinal Beaton, by then Archbishop
of St Andrews, and burned as a heretic outside St Salvator's College.
The ceremony lasted six hours, and did nothing for Beaton's beastly
reputation, but he survived the public disgust.

Twenty years later he passed the same sentence on George Wishart,
who had dared to preach against him personally. Wishart died at
the stake in front of St Andrews Castle, while the Cardinal watched
in comfort from a convenient window.

Murder generated murder. A few weeks later a band of Wishart's supporters swept into the castle brandishing swords and surrounded Beaton in his bedchamber. 'I am a priest, I am a priest,' the cardinal screamed. 'You will not slay me!'

They did.

On his evangelistic tours, Wishart had usually travelled with a bodyguard, a thick-set little man who stood beside him with a great two-handed sword. Wishart ordered him to flee and save himself when he knew he was about to be arrested. He obeyed unwillingly, and lived to fight many other days and turn Scottish religion on its ear. His name was John Knox.

Knox was a teacher by trade, but in his time there was no great distinction between teacher and preacher. He was a curious, complex man. His simplest characteristics were courage and a rock-hard belief in himself and in reform. In the more tolerant atmosphere following Beaton's death, he stumped the district calling for an end to Romish practices, and administering Holy Communion in the style of the European Protestants. He was among the reformers captured by a French Catholic invasion force in St Andrews in 1547, and spent two years as a galley slave without changing his opinions by a comma. He was erudite enough, and forceful enough, to find a job in England, as tutor to Edward VI, but when the Catholic Mary Tudor succeeded Edward he left for Geneva.

Geneva was the centre of the new faith, and John Calvin was its prophet and master. Knox met and admired him, and was delighted with the Protestant Utopia Calvin had created in Switzerland, impregnated with learning, and austerity, and law and order. As is common when political authority is combined with ideological rectitude, the penal code was a no-nonsense affair. At the more trivial end of the scale, a child who struck a parent had the offending hand cut off.

Back in Scotland, the situation continued to be confused and exasperating. The country had an infant queen, Mary, who was being raised in France while her mother, Mary of Guise, acted as Scottish regent in the style of a good Roman Catholic. She was in fact a fairly tolerant woman, but the prelates under her retained a wee touch of the Beatons, and pursued blasphemy and heresy with dedicated gusto. Some of the Scottish lords had become infected with the new Protestantism, and they were too big to punish, but ordinary dissidents were still brought to heel by the traditional process, including Walter Myln, who was put to the fire at the age of eighty-two. This provoked the routine Scottish revulsion.

Knox came back home and found wide support for the new, spare, anti-Roman form of church service. At one church in Perth, a priest cuffed a small boy for shouting at him, and the child threw a stone at him. It missed, and struck an ornament on the altar. The congregation were inspired by this blow against popery, and in no time churches all over Scotland were being vandalised and ripped apart and even demolished. Knox himself called the new enthusiasts 'the rascall multitude', but even he couldn't stop the destruction.

This perverted form of Knoxian reform pushed Presbyterianism along the road to Philistinism, and helped to confirm the idea that in religion, or anywhere else, anything that was ornate, or beautiful, or fun, was an abomination in the sight of the Lord. Even music became suspect, unless it was stripped of every embellishment and reduced to an unaccompanied precentor singing each line of a metrical psalm, followed by the congregation repeating it. This is a truly mournful exercise; and the metrical psalms themselves, hammered into rhymed quatrains by a Cornishman, are often limp and leaden-footed. But they suited the converted.

The later tussles between the old and new religions sometimes evoked dignified courage on both sides, sometimes pigheaded absurdity, and often viciousness. When Mary Queen of Scots arrived in Edinburgh in 1561 to take the throne, she was a beautiful, naïve, Roman Catholic nineteen year old. She had no prejudice against Scots who preferred the reformed faith. She had some difficulty in asserting her right to worship in her own way. Knox, who cared nothing for secular authority, harangued her regularly, and at enormous length, about the evils of the papacy, but his thunderings passed her by. The two were like creatures from different planets. But the new Kirk was forging ahead in any case. Knox replaced the hierarchy of the bishops by organising the Church into representative assemblies, power from the bottom up. This is the structure of the Presbyterian Church to this day, but there was still dissension and persecution and blood ahead of it.

Mary passed from the scene when she took refuge with her cousin Queen Elizabeth in England during a little civil war, and was judicially murdered after long years of imprisonment.

She had one son, to Henry Stuart, Lord Darnley, a petulant popinjay of the Scottish nobility. As James VI, the child inherited the English throne and became James I of England in 1603. Working from London, he furtively restored bishops to the Scottish Church, but his orders to restore Roman forms were generally ignored. His son Charles I, who displayed much of the myopic stupidity of the Stuarts, tried to push the Roman line harder, and his rebellious subjects drew up the National Covenant, a Presbyterian act of faith.

Charles II went further, and made it an offence to stay away from church. Some of the more fervent covenanters marched on Edinburgh to protest. They were chased and captured by troops. Thirty were hanged and the rest sent to slavery in the colonies.

The faithful, strengthened by anger and righteousness, took to holding their own church services out of doors, in the remote hills, where they were pursued, sometimes found and hacked down, by the king's troops. James II, the next Stuart king, was even more mulish and stupid, and declared the covenant treason, punishable by death. He was overthrown in a particularly silly war, and William of Orange came to the throne.

William had no time for religious factionalism. The passionate Presbyterians expected him, exhorted him, to establish their faith everywhere, persecute the Catholics and the Episcopalians and drive their evil practices from the earth. He simply couldn't be bothered with this new bigotry. He wanted peace, and the Protestants, who had hoped for power, had to put up with it.

In spite of that, William of Orange remains as a heroic legend to Protestants who have not read history—William, and the Battle of the Boyne, in which he routed James's forces in Northern Ireland. To William himself, this was a military exercise. To the faithful, it was the peak of a religious crusade to overthrow popery. William had no idea he was being turned into a nonconformist saint. He had Roman Catholic troops fighting for him at the time. Before he came to Britain, he had enjoyed the most friendly relations with the Catholic Church, lived in monasteries when he was travelling, and made generous gifts to religious orders. In the description of one historian, 'a wise and tolerant prince'.

But people who need a myth will find a myth. Today, King William is the cult figure of the resolute band of Protestants organised in the Loyal Orange Order. Many of the non-Catholic residents of Ulster at the time of the Boyne were colonists from Scotland. Ulster in turn created, and gave to Scotland, the tradition of the Orangemen, whose battlecry 'No Surrender' means no surrender to the power of Rome, and who preserve the old fervour in such songs as,

> King Billy slew the Papish crew
> At the Battle o' Boyne Water . . .

In Ulster itself, the folk memory, both bitter and twisted, has provoked a response equally bitter and twisted and made the province a tragic battleground. The Scots, magically, have contrived to nurse old suspicions and keep their senses at the same time.

The suspicions are pathetic. They would probably have petered out, but for the mass immigration of penniless Roman Catholics from Southern Ireland during Victorian times. Ireland was a subsistent peasant economy, crazily dependent on a single food crop, the potato. In the 1840s, potato blight swept the island and ruined it. The fatuous negligence of the British Government speeded the ruin. Hunger and death ravaged the island. Energetic survivors left Ireland altogether, for America, England, Scotland.

In Scotland, especially in the south west, the influx created anew the old hostilities. The newcomers were clearly alien, they were Roman Catholics, many could not even speak English, they had big families and they were prepared to work for low wages and undercut the native working class. In the meantime, the Irish who remained in Ireland had started their struggle for independence from Britain, the subversive Fenian movement was growing. The inoffensive Irish Catholics who came to Scotland were regarded impartially as Fenians and probably dangerous.

Generations later, they have assimilated. It is not possible, as some belligerent Protestants claim it is, to recognise a Roman Catholic at twenty paces by his face. Outside the lunatic fringes, Protestant and Catholic live at peace, and there is a vigorous movement among the clergy for conciliation. The lunatic fringes are quite spectacular, all the same. They are visible principally in the support of Scotland's two premier football teams, Glasgow Rangers and Glasgow Celtic, whose dafter fans drink themselves into savagery at big games and damage one another. However, considering the violence that disfigures football in England and elsewhere, it is hard to blame religious fervour as the single cause of the Rangers–Celtic feud. Some people enjoy feuds and fights. They will find reasons for them.

Scotland is fairly unusual in having separate schools for Catholics. These are the product of an act of unusual tolerance by which Scottish local authorities maintain particular schools to be administered by the Catholic community, for the protection of the Catholic faith. Arguments have raged round them in recent years. They are accused of fortifying old enmity and increasing old divisions. They are defended by Catholics who see them as necessary safeguards in a Godless age. Some chaplains in the Catholic schools find that their adolescent charges are more Godless than their parents, regardless. The controversy will go on. In a way, Scotland needs it.

There are only a few thousand Jews in Scotland, descendants of the fugitives from European pogroms. They keep up the Jewish family-tribal tradition. Most of them live in the Glasgow area. As well as maintaining their own ancient faith and their own churches, they are involved in the general community. There has never been any noticeable anti-Semitism in Scotland. The Scottish Jews consider it to be the most tolerant country in the world.

More recently, immigration from Pakistan has brought Islam. The Pakistanis are more easily recognisable as incomers than other arrivals. They too enjoy an easy tolerance in their adoptive country. There is a saying that nobody objects to Muslims, unless they're Catholic Muslims.

The mainstream Protestant faith is alive and kicking, and the Church of Scotland would not actually offend John Knox too deeply if he could see it today. It is organised on the lines he himself laid down. The power rests with the people. Ministers are not appointed to parishes from above but, in principle at least, elected by the congregation. Decisions on Kirk policy are made by a parliament known as the General Assembly meeting once a year in Edinburgh, and it is presided over by a Moderator who is a perfectly ordinary minister elected to the supreme office for one year only. At the end of that year he returns to his parish duties.

Certainly Knox might jib at the amount of tolerance that has crept into the Church. Congregations sing to organ music, and quite nice ornamentation has appeared, to soften the stark austerity; stained glass windows, even. But all this has been done with the consent and approval of the humble parishioner, and that is the real point. Knox's Church was founded on democracy, and democratic pioneers can't complain if the people want their own way.

The Free Church would seem more familiar to the great democrat. Still strong in the Highlands, the Free Church has set its face against fripperies. It lives by the Word and has no truck with modern decadence, like whistling on the Sabbath. In many fundamental ways, in fact, the rigorous adherents of the Free Church cleave to a faith that is largely Judaic rather than Christian. They don't like crucifixes, they are suspicious of Christmas as a Romish rite, and they accept the Old Testament as literal truth. They do not so much cope with the facts of modern life as dismiss them.

Since the Protestant creed is that every man is in direct touch with God, it is natural that different men may get different messages from the Deity; especially different Scotsmen. So there has been a lively history of schism and fission. In the nineteenth century, two brothers Erskine rebelled against what they felt were the slipshod habits into which their church had fallen.

They walked out, and took a sizeable congregation with them into the wilderness, or promised land. In no time, the brothers themselves disagreed about whether their adherents should take the Burgher's Oath (a question which is too obscure and trivial to deserve lengthy explanation—if it hadn't been the Burgher's Oath it would have been something else). They and their followers split into two separate bodies, the Burghers and the anti-Burghers.

New controversies racked both churches. Each of them split into warring factions known as the Auld Licht and the New Licht. There were now four Erskinite churches, each possessing the only true gospel. In each of them, arguments arose over a minute element of ritual known as Lifting. The Lifters and the non-Lifters turned their backs on one another to form separate congregations.

In the words of an eminent modern divine, the Reverend Andrew Herron, a Scotsman who was an Erskinite, anti-Burgher, New Licht, non-Lifter, must have been the ultimate in individualism and dissent; and very very Scots.

There is an old tale of a Presbyterian who was cast away alone on a desert island, and rescued after a lapse of years. He had got everything properly organised, built an austere but habitable bungalow, and two small churches.

'Why the second church?' he was asked.

'Oh, that's the one I don't go to.'

(*above*) Contemporary portrayal of an historic meeting: 'Dr Livingstone, I presume?'. Stanley on left, Livingstone, right (*Mansell Collection*). (*right*) John Paul Jones shooting a sailor who had tried to strike his colours in an engagement (*from a picture by John Collet, Mansell Collection*)

Andrew Carnegie didn't make steel or railroads; he made money (*Mansell Collection*)

23

SWING
CRAZY

A T ABOUT the same age when I was suffering the trivialities of
James Boswell, and writing off Sam Johnson as an ill-tempered
old trout who was not merely boring, but English to a fault, another
Scottish phenomenon was forcing itself on me, and I couldn't stand
it at the time.

Like Boswell, it was unpredictable. Like Boswell, it made no
obvious sense. Like Boswell, it was stupefyingly boring. It was designed, like so many other national products, to induce madness in
the natives and in the world at large.

A few years later I went into partnership with a newspaper sub-
editor whose hobby was training lions, and we formed the Anti-Golf
League in a Glasgow newspaper office. I suppose it was not golf itself
that enraged us, but golfers, who are even more boring than the
game itself; and we were surrounded by them. We briefly considered
a serious campaign against the game, like recruiting other crusaders
to lie on fairways, or put noisome engines in holes. But we were
essentially intellectuals, and therefore indolent and cowardly, and we
concentrated on a literary campaign on the office noticeboard, where we
posted hurtful aphorisms such as GOLF EQUALS LINKS PLUS MISSING LINKS,
and paraphrasing Oscar Wilde: GOLF IS THE ATTACK ON THE UNEATABLE
BY THE UNSPEAKABLE and GOLFERS SHOULD SWING FOR IT.

One day the president of the league came into the office without
any of his lions, and he was cornered by the most boring golfer on
the staff, a man with bulging veins, white nostrils and a skull of solid
teak, who snarled, 'If you looked through enough books you could
get quotations in favour of golf!' Since the leisure of this oaf was
completely filled with golf and with talking about golf, he had not
himself read a book. But in his moronic way, he was right. It isn't
only golf that has become a global industry. The making of books
about golf is even bigger.

So is the making of golf jokes, and if the world owes Scotland
nothing else, it is under a deep debt for a lot of laughs.

'I had a miserable experience last Friday—old Charlie had a coronary and dropped dead on the fifth tee.'

'My God—what did you do?'

'Well, from then on it was hit the ball, drag Charlie, hit the ball, drag Charlie . . .'

There is also the ultimate definition of unpopularity in the dialogue:

'Any chance of a game on Sunday, Hugh?'

'Sorry, Dick, we've already made up a three.'

Like all basically absurd things, the game is also infinitely solemn, and perhaps even purges the soul, if golfers have souls. Saint Peter glanced down from Heaven one Sabbath morning and called God's attention to a Free Presbyterian minister, on holiday far from his parish and sneaking out to play a round on his own. A thunderbolt, Peter thought, would be in order.

'No no,' said God. 'Off the next tee I'll give him a hole in one.'

'But that's no punishment.'

'Who can he ever *tell*?'

Men were hitting balls with sticks before history was recorded. It is possible that Belgians were doing it formally and competitively ten centuries ago. It is possible that the Chinese were at it even earlier, since most things are ascribed to the Chinese. The ascriptions are in error since, as we know, the Scots invented everything.

They did invent the game as we know and fear it. Two centuries before Cromwell prohibited games in England because they diverted young men from the practice of arms, the Scottish Parliament had put a ban on golf, presumably for the same reason. As America discovered during Prohibition, the ban merely added to an already hypnotic pursuit—the sweetness of forbidden fruit. James IV, the grandfather of Mary Queen of Scots, finally had a go at the sport himself, and his son had a golf course made for him. When Mary's son ascended the joint English–Scottish throne in 1603 he took the game with him to London, and the English have never been the same since, either.

The original game was fairly formless. Fanatics walloped a small object, roughly spherical, over any moors or meadows available, rather like Americans in the current craze for orienteering or point-to-point golf; and from time to time they dug a hole and tried to steer the ball into it. Like all the genuinely worthwhile and thera-peutic activities of mankind, the process is revealed as fatuous, futile and fruitless when subjected to pseudo-logical analysis. But the only legitimate criterion for any human activity is: do people like doing it?

By the seventeenth century, formal golf courses were beginning to appear in Scotland and the south of England. Golf balls could then be imported from Holland, which might suggest that the Dutch were into the game just as early, or earlier. Such a suggestion will be ignored in this book. So will the delusion, enjoyed by some Englishmen, that the whole thing started there. Such claims are as absurd as the heretical notion that the Greeks invented the kilt.

The early balls were 'featheries', fairly horrible little objects manufactured by a ludicrously cumbersome and painful process. The artisan sewed several bits of leather together into something resembling a sphere, which he then 'flyped' through a small gap in the stitching. *Flype* is the crisp Scots word for turning inside out.

To his chest he attached a bit of wood with a hemispherical dent in it. The leather purse was pressed into this hole, and the man took a great heap of goose feathers and proceeded to ram them through the tiny gap in the stitching with a metal rod. It was agony.

When the ball was stuffed with more feathers than physical science would believe possible, the gap in the stitching was sewn shut, and he was left with a golf ball and a fearful bruise on his chest. The ball was clouted over the Scottish scenery by aficionados wielding things like hockey sticks. Then came the brilliant Scottish trick of carrying more than one of these implements, each with a different slope on the striking surface in order to vary the trajectory of the ball, and the world was set for its plunge into the true insanity of golf, its crazy subtleties and its proliferation of gadgets and cure-alls.

The pioneer golf organisation is the Honourable Company of Edinburgh golfers, which was created as a loose organisation in 1744 and formalised twenty years later. It drew up the first set of rules in what had been a free-for-all game. At St Andrews, a group got together in 1754.

But for well over a century the sweet madness was very much a minority pastime. Britain was edging into the expansive years of the Industrial Revolution, but the new wealth was a minority pastime too. By the middle of the nineteenth century there were only a few dozen clubs scattered over Britain, and they were confined to the upper classes, who introduced pleasantly daft and very Victorian social conventions into their ritual, and dressed up in popinjay uniforms to display their superiority to the common ruck of toiling mankind.

The 'gutty ball', still remembered affectionately by elderly golf bores, arrived around that time. It was a homogeneous structure made simply by moulding gutta-percha into a sphere, and was a miraculous boon to the chest bones of ball makers. It was also tougher and more durable than the feathery, and golfers started hitting it with clubs with iron heads.

Fifty years later, towards the turn of the century, the rubber-core ball arrived. It was invented by an American. Well, the Scots can't be expected to originate every little detail, when they are concerned with the great sweep of golfing history.

Well into this century, the standard golf implement, whether with a wood or iron head, had a shaft of hickory wood, and mighty deeds were done with these rigid clubs, though they transmitted the impact of a mishit with the speed of radio waves through the player's hand and up to his clavicle and left him clanging like a brass gong. Scottish know-how had to find something better. It did, and it is one of the sad little stories of golf history and an interesting reflection of the Scottish thing.

By this century, St Andrews, although its golf club was a Johnny-come-lately beside the Honourable Edinburgh, was established as the home of golf, the shrine, the mount from which tablets of stone descended to teach the faithful all over the world the way they should go. The Royal and Ancient was, and is, the only true prophet. It is also very Scots and very canny and will rarely leap before it looks. In the 1950s, for instance, it went into a dignified panic when an American woman golfer proposed to enter for the Open, and compete on level terms with the men who had always had that venerable contest to themselves. The thing had never even been considered a possibility when golf was growing up, and since nobody legislates against an unthinkable possibility, the rules did not actually prohibit such blasphemy.

The committee deliberated long and conscientiously and decreed that, interpreting the spirit of the law, it had to turn the lady down. Writing at the time, I applauded this judgement on these simple grounds: women are smaller than men, frailer than men, probably less intelligent than men, and less competitive than men; and they must be discouraged from matching their prowess against men in open combat, in case they win.

Some years before, during the last war, I had encountered the story of Tom Horsburgh, an elderly Edinburgh gentleman and lifelong golf maniac, who had also suffered disappointment. In his prime, he bent his mind to the business of the hickory club, and produced a replacement with a tubular steel shaft, splendidly resilient and whippy and unbreakable. He took out a patent and waited to become a millionaire. He reckoned without the caution that soon pervades any newfangled Scottish institution.

The Royal and Ancient deliberated even longer over his innovation. Much was at stake, including perhaps mass unemployment in the hickory forest industry. The deliberations went on so long that Mr Horsburgh accepted defeat and let the preliminary patent run out.

Almost instantly, the Americans seized on the idea and started experimenting with steel tubes. They were so good that an industry sprang up. Golfers across the Atlantic bought the new clubs in hundreds, thousands, and played with them. The steel shaft proliferated in such numbers that it was clearly impossible to reverse its tide. The R & A sensibly accepted the reality of the situation and sanctioned the new design. This gave some wry satisfaction to Tom Horsburgh who, as I have said, was a gentleman and never complained; thus demonstrating the other Scot characteristic, of stoic acceptance.

The American triumph echoes the history of the game of golf itself. Having invented golf, or received it as a divine inspiration, and given it to the world, Scotland left other nations to take it up and win. It is true that there are more Americans than there are Scots, and by the law of random selection the larger group will produce more champions than the smaller. (If the Chinese ever take up golf everybody will be in trouble.) But many patriotic Scots detect in their own countrymen a reluctance to win. The Scot tends to be at his best when he is struggling against impossible odds. In sight of victory he tends to lose interest.

It may be because the game is an intensely Presbyterian activity. In golf, you do not play against an opponent. You may play alongside one, but he can't touch your ball or interfere with your swing. You are on your own, one man matching his effort and his conscience against the enigma of life. You may lie about the number of strokes you took to kill a snake in the heather; but you know, and so does the Big Handicapper in the Sky from Whom nothing is hidden.

The game also involves the Doctrine of Election. Honest, conscientious players who obey all the rules, and follow teacher's instruction, can swing into disaster, while feckless fools hole out in one. The explanation clearly lies in the sins or virtues of their ancestors and each has entered the world predestined to divine favour or contempt.

Where the Scots have clung to the best in their national tradition is that in the land of its birth, golf is a sport for anybody. The first time I was taken to an American country club, I discovered that the entrance fee was more than I earned in a year, and I thought I was doing quite well. In Scotland in the 1980s, tens of thousands of players will expect to pay annual fees of less than £100.

When it comes to nations late in the game, the situation is perfectly insane. A Japanese lucky enough to be allowed into a club may pay £75,000 for the privilege. For that money, he should logically get 750 times as much fun as a member in a good artisan club in the West of Scotland.

He will not. There is no such quantity as 750 times the fun that even the most erratic, choleric, incompetent Scotsman derives from duffing a ball round eighteen holes. Other nations may win championships. They may inject the game with killer instinct. They may smother it in temples and alien rituals and irrelevant swimming pools on the side. The Scot knows who belongs to golf. He and his stern God play it together. They don't spend a fortune on it, because that would spoil the fun entirely.

24

THE
BONNIE BOY

FROM THE royal and ancient sport that refuses to die to the royal and ancient sport who did. He is still the source of angry argument after two centuries. If his only legacy is something to argue about, he has done some service to his country.

To some he remains Bonnie Prince Charlie; to others an egotistical degenerate. He was both, but not at the same time. And his detractors would have nothing to argue about if he had not exercised a prodigious charm and evoked an affection hardly short of idolatry. He was flawed, as men are flawed. He was a bonnie prince too.

To anyone who believes in an hereditary monarchy, Charles was as much entitled to the British throne as anybody else. The fact that he was born and raised in Italy, and never set eyes on Scotland until his twenties, can be dismissed as irrelevant to the hereditary principle.

His grandfather was the Roman Catholic King James II, overthrown and replaced by William of Orange, who was incidentally James's son-in-law. James died in exile. His son, also James, was styled by himself and his friends as James III. He is better known in history as the Old Pretender, who landed in Scotland in 1715 in a doomed effort to recover the throne by force. After this failure he abandoned his own hopes and passed them on to his son, Charles Edward Louis John Sylvester Maria Casimir Stuart.

The boy was bright and attractive. There are stories that when he in turn arrived in Scotland he could scarcely speak English, and preferred Polish (he was related on his mother's side to the King of Poland). The stories can hardly be true. Before he was ten years old he was fluent in English, French and Italian. He was a useful horseman and marksman, he played tennis and golf. He grew up tall and handsome and altogether well qualified for one of the great romantic roles of history.

His crusade went well, and badly. He expected a lot of help from the French king, and got virtually none. In 1745 he found himself two ships and a few hundred men, and sailed from France to invade

Britain. A few days out they encountered a British man-of-war. One of Charles's ships was disabled and had to turn back, with most of the military equipment and men. Charles, on the other ship, pressed on with his voyage of conquest. His force now consisted of one small ship and a dozen men.

They landed in midsummer on the Isle of Eriskay, in the Hebrides, and made contact with a few sympathisers. The sympathisers were not all enthusiastic or hopeful. One of them sized up the situation and advised the Prince to go home. Charles's reply was that he *was* home.

Messages sent to the clan chiefs got discouraging replies. They had expected to rally to a huge force of French soldiers. Rallying to a dozen men was quite different.

But the Prince was not prepared to give up after coming so far. He travelled to the mainland, and some of the loyal Jacobites did turn up to support him, French soldiers or no French soldiers. During the following months, the little army of Highlanders displayed that a lot could be achieved by sheer energy. A government force under Sir John Cope bypassed the rebels out of pure nervousness and went to Inverness. Charles and his men went south and took over the town of Perth. His army grew to two and a half thousand, and a few weeks later, with only petty skirmishes, occupied Edinburgh, virtually without striking a blow.

General Cope managed to get his inexperienced troops into the area, and the first real battle of the rebellion was engaged at Prestonpans. The rebels won outright. They won principally by reckless determination. Cope's soldiers, trained in formalised battle tactics, were baffled by the Highlanders' custom of firing a musket volley, throwing away the muskets and charging with swords. They had another unexpected trick when facing a cavalry charge. They ignored the riders and struck the leading horses on the nose, which induced the horses to wheel in panic and crash into those behind. For General Cope, it was a shameful rout. In a very brief space, Prince Charles was, in the words of a supporter, entirely master of Scotland. He was able to rest, and the ladies of Edinburgh found him quite enchanting, though there were no scandalous amours.

It was now a question of sitting pat, or moving south to conquer England, where there were plenty of Jacobite sympathisers. He decided to move south.

Not all the Highlanders under him were anxious to go so far. Even the Lowlands of Scotland were alien territory to them. There were sporadic desertions. Nevertheless, the rebels took the English town of Carlisle, without difficulty. The principal problem of the Prince was that his two commanders, Lord George Murray and the Duke of Perth, were incompatible, and that he himself tended to disagree with Murray. However, in November the rebel army occupied Manchester, and celebrated with bonfires. They were received and welcomed by the people of Derby.

Derby was the turning-point. Charles himself was convinced that if he advanced, he could conquer London and win the war. It is possible that he was right. The Government was in a panic, and King George was in half a mind to emigrate. But there is no point in speculating about what might have been. The Prince's enthusiasm was overborne by the superior age, experience and pessimism of Murray, who insisted that they should return to Scotland and con-solidate. It is true that large numbers of supporters who had been thinking of joining what looked like a winning team decided not to when they discovered the team backing away. And on their way home, the Highlanders found that people who had cheered them on the southward journey had now turned against them, since nobody likes a loser.

And although there were odd skirmishes in which the rebels came off on top, the retreat was positively a retreat. And Charles's main enemy now was the very capable Duke of Cumberland. The English later gave his name to a flower, Sweet William. To the Scots, he has always been known as Butcher Cumberland.

The final battle of the uprising was at Culloden, where Charles's army was smashed by Cumberland. It was a literal massacre. Cumberland had put out a forged order suggesting that the High-landers' policy was to take no prisoners and spare no life, and this justified his own savage orders. Wounded rebels were slaughtered, and more than that; when victory was complete and the Jacobite fighters dead or scattered, the duke went through the Highlands murdering anybody who might look like a rebel sympathiser, regardless of sex or age.

The Prince escaped with a few friends, and then endured a hellish period of fleeing and skulking in the bitter Scottish winter. He slept in caves, starved some of the time, and was nearly always cold. His little party skulked miserably from island to island in the Hebrides. right into the summer of 1746, and Government parties hunted them all that time. From the time of his arrival in Scotland, there had been a reward of £30,000 for his capture. During all his days as a fugitive, no Highlander ever tried to collect it. This says something for the Highland sense of honour. It says something too for the personality of the Prince. At twenty-four he seems to have had no interest in sexual adventure (his detractors have jumped to dark conclusions

about that, too) but women as well as men found his charm irresistible; and at the worst moments of hiding in some freezing hovel, he
didn't complain.

More and more, however, he turned to brandy and whisky to
keep the cold out and his spirits up. 'In my skulking,' he told one
host, 'I have learned to take a hearty dram.'

It was on the island of South Uist that he met by chance the
Highland girl Flora Macdonald, and his friends suggested that she
should take the Prince for safety to her mother's home on the Isle of
Skye. Before it could happen, she was arrested by the militia for
travelling with no passport, but as their captain was her own stepfather she was able to get from him a passport for herself, a man-
servant, and a woman servant, Betty Burke.

By this time the islands were crawling with hunters in search of
any Jacobites, but particularly Charles. He hid out alone in a
deserted shed for some time, at exactly the time a French ship was
trying to make contact with him an another island.

Eventually he was able to slip away from the Uists in a small
sailing boat. He was travelling as Betty Burke, in women's clothes.
Even after reaching Skye, they were constantly in danger of discovery, and the tall, long-legged Prince gave a very poor performance
as a woman. But Flora got him to the little town of Portree and said
her last farewell there. It was not a tearful or a romantic parting. In
fact, Charles was more overcome with emotion in saying goodbye
to his male comrades than when he left Flora. She was no more than
a good and resourceful friend who had helped him through a
difficult time.

There were other difficult times ahead of him, and other nights
in the cold heather, recurring bowel trouble and close encounters
with his pursuers before he boarded a French ship, *L'Heureux*, to
leave Scotland for ever.

Flora Macdonald was arrested and taken to the Tower of London,
but she was freed in 1747 under a general amnesty and married three
years later.

In France, Charles had a hero's welcome. King Louis greeted him
with affection, and the Prince settled in Paris to the life of a social
lion. He became a nuisance to the French king, but he refused to
leave Paris, where he had an aristocratic mistress and various other
lady admirers. He was finally kidnapped and removed physically
from the capital.

From then on, his life was downhill most of the way. For a time
he vanished from public view and travelled aimlessly in secret. He
tried to organise a gunpowder plot in London, but the British

Government forestalled it and executed the Prince's agent. He started living with Clementina Walkinshaw in 1752 and she bore him a daughter, his only child. Clementina soon found him unbearable. He drank, he beat her, and his moods were unpredictable but usually unpleasant. All his old friends and supporters were turning away from him.

When his father James wrote to him from Italy, badly ill, and begged him to visit him, he ignored the letter. When he at last did go to Rome on learning that the old man was dying, he arrived too late.

In 1772 he married Louise, daughter of the Princesse de Stolberg, and for a time he gave up drinking; but not for too long. The dashing young prince was now encased in a sick, obese body, his complexion was overripe, he often slid into a drunken sleep in public. This is the degenerate Charles of hostile legend. He seems almost a different person from the cheerful warrior who endured so much in Scotland. Louise left him. In 1788 he had several strokes and died. His brother Henry, now a cardinal, conducted the service, and Charles was buried as King Charles III. His daughter Charlotte died in the following year. The line of the Stuarts, charming, romantic and strangely stupid, was ended.

25

THE
ROYAL PURPLE

IT MAY SEEM a far cry from a prince of the blood to two simple peasants from the Hebrides. It is not. Goethe warned us, 'Connect, always connect.' Scottish history connects.

In the year of 1898, two brothers from the Isle of Lewis were admitted to the Western Infirmary in Glasgow, each with the same puzzling ailment. It had started in childhood. Now, as adults who worked as fishermen, they were still plagued by it. As soon as they exposed themselves to sunlight, their faces, ears and hands began to itch and burn, and inside twelve hours would blister. At the same time, their urine ran the rich colour of red wine.

They were examined by Sir Thomas McColl-Anderson, Regius Professor of the Practice of Medicine, who concluded that the symptoms were interconnected. His findings were an early start to one of the most curious detective investigations in medical history; the pursuit of porphyria.

Not one layman in 10,000 has even heard of porphyria. Only one in 50,000 is likely to meet it personally. But modern speculative research makes it at least possible that porphyria was for centuries a curse on the British ruling house and, in short, that King George III was not mad at all.

Certainly the health of George III has fascinated doctors, during the king's lifetime and afterwards. Twenty years after his death, an American psychiatrist read through the available evidence and had no hesitation in describing his findings as 'The Insanity of King George III'. Another American psychiatrist a century later was just as confident in declaring that 'in all probability the disorder was purely mental and the clinical reports were falsified', and that, 'physical symptoms were invented or, at least, exaggerated further to fool the public.'

If the king's physical symptoms were exaggerated, his physicians have left enough written reports to indicate that they were fairly horrible to begin with, and his mental symptoms were quite enough to rock the British constitution for several years. The possibility of having a lunatic on the throne sent Parliament into a continuing panic. Accepting that he was mad, the Commons actually passed a Regency Bill in 1789, to unseat the monarch and put the Prince of Wales in his place. Before the bill could reach the House of Lords, the king recovered; without a lot of help from his doctors; and the bill was dropped.

The attack that started this panic happened in 1788, in the summer, when the king complained of severe pain. This was professionally ascribed to 'biliary concretions in the gall duct'. The patient was over-excited, and a few months later had colic, various pains, weakness, stiffness, lameness, cramp, accelerated pulse rate and hoarseness, followed by logorrhoea, confusion, persistent insomnia, and fits. It does seem like an excessive group of symptoms for a doctor to invent.

However, in our own century we can at least understand what the symptoms were from that description. The diagnoses of his time are more puzzling, since they were written in a medical language that sounds like mumbo-jumbo. One eminent physician wrote in 1788:

> The cause to which they all agree to ascribe it, is the force of a humor which was beginning to show itself in the legs, when the King's imprudence drove it from thence into the bowels; and the medicines which they were then obliged to use for the preservation of his life, have repelled it upon the brain. The physicians are now endeavouring to bring it down again into the legs, which nature had originally pointed out as the best mode of discharge.

The process of moving a 'humor' from the brain to the legs would daunt the most arrogant of modern doctors. Unfortunately, Parliament was not too worried about the king's physical condition, merely about whether or not he was mad. So his treatment was increasingly put into the hands of specialists in insanity, and his bodily troubles were pushed into the background. The 'mad-doctors' were on to a bonanza.

One of them delivered a lengthy dissertation in which he tried to distinguish between 'insanity' and 'delirium'. To a modern reader, his report sounds like the semantic quibbling of a pompous fool with a confused mind, and he hedged his bets by suggesting that the king's condition fell somewhere between the two definitions and could properly be called derangement of mind.

A later mental specialist produced the retrospective diagnosis of manic-depressive psychosis. Another blamed the trouble on something like a guilt complex, though that piece of jargon hadn't yet been invented. 'Self-blame, indecision, and frustration destroyed the sanity of George III,' he said. 'Had he been a country squire, he would in all probability not have been psychotic.'

In the meantime, the monarch was having a ghastly time fairly regularly. On top of his own troubles, he had his doctors. One of them, Francis Willis, had boasted that he approached patients like horses in a *ménage* and 'broke them in'. During a particular attack, the king confessed to Willis's son that he had prayed either for a cure, or for death. If neither occurred, he added, 'for God's sake keep me from your father'.

Willis stood for no nonsense, even from a royal patient. If the king refused his food, or didn't want to go to bed, he was wrapped tightly in a sheet, or strapped in a straitjacket and had his legs tied to the bedposts. He was dosed with emetics and purgatives, he was bled with leeches and blistered. To cure his excitement he was put in solitary confinement for lengthy periods. Any resistance to these treatments was taken as fresh evidence of mania. His dislike of Doctor Willis was dismissed as a delusion.

Another medico did suggest that there might be a physical cause of the trouble—'morbid matter, or acrimonious particles settling on the brain'.

The king was of course German, and his doctors were English. The Scottish connection occurs long before his birth, and long after his death.

Long after his death, McColl-Anderson made a dispassionate physical study of those two Hebridean fishermen. His work has continued in his department, and his present-day successor, Professor Abe Goldberg, still studies and treats porphyria, or rather, the group of diseases known as the porphyrias.

They are usually hereditary. We shall come to that later. In a learned paper, Professor Goldberg has explained that, in one form, the only trouble is hypersensitivity to sunlight. In others, there may be excruciating abdominal pain, paralysis and mental disorder. The cause is an inborn error of metabolism.

Porphyrins are purple pigments essential to the human organism, and indeed to more primitive organisms. They exist in every cell of the body and give us our natural pink colour. In the porphyria victim, the body simply produces too many of them. Proneness to prophyria is passed from parent to child, but in some cases it may be dormant until it is stimulated by some drugs, including bad alcohol.

In acute porphyria the symptoms can be distressing and dramatic, with fits resembling epilepsy. Even today, some patients have been certified insane.

The painstaking investigation into the affair of George III was conducted by Dr Ida Macalpine, her son Dr Richard Hunter, and Professor Rimington of London. Their study was enough at least to raise enormous doubts about all the diagnoses of insanity. When they spread their study to other members of the royal line, one of the great dramatic figures of Scottish history burst upon the scene— Mary Queen of Scots.

Now it emerged that Mary's medical history was as harrowing as her public life. From adolescence, she was subject to regular attacks of abdominal pain, lameness and mental upsets. One such attack left her blind and speechless for hours. Some of the people around her concluded that she was faking illness to gain sympathy. In the words of the investigators, women suffering the pains of porphyria tend to be considered hysterical, while men are regarded as hypersensitive.

Mary's son, James I of England, did not enjoy untroubled health; melancholy, insomnia, vomiting, limb pains, nameless dread, sensitivity to pain, lameness, were his recurrent companions. And he often passed urine 'red like Alicante wine'.

George III was descended reasonably directly from Mary Stuart and James I. Some of the branches on the way down seem to provide evidence of other victims. There is of course no certainty. It is not possible to diagnose with certainty without having the actual patient available, as opposed to second-hand reports.

But even monarchs are entitled to a fair judgement by history; and when we consider the madness of George III, and place it beside the symptoms recorded by Mary Stuart, and the modern studies that began in Glasgow Western Infirmary, the king is at least entitled to that tentative Scottish verdict: 'Not proven'.

26

THE
PADDLERS

THE HIGH and mighty are always interesting spectacles, especially when they are in trouble. The totality of Scotland, however, demonstrates the proverb that God must have loved the poor, because He made so many of them. In real terms of the human condition, it is more exciting being poor, because any fun is a startling surprise. The ordinary joes in the City of Glasgow, for instance, invented summer holidays for the working man. As so often happened in our tortured history, the motive, the means and the opportunity converged on one moment.

The opportunity was embodied in the Firth of Clyde, unquestionably the most beautiful body of water in the world. The motive was the incurable restlessness of the citizens. The means arrived in the shape of the paddle steamer. Taken together, these three factors created a genuine golden age of romance and adventure such as the world has never seen, nor will ever see again.

The river Clyde grew to world stature as the home of shipbuilding, and this in itself is a pleasant absurdity. It is wildly unsuitable for shipbuilding. It is narrow and it is shallow. Until it was dredged in the nineteenth century, no ship of any size could navigate as far up as Glasgow, and the little town of Port Glasgow, farther downstream, was designed literally as the port of Glasgow.

Even in the boom years of shipbuilding, the process was insanely complicated by the shape and size of the river. Ships had to be launched down slipways with thousands of tons of drag-chain fastened to their hulls, to prevent them from skimming across the river and ploughing up the opposite bank. There were other occasional difficulties. In quite recent years one sizeable vessel was dispatched into the water in the upper reaches and instead of floating, simply went on going down like a stone. It was wildly cheered.

But whether or not the Clyde was ideal, it was the cradle of the trade, and Clydesiders were in no doubt that it was the greatest. 'Clyde-built' is the ultimate token of high quality.

The river has always dominated the consciousness of the Glaswegian, and he finds enchantment even in the bridges and ferries that cross it. There was until recently, for instance, the Govan car ferry, an incredible structure resembling the steel frame of a two-storey building, with a propeller at each corner for tricky manoeuvring. The Renfrew ferry, downstream and outside the city proper, still functions today on the chain system. Two heavy chains lie across the river, fastened to both banks, and passing through tubes in the boat's hull. It travels by pulling the chains in at the front and pouring them out at the back, and the natives are rightly proud of this brilliant piece of Scottish knowhow.

There is a jokey quality about the ferries too; and a few years ago, a master was fined for being drunk in charge of the Renfrew ferry. It happened on New Year's Day, always a perilous period in Scotland. Successions of passengers venturing across the river on First-Foot missions honoured the tradition of offering a dram to the passing stranger, including the ferry captain, and some time during the afternoon the ship was seen to be sitting, in a confused state, in midstream, blocking traffic and uncertain which direction was which.

In pre-steam days, the river was more prolific of minor calamities. There was some up-and-down traffic conducted by fly boats, simple shallow-draft sailing vessels, with oar power added for emergencies. They ran aground quite regularly, and nobody worried too much about it, even when it happened in the dark. There was one exciting night when a fly boat set out from the heart of Glasgow for a downstream voyage; the crew pulled manfully on the oars and the captain stared knowledgeably into the pitch dark ahead, adroitly keeping to the channel he knew so well. As day began to dawn he announced that they were just abreast of Dumbarton Castle, just taking shape in the mirk. In full light it became clear that they had been rowing mightily with the boat still tied to the wharf.

But steam was the glory, steam was the explosion of Clyde traffic and the progenitor of a true splendour.

Nobody can positively claim credit for the first steamship. Glasgow was early in the game, with the *Charlotte Dundas*, built in 1802 for plying on the Forth and Clyde Canal, which it did briefly and was then laid up. There had been a previous effort on the Delaware, with a crude and complicated vessel called the *Steamboat*, which actually had steam-driven oars.

The American Robert Fulton put a steamboat on the Hudson River in 1807, and is probably entitled to the credit for the first successful commercial operation. Five years later, Henry Bell had the *Comet* built and launched on the Clyde. It was not the first, and it was merely a development rather than an invention; but the name still rings with pride, and the *Comet* was a real beginning of something big.

Within a few years, energetic businessmen were ordering new steamboats and hurling them into the waters of the Clyde. The fine madness was on the place. Over the next century, the Clyde paddlers were to become a legend, and the Firth fairly seethed with them, all competing for passengers. Speed was the thing. The Glaswegians realised what richness was opening for them, and they wanted to get to the delights of the Firth without wasting a second.

The Firth is open, but sheltered. It is a complex jigsaw of broad water, narrow sea lochs, hills and islands and endless variety, and many of the delightful towns and villages on its shores were created by the stream of tourists carried downriver by steam. Before steam, the area had no more than a few tiny, scattered hamlets, and when the *Comet* first appeared in the West Highlands, local people stared at her in pure terror, or fled to the hills to escape the devilish machine.

We can say, in fact, that the Firth of Clyde invented the paddle steamer, and the paddle steamer invented the Firth of Clyde. There were teething troubles, naturally. In 1825, the *Comet* (a second vessel plying under the historic name) was heading up towards Gourock in the dark when another steamer, the *Ayr*, was churning in the other direction, and they collided head-on at full speed. The *Comet* sank in minutes and seventy people drowned. But boiler explosions were a commoner form of hazard in the apprentice days of steam. The *Earl Grey* burst hers at Greenock, splintering the decks and killing ten people. At Helensburgh in 1842, the *Telegraph* had barely started her engines when her boiler burst and scattered the vessel in fragments. A score of people died in the blast. The *Plover* blew itself to destruction in the middle of Glasgow one morning, killing two of the crew and flinging massive bits of metal clear over high buildings nearby.

It says something about the national character that none of these incidents affected the customers' enthusiasm for paddle-steamer travel. Hundreds of boats were built, and filled, faster and faster—fifteen knots was common, and passengers expected their skipper to plough ahead of rival boats. They lined the rails and screamed abuse at other craft, and yelled for more steam. Now and then, steamers in a hurry crashed into piers or piled themselves on rocks. It was all part of the game.

Many of the Clyde paddlers, suitably bribed, furtively departed from the Firth and served as blockade runners into Confederate ports during the American Civil War. They were capable of anything. They even made a serious dent in the rigid observance of the Scottish Sabbath.

In the 1850s, the owners of the steamer *Emperor* announced a Sunday cruise to the village of Kilmun. The Kilmun natives were strict Sabbatarians, but they accepted the event without too much hysteria. In Rothesay, on the island of Bute, there was fury and panic. This was a town where the people took Sunday so seriously that pump wells were padlocked all day in case anybody should profane the Sabbath by having a drink of water. The idea of a pleasure cruise on the Lord's Day was too much, and plans were made to prevent any ship from calling. The *Emperor* ignored Rothesay, and the virtuous islanders were landed in an anticlimax.

The real war broke out at Garelochhead, which was owned by Sir James Colquhoun. At the first hint of a Sunday-breaking cruise, he put on his other hat as lord lieutenant of the county, called out the local police and reinforced them with his own servants, and prepared to repel boarders. When the *Emperor* approached the pier, the captain was told that he would not be allowed to tie up. The captain was not to be put off. Mooring lines were thrown ashore. They were thrown back at once. Somebody on the boat got a long pole to prod the pier defenders out of the way, but it was wrested ashore and used to push the steamer off.

The captain made a second approach. This time both crew and passengers were mad for battle. They fired lumps of coal, bottles and vegetables at the defenders to drive them back. An advance party leapt from the steamer on to the pier to engage in hand-to-hand fighting, and the villagers retreated in humiliation.

There was talk of prosecution, but nothing came of it. The pleasure-mad heathenish Glaswegians had triumphed against the stern Presbyterian God of the West Highlands, and nothing was ever the same again.

The Clyde paddle steamers dominated the imagination of travelling Scots up to and beyond the middle of this century. There was a great fleet of them, and they plied to places whose very names were music—Kirn, Hunter's Quay, Innellan, Lochranza, Tighnabruaich and Lochgilphead. They were the personal pride of the Scot, and connoisseurs prided themselves in being able to recognise and name them at a mile's distance. Well into our time, they were the finest, the only acceptable form of transport to holiday delights.

The engines were almost as glamorous as the scenery; titanic workshops filled with great cranks as thick as a man, cams and levers working in strange harmony with the fragrance of sweet hot oil. The automobile finally destroyed them and a glory passed from the earth. But in their time they were unique in the world. If the Clyde did not invent the steamship, it did create something wonderful with it, and the man who has not taken ship by paddler to the enchantments of the Firth of Clyde is a man deprived and pitiable.

27

MERRETT

(Criminal Compendium 5)

I F YOU SEEK a seafarer even crazier than the wildest of the Clyde captains, look no farther than Chesney. He was born John Donald Merrett; and there is a touch of bravura, or nonchalance, or maybe pure stupid arrogance, about the history of Merrett that picks it out from the routine annals of mayhem. There is also the fact that, like Madeleine Smith, he got away with it. Well, he got away with it once. Unlike Madeleine, who went on to a respectable old age, Merrett never threw off the habit.

Edinburgh, again—it is entirely suitable that the douce, almost mim-mouthed capital city should provide the fruitful soil for so many felonious flowerings. It was to Edinburgh that the well-bred widow Mrs Bertha Merrett brought her adolescent son in 1926, so that he could enrol in the university there and study under her eye. The boy was a brilliant scholar, and she intended him for the Diplomatic Service; but he had wayward tendencies and his mother didn't want to let him attend a residential university where he might get up to anything, out of her sight.

She had an income of £700 a year. In his definitive analysis of the case, the great Scottish criminologist William Roughead evidently regards this is as modest to the point of hardship, and says that it needed all Mrs Merrett's ability to maintain herself and the boy in comfort. He overstates the hardship. In 1926, when skilled tradesmen were earning less than £3 a week, £700 a year was really very good. Mrs Merrett's situation made her worth plundering, and her son rapidly plundered her.

He was soon living a double life. Having started an Arts course at Edinburgh, he attended classes for a couple of months. After that, he left home with his books every morning and found pleasanter things to do with his days. He also crept out of the house in the evenings and went to the Dunedin Palais de Danse. He got friendly with Betty Christie, one of the instructors. He spent a lot of money on Betty, entertained her, and bought her jewellery. His pocket money was ten shillings a week, but in addition to his outlays on Betty Christie, he bought first one motorbike and then another with sidecar, and generally lived the life of a man-about-town.

The Merretts lived in a flat at 31 Buckingham Terrace, and had a daily maid, Mrs Henrietta Sutherland. On 17 March, only a few months after their arrival in the city, Mrs Sutherland arrived as usual and her mistress let her in.

The maid last saw mother and son in the sitting-room; Mrs Merrett writing, and Donald at the other side of the room reading a book. A little later, while she was lighting the fire in the kitchen, Mrs Sutherland heard a shot, a scream and the sound of a falling body. Then Donald came to the kitchen and said, 'Rita, my mother has shot herself.'

The two went back to the sitting room. Mrs Merrett was lying unconscious, bleeding from the left ear. On the bureau was a pistol.

They telephoned the police, who came with an ambulance and took Mrs Merrett to the Royal Infirmary.

The story now became quite silly. Accused of attempted suicide, the lady was examined and then put in a room with barred windows and locked doors. A police sergeant wrote formally to the Infirmary describing her as 'a prisoner charged with attempted suicide'. This in itself is curious, since suicide is not a crime in Scotland. But the victim was held incommunicado. Staff and visitors were forbidden to tell her what had happened.

When she did finally succeed in speaking to a doctor, she said, 'I was sitting down writing letters, and my son Donald was standing beside me. I said, "Go away, Donald, and don't annoy me"; and the next I heard was a kind of explosion, and I don't remember any more.' This worried Dr Holcombe. He called the police, and on the next day Inspector Fleming visited the infirmary and spoke to him; but he didn't think it necessary to see the patient, though she was critically ill. It was left to the doctor to question Donald Merrett about the incident, and his version was that his mother had told him to go away, that he had gone to the other side of the room, heard a shot and turned to see his mother falling, and a revolver falling from her hand.

In the meantime, Inspector Fleming had visited the Merrett home. He was obviously making purely formal inquiries in an open-and-shut suicide case. This time, Mrs Sutherland the maid had a different version of her story. She had many versions, in fact. The second was that she had heard a shot from the kitchen, gone to the hallway and seen Mrs Merrett falling off her chair, and a gun falling from her hand.

On the bureau in the sitting room, the keen-eyed inspector saw two letters to Mrs Merrett from the Clydesdale Bank, informing her that her account was overdrawn. These also helped to convince him he was dealing with suicide.

On 1 April, the patient died after several days of unconsciousness.

While she was in hospital, Donald managed to make some kind of social life. In fact, when a nursing sister asked where she could call him in emergencies, he gave her the telephone number of the Palais de Danse.

Inspector Fleming did get round to interviewing him, for the first time, on the day before the death. Donald described how he had loaded his pistol (he had bought the pistol quite recently and didn't conceal that it was his) because he planned to visit the Braid Hills and shoot rabbits. His mother had taken the gun from him and put it into a drawer of the writing bureau, and he never saw it again, until the day of the incident.

After this, the sad case was virtually forgotten. Following the terms of Mrs Merrett's will, the Public Trustee asked her sister, Mrs Penn, to stay at Buckingham Terrace with her husband to take care of Donald while he carried on his studies. Donald carried on much as before, and was eventually dismissed by the University for absenteeism.

The police had not quite abandoned the affair. Somebody must have noticed something slightly unsatisfactory in the reports. Nine months after the death, a warrant was issued for Donald's arrest, on two charges: murdering his mother, and cashing cheques on which he had forged her name.

Mrs Merrett died on 1 April 1926. The trial didn't open until February 1927. On the charges of forging cheques, the prosecution had no great difficulty, although the evidence was lengthy and laborious. It became perfectly clear that the lad, sitting in the dock completely at ease and looking mature beyond his seventeen years, had consistently been paying for his expensive lifestyle by robbing his mother.

The murder charge was tougher to prove. Mrs Sutherland, the key prosecution witness, had changed her story so often that it was hard to believe any version. Long-drawn-out scientific evidence proved practically nothing. The whole business was muddied by the lapse of time and the ludicrous short-sightedness of the police from the first moment they were called into the case.

The jury were out for barely an hour. On the charge of uttering cheques, the fifteen members voted 'Guilty' unanimously. On the murder charge there was a majority verdict of 'Not proven'. The minority, five men, had voted 'Guilty'. In other words, although ten jurors wouldn't, in conscience, uphold the charge on the court evidence, not a single member was able to declare that Merrett was innocent.

He was sent to prison for twelve months. Like other eminent figures in crime, he should now vanish discreetly from history.

It was not in Merrett's nature to do anything discreetly, though the name Merrett did disappear from the scene.

In 1954, twenty-eight years after the distressing incidents in Edinburgh, London police made a harrowing discovery at a house in Ealing. It was run as a home for old people by Mrs Mary Bonnar and her daughter Mrs Vera Chesney. Officers who were called to the house opened a locked bathroom and found the younger woman dead in the bath. In an unused room in the big house, half-hidden behind lumber, was the bloodstained corpse of the mother, strangled with one of her own stockings. It was obvious that she had fought her murderer frantically before she was overcome. The double crime, ideal material for newspaper stories, was given an extra touch of colour by Mrs Bonnar's habit of styling herself 'Lady Menzies'.

Inquiries quickly concentrated on young Mrs Chesney's estranged husband Ronald Chesney. By then, he was in Germany. He was also John Donald Merrett.

After his release from prison in Scotland, young Merrett had never actually settled to the dull routine of working life. Mrs Bonnar, a friend of his mother's, had maintained an interest in the boy, and he travelled to Hastings to enjoy her hospitality; an altogether evil day for the generous lady. He first seduced the teenage daughter, Vera, then eloped with her to Scotland for marriage under the tolerant Scottish law. He even took his bride to Edinburgh, but he had already changed his name to Chesney, and he avoided his old haunts and his old companions.

It was the beginning of an interesting and exhausting life for Vera Bonnar. During the honeymoon the young husband kept her constantly travelling, leaving a trail of bad cheques behind him. He was arrested in Newcastle and sentenced to six months in Durham Prison. But he was irrepressible. He still had the income from his mother's estate, and on his twenty-first birthday he inherited his grandfather's fortune of £50,000. He lived in lavish style, installed the two women in a house with six servants, bought a fast boat and a small aeroplane, and went into the smuggling trade.

In 1940 he joined the Royal Navy as a trainee officer and enjoyed an interesting war, including a spell in a German prison camp. He was known in the navy as 'Crasher' Chesney from his habit of driving too fast and hitting things.

The boy who had swindled, and certainly killed, his mother, had matured into a swashbuckling character addicted to drink, women and easy money. In postwar Germany he was an enthusiastic and successful operator in the black market, and a prison sentence for stealing a car from the navy was only a temporary setback. He was soon in prison again, in England, for smuggling nylon stockings. It was there that he decided to kill his wife.

Some years earlier the Public Trustee, who still overlooked the maternal estate, had advised him to make a settlement on Vera, of over £8,000. By now, he wanted that £8,000. Back in Europe with the latest of many girlfriends after his release, he laid his plan, bold, ingenious and very, very crude. He travelled back to London on a false passport, visited the house at Ealing and drowned her in the bath. His mother-in-law surprised him and he disposed of her.

Aside from recurring visits to prison, Merrett had spent his adult life getting away with most of the enterprises he tried. When he read newspaper reports of the murder hunt, he realised that the time of getting away with it was over. He walked from Cologne railway station to a wooded park in the city, put a pistol to the roof of his mouth and destroyed himself.

It is not completely fair to claim John Donald Merrett as a Scottish criminal. He was born in New Zealand, and the main part of his illegal career was conducted in England and continental Europe.

Still, he served his apprenticeship, as it were, he made his first discovery of the process, in the fruitful environment of Edinburgh. That must count for something.

28

BIG
JOHN

How can a Scot have ideas above his station, when the nation doesn't recognise the existence of stations? The answer is that we like to have it both ways. But the presumptions of a Merrett shrink to nothing when we come to the case of John Brown.

A cat may look at a queen. A Scot may go much, much further than looking. And as the cat is an enigma, so our hero is a bafflement. John Brown was a simple peasant lad who took employment as a stable boy. While more ambitious youngsters might strive to heave themselves out of the backwoods and seek fame and fortune in the south, John Brown just sort of stood there and let them come to him. He managed, in his own odd way, to become one of the most important people in the kingdom; he was the centre of a national scandal and he strode through it all completely impassive and impervious.

What he was thinking about all the time, nobody knows. What he was up to in private still provokes feverish speculation and argument after more than a century.

And it all happened because, by chance, the place where he found himself tending horses was Balmoral Castle. And Balmoral Castle became the favourite resort of Queen Victoria. She and the Prince Consort, Albert, leased it for several summers and then bought it. And John Brown came with the package.

It is possible that his inclusion made the package more attractive in the first place. About that, we can only speculate, which is quite amusing. If it is true, then young Brown has more to answer for than merely causing a little royal scandal. He has to take the blame for the bizarre development of the Highland Games industry, because it was at Balmoral that the first Highland gathering was held, and from that small beginning the thing has gone berserk.

The first gathering was a little family affair. Queen Victoria, besotted with Scottishness, commanded a modest entertainment at which some of the Balmoral servants played pipes, danced and showed their prowess in simple games. It was no more spectacular than a village fête.

The royal approval of such proceedings encouraged a tradition to spring ready-made out of the ground. Highland gatherings were organised all over the place, large-scale promotion and razzmatazz were injected, and now we have crowds of thousands, enormous booze-ups, sweaty men in kilts heaving one another round rings, pipe band competitions, little girls leaping about, and hairy giants trying to throw trees in the air. It is all marvellous, and it has as much connection with ancient Highland tradition as a massed choir has with an old woman crooning to her cow at milking time.

And it all started with Balmoral; and Queen Victoria; and John Brown.

He was a well-set-up youngster of twenty-one when he first caught the royal eye, and Prince Albert himself picked him out as the steady sort of chap who could be trusted as the Queen's ghillie, or personal helper. She was twenty-seven years old; tiny, solemn and self-willed. Brown, at least on the surface, was grave enough and heavy enough to suit her. He took his promotion very seriously and grew into it, a taciturn man who knew his own importance and regarded the queen's comfort and safety as his personal property.

He was a faithful, slightly priggish servant to Her Majesty for a few years, and then Prince Albert died. The queen went into profound mourning and never came out of it. This is the Queen Victoria whom history remembers—the Widow of Windsor, the stern, humourless little lady who impressed her stiff code of moral propriety on an era. The latter half of the nineteenth century was the Victorian age, when pleasures were taken glumly, sexual shenanigans were 'out', and a bourgeois mother's advice to her daughter on how to cope with the wedding night was, 'Grit your teeth and think of England.'

Meanwhile, back at Balmoral, there was only one person capable of cajoling the widow out of her hermit desolation. John Brown was there when she needed him; solicitous, correct and absolutely reliable.

The relationship slid on to an even more interesting plane when a psychic medium announced that he had been in touch with the shade of the dead prince. Victoria consulted him and asked to be put through to the consort. The answer was that owing to the peculiar set-up of communications with the other world, Albert couldn't make personal appearances, but would work through somebody handy on earth. And there was nobody handier than John Brown.

Or so the story goes. It is a nice enough story, and even if it isn't literally true, that is how things worked out. From being a useful fellow about the house, John became the inseparable companion of the queen. He hardly ever left her side in waking hours, and slept in an adjacent room. Till the day he died, he never took a holiday from his duty. The queen's ministers might resent the eternal presence of this quietly arrogant Scottish ghillie. They had to put up with it.

Irreverent newspapers of the time assumed the worst, or at least the most interesting. The relationship was public and visible. Brown could be seen leading the queen's pony when she took the air, with an authoritative manner suggesting that he owned both. Lampoonists referred to the queen as Mrs Brown.

Since Brown was at her side for over twenty years, from the prince's death in 1861 until his own in 1883, there was plenty of time for spicy bits of gossip to trickle out. One was that another servant had seen Brown leaving Her Majesty's bedroom in the middle of the night, and that the queen imperiously informed the woman that nothing improper had happened.

The rumours are still trickling out. A modern writer has suggested that the pair were secretly married and had a boy-child who was smuggled out of the country to be brought up in France.

The documentary evidence for these and other tales is feeble. But as the speculators point out, documentary evidence in Victoria's circle was severely censored. Even the queen's journals were heavily edited and altered by one of her daughters. Another story is that her son Edward celebrated his accession to the monarchy by heaving out of Windsor Castle every object that might remind him of John Brown. Edward was sixty when he became king. He had spent most of his mortal life despised and domineered and treated as an irresponsible adolescent by his mother. Like many ordinary people in Britain, he must have thought the old lady would never die and, for a good part of that time, the affection and respect that should have been given to a son and heir was reserved for a Scottish ghillie with ideas above his station.

It is possible, since anything is possible, that John was lover as well as hired help. It probably isn't really important. What is absolutely clear is that John Brown gave every evidence of having what he wanted. And although he would have been careful never to use the phrase in the queen's hearing (or who knows? maybe he had licence in that field too) he didn't give a damn.

29

THE FLYING
SCOTSMAN

For THE REAL high flier, however, the palm must be awarded to Percy Pilcher.

Everything in history of any importance happened first in Scotland. In Scotland, man conquered the air. Percy Pilcher flew.

Certainly, he died young. He died in the air. Young Percy Pilcher knew that a man could take off in a heavier-than-air machine, and he did it. He was a humble worker on the staff of the naval architecture department of Glasgow University, and he knew that man could and would fly. He thought up, and made with his own hands, the machine that Leonardo da Vinci had dreamed of and never quite managed. Percy built a glider, and it worked.

He knew it would work. He was a Scot, who worked out the snags, and circumvented them. Another thing nobody knows is that this young man solved problems that would not arise until decades after his death. The undercarriages of modern intercontinental aeroplanes are based on his predictions. He thought of shock-absorbing springs. He thought of nearly everything. And he flew.

Pilcher piloted the first heavier-than-air, man-operated machine that ever took off the ground in Britain. It was his own handiwork. He got into the driving seat and flew this thing, beautifully. The system of launching gliders and sailplanes has not changed much since he worked it out before the turn of the century. It is all his.

Pilcher (the name does not sound excessively Scottish, but Scotland is where he was, and where he did it) first took a kind of aeroplane off the ground near Dumbarton in the year 1895.

Four years later, in 1899, he got ambitious. He fitted a petrol engine to one of his machines and invented the powered aeroplane. It got off the ground, several years before Wilbur and Orville Wright.

The end is a sad story. Percy took a powered machine into the air. It worked. A control wire broke. The machine turned upside down and crashed to earth. It was destroyed, along with the pilot-designer.

It would be four years before the Wright brothers, who had never heard of Percy Pilcher, or maybe they had, took their little machine into the air and imagined they had invented the aviation industry. There is no need to steal the glory from Wilbur and Orville. They did it, and they didn't get killed. Three cheers for the Wright brothers.

Four cheers for Percy Pilcher.

30

THE
WORLD SHAKERS

THE MOST worrying Scottish flights, certainly in the eyes of our
southern neighbours in England, are mainly oratorical. In that
area, we have rarely touched down. To the outsider, Scottish
political history means two things, and both of them are terrifying:
the Red Clydesiders, bent on hurling the country forward into Red
ruin; and the hairy-kneed Scottish Nationalists, determined to turn
back the clock and restore the golden age of rugged independence so
bloodily won under Robert the Bruce at Bannockburn in 1314.

There is truth in both myths, if they are taken with a pinch of salt
and not too solemnly. In infancy, Scotsmen still absorb into the
bloodstream the valiant words of Burns:

> Scots, wha hae wi' Wallace bled,
> Scots, wham Bruce has often led,
> Welcome to your gory bed,
> Or to victory!

The victory of the dream is, of course, victory against the evil
English and for liberation. In the weave of the Scottish psyche, it is
still a thread of strong colour, even if sophisticated Scots explain it
away as symbolism or folklore, and carry on having a dram with
their English friends.

The truth is, anyway, that from the time of the Union of Parliaments in 1707, Scotland made very little mark on the British political
scene. It was largely irrelevant. Politics was a Whig–Tory seesaw.
Whiggism and Toryism were English inventions, and Scottish
Members of Parliament mostly found a small space on either end
of the seesaw and bobbed up and down with decent humility in the
company of their English betters.

This in itself helps to explain the sense of grievance that lurks in so
many Scots. The parliamentary time-servers might be content to
enjoy the dignity of Westminster and an occasional favour from the
great and powerful. The ordinary Scot very often thought of the

proud history, the Scottish creation of religious democracy, the endless output of original intellects, and the martial music of Robert Burns, and felt that the country's great traditions had been pushed aside, and the Scot reduced to an inferior citizen.

Add to this the ingrained egalitarianism of the Scot ('We're a' Jock Tamson's bairns') and it is quite hilarious to find that the pioneer champion of Scottishness and the equality of man was a thoroughbred aristocrat, descended from generations of the same and tracing the family line back to King Robert II of Scotland. Robert Bontine Cunninghame Graham was practically everything that no radical politician would dream of being, or could hope to be: one of the finest horsemen of his time, a master swordsman, adventurer, explorer, entrepreneur and, luckily for us, an author of superb talent.

Oddly enough, it all fits together. Don Roberto was a man completely integrated and annealed. Everything he did in life he did because it was there, and was the right thing to do at the time.

He was born in 1852, son of a Scottish father and a mother with Spanish and Italian blood. He grew up in the expansive comfort of the landed gentry, spent time visiting Spanish cousins and learning the language, went to school at Harrow, learned to ride, carried on his education in Brussels, learned French and fencing, and emerged, evidently, as the finished young aristocrat. He was barely seventeen.

Almost immediately he was offered the chance of sailing to the Argentine to take a partnership in a ranch. He arrived there in 1870, and spent most of the next ten years racketing about in the Americas, unconsciously studying animal and plant life, being swept up in revolution and disaster. If we are to believe his biographers (and why not?) he went through all this, he went through his entire life, without a trace of fear; a very parfit gentil knight.

When the ranch lost money, he took up trading in horses and cattle, in Uruguay and Chile, and lived out his own Wild West legend. His trading journeys stretched over hundreds of miles, and when he rode alongside the few gauchos who were his crew and his only companions, he rode harder than any. Even to those hard-bitten plainsmen, the gently bred adolescent was a legend, a gaucho among gauchos.

He first returned to Britain on hearing that his father was dangerously ill. His father had been thrown by a horse and the accident left his brain badly affected, and on his death, the responsibility of the family estates would fall on R.B. However, he survived, though still affected, and there was nothing for the boy usefully to do, so he left home again to travel in Europe. In Paris, he entered for an inter-

Americans are probably entitled to claim Alexander Graham Bell as their own but the Scottish connection is firmly established. Being tubercular he emigrated to Canada for his health and it was in Boston that the first magnetic telephone was produced in his laboratory (*Mansell Collection*)

On 'Bloody Sunday' a small quantity of the blood was Don Roberto's – R. B. Cunninghame Graham's (*above left*); (*above right*) James Ramsay MacDonald whose triumph was a tragedy; (*below*) Keir Hardie, the first Labour member of the House of Commons with (*left to right*) Mrs Bernard Shaw, Geoffrey Ramsay, a local supporter, and George Bernard Shaw, during the General Election, 1910 (*Mansell Collections*)

national fencing competition, and was well placed among the best. He also almost rode down a beautiful nineteen-year-old girl in a Paris street, made her acquaintance, and almost immediately took her to London to marry her.

Their marriage would have been easier, and less exciting, if he had been acceding to the family estates, but although his father was now virtually out of his mind he was still physically sound. Don Roberto took his bride to Texas to seek his fortune.

On the mere facts, the expedition was a disaster. They took a partnership in a ranch. Hostile Indians raided it and wiped it out.

Graham and his wife Gabrielle organised a shipment of cotton in San Antonio and set out to haul it to Mexico City in covered wagons. They survived a hideously cold journey through country infested with belligerent Indians and reached Mexico alive. During their trip, the price of cotton in Mexico City had collapsed and ruined the enterprise.

Nothing in life was capable of discouraging Don Roberto, or his wife, and they both turned cheerfully to odd jobs. Gabrielle took pupils in French and music. Graham drove cattle for a cowpuncher's wages, trained horses, and set up a school as 'Professor Bontini', fencing master. As always, he survived.

His father died in 1883, and the young couple came back to Scotland; but not to wealth or idleness. His father had run up enormous debts and Graham had to pay them off, partly by managing the estates and partly by selling off some of the inheritance. But managing the land didn't offer enough excitement for his nervous energy, and he went into politics.

It was inevitable that when he did go for politics, they should be radical politics. He was too independent to swim with any tide, and he formed his own judgements without reference to his class or his background. In his American adventures he had met and lived with the high and the low, and judged every man as he found him. As a boy, he had once decided that there were only two classes in society, 'the genuine, and the humbugs'. He had a temperamental passion for justice and the rights of the underdog. The Liberal Party of his time was his natural home.

In 1886 he was elected as Member for North-west Lanarkshire. He was not, however, a great parliamentarian. Westminster worried him, bored him, exasperated him. Graham had the laudable, but naïve, idea that Parliament was there to right wrongs and abolish the terrible injustices of Victorian Britain, preferably at once. When he rose to speak in the House it was usually as an avenging angel— an angel with a rich command of salty, un-parliamentary English.

It would be hard to claim that Don Roberto had any important influence on the course of British politics, because at heart he was unpolitical. He was a maverick, with no taste for power groupings and backroom manoeuvres. His value—and maybe it is enough—was that he enlivened political life and that he was the voice of conscience. Every age needs such a man, and few ages find one so richly coloured.

He had spent one spell in prison in South America in fear of his life. He did his time in a British prison too.

On 13 November 1887, there was a working-class protest demonstration in Trafalgar Square, which was attended by several non-proletarian notables sympathetic to the underprivileged—George Bernard Shaw, Mrs Annie Besant, Prince Kropotkin, John Burns and others; and R. B. Cunninghame Graham. In working-class history the day is known as Bloody Sunday, and a small quantity of the blood was Don Roberto's.

When the police made a baton charge, they ignored most of the important people, but perhaps Graham's appearance itself was provocative. He dressed like an adventurer, with a dark cloak and a theatrical broad-brimmed hat, and he attracted attention when he wasn't even trying to. He was clubbed down by the police, and John Burns was arrested with him. Each was sent to prison for six weeks for unlawful assembly. He survived this as cheerfully as he had survived Indian raids and bankruptcy.

Although a Liberal Party member, Graham described himself as a socialist. The word has been used by so many people of contrasting opinions that it isn't easy to tell what it meant in his case. Basically, no doubt, an unshakable passion for social justice. In any case, his parliamentary life was fairly brief. He was a Member for only six years before he returned to the life of adventure, and later found his strength as a writer.

This is not to say he became apathetic or disillusioned. He simply put his energies where they flourished best. His wife died young, they had no children and he had no ties, but he never lost interest in the affairs of Scotland. In 1928 he was elected first President of the Scottish National Society.

At the age of seventy-three, Graham travelled up the Orinoco and then set out on horseback, alone, to explore the plains of Venezuela. On a later journey to South America, at the age of eighty-four, he died in Buenos Aires.

Long before that, however, one brief incident in his parliamentary life links him with the mainstream of the Labour movement.

During his time in Parliament the Liberals, for want of anybody else, were the spokesmen for labour and the working class. Politics was a middle-class or upper-class affair, and the idea that working men themselves might enter Parliament was novel and even absurd. But working men were active in the Liberal Party, and a campaign was beginning to show itself. In 1888, when the Liberal Member for Mid-Lanark resigned his seat, there was a Labour politician available and very willing to take his place.

It was R. B. Cunninghame Graham who was urgently called to the district to use his persuasive influence on the local Liberal Association to back the working man. Graham was the man, if any, who would support Labour representation.

He hurried to Mid-Lanark and did his best to encourage a historic decision. Unfortunately, the politicians had already been at work, and another decision had been made on the quiet. There were bitter arguments, and some more of those back-room manoeuvres that were alien to Graham, but the local association in the end were attracted to an elegant Welsh advocate, and the Labour hopeful was discarded.

In the end, the decision proved ironic. The man who was so fiercely disappointed was to become the pioneer of Labour representation in the House of Commons, and launch the destruction of the Liberal Party itself. His name was James Keir Hardie.

Keir Hardie's name has acquired the status of sainthood among later generations of Labour enthusiasts; or perhaps he comes down as a blend of saint, Jack the Giant Killer, and Samson bringing down the temple in ruins. And the most vivid image in his struggle is of his eventual and triumphant arrival at Westminster, sitting atop a two-horse charabanc, defiantly wearing a cloth cap instead of the obligatory bowler hat, and with a bugler announcing his coming. Reporters were startled. Middle-aged Conservative citizens trembled at the harbinger of the Apocalypse. The End, the absolute End, was at hand.

It wasn't, of course.

If it is possible at this date to stand back and see Keir Hardie clearly (and it is not easy for a Scottish writer who grew up in the Labour movement in the fierce glow of the Hardie legend), the spectacular assault on Westminster, the bastion of capitalism, was just a bit of a show and, apart from precipitating some paroxyms in White's Club, it did no particular harm and has provided a lot of innocent amusement to Labour supporters ever since. The bastion failed to fall. There was perhaps a hint of localised crumbling, but generations of struggle, advance and recoil, were to pass before the upper-class monopoly of power in Britain was to be cracked.

Keir Hardie certainly had the childhood qualifications for a radical reformer. His father was a carpenter, sometimes on land, sometimes at sea, and often nowhere because of industrial depression. James was born in a mining village near Glasgow, in 1856, and spent his childhood in the city itself, in conditions which it is not easy to imagine for anyone raised in modern times in a western country. Victorian Britain, proud of its technical genius, its leadership of the Industrial Revolution, its imperial magnificence and its dedication to Christian charity, was also a profoundly callous society by our standards. It was both convenient and natural for the prosperous bourgeoisie, or even the successful proletariat, to equate unemployment and poverty with sin, the sin of the unemployed and the poor.

Charity was of course a virtue, and could help a generous donor into Heaven. As more than one cynic has said, philanthropy is the millionaire's form of life insurance. But those who needed charity had certainly themselves to blame and were no better than they should be.

I am of course oversimplifying this. We usually oversimplify when we discuss the Victorians. There were men (like Don Roberto, to mention only one) who had a quite different view of social ills. But the oversimplification has truth in it.

It was also a stratified society. Intelligent Victorians could believe simultaneously that society was progressive and mobile, for *them*, and that it was their right and their duty to improve their lot; and that society was also stable and should not be upset; the people at the bottom should not start pushing and disturbing the balance.

Remember that moving Victorian hymn, 'All things bright and beautiful', and its ominous third verse which reads,

> The rich man in his castle,
> The poor man at his gate,
> God made them, high or lowly,
> And ordered their estate.

This was the charitable, smug, unimaginative culture in which young James saw the light of day. As a child, he had to help the family out by working as an errand boy, and we have the record (presumably from Keir Hardie himself) of an early experience of brutal nineteenth-century capitalism.

Leaving the family hovel, where there was rarely a crust to spare, the boy arrived hungry and a few minutes late at the bakery shop where he worked. He was summoned to the parlour, where his boss was sitting down to a hearty cooked breakfast, the very smell of which stunned young James.

The baker, without interrupting his meal, delivered a sarcastic harangue on Keir Hardie's worthlessness and threatened to throw him out without pay if he was late again. After trying to mumble a defence, the boy stood humbly and tried to keep his mind off the egg and bacon on the table. Soon afterwards he turned up late for work again and was fired on the spot, without the wages due to him.

An experience like this is the stuff of which revolutionaries are made, and James's sense of injustice was bolstered by his father, who was embittered against society and religion by his own misfortunes.

In his youth, Hardie and his brothers found work in the coal industry in Airdrie during the desperate depression of the 1870s, when wages were at rock bottom and the coalmasters intended to keep them there. James became one of the miners who were prepared to speak out against the wretched conditions in the industry, and his bosses reacted as firmly as that Glasgow baker. When he and his brothers turned up for work one day the entire family was ordered out of the pit. The brothers, who had done nothing, were guilty by association.

From that moment on, Hardie was set on the path of a professional radical. Though he managed to scrape a living as a small shopkeeper, his enthusiasm went into acting as local correspondent for a radical Liberal newspaper, the *Glasgow Weekly Mail*, which gave him a grounding in journalism and made him a dedicated propagandist.

He was not, certainly not at that time, the conventional embodiment of the social revolutionary, devoted to destroying capitalist society and ushering in the 'red dawn'. He didn't even think of himself as a socialist. In fact, he was both simple and complicated. He read Robert Burns rather than Karl Marx. He was also, in spite of his father's outspoken atheism, an earnest Christian. He had been 'saved', during the ferment that followed the Moody and Sankey revival, and attached himself to a small Presbyterian sect. He was also a vigorous advocate against drink, the curse of the working classes. He was a man of his time.

His religion was the religion of a natural dissenter. Mainstream Calvinism in his time was strong on the curious Doctrine of Election, which holds that salvation is reserved exclusively for the chosen few, and that the non-Elect are bound for Hell no matter how hard they try to be good. Hardie and his friends in the splinter church of the Morisonians would have none of this. He believed that salvation was for everybody; and if heavenly bliss was available to all, the same should apply to earthly comfort.

With his little shop, and his standing as a radical journalist, Hardie became a central figure in the anti-boss movement in the district. He was invited to organise a strike against a reduction in miners' wages, and did it well. The strike failed, but he was invited to work as an organiser by the miners of Ayrshire. He moved to Cumnock, where he married and raised a family and which was his home till he died; and where he is still remembered as something almost more than human. Almost at once he was leading the Tattie Strike of 1881, a miners' stoppage that stuck out for over two months on a diet of potatoes, because they had no money and potatoes could be had free. The strike collapsed, virtually of malnutrition, but soon afterwards there was an upsurge in the national economy and wages were improved. The miners felt they had won, and Hardie was their man.

He found work with a local newspaper, became secretary of the Ayrshire Miners' Union and a local power in the land. With this standing, and a reasonably settled way of life, he began to think of national politics, and saw his chance to do something about it. The Liberal Member for North Ayrshire, the Hon H. F. Eliot, defected to the Unionist Party, and a Liberal candidate was needed to oppose him at the next election. Keir Hardie submitted himself to the Liberals for the nomination.

He was turned down.

There were probably many reasons for the rejection. The Liberals were having enough troubles in the country without risking their money on a newcomer whose record might antagonise douce Liberal voters. But Keir Hardie took the dismissal as a deliberate snub to the working classes (because the successful nominee was a rich baronet) and to himself.

One irreverent biographer has suggested that Keir Hardie was a simple man with an inferiority complex who went through life looking for insults, braced to receive them and determined never to forgive them. The judgement is probably harsh. Nobody likes to be rejected, and he could claim that he had devoted his life to the Labour cause and was the right man to represent it in Parliament. And more snubs and rejections were in store for him.

Another Liberal MP, Stephen Mason, resigned his seat at Mid-Lanark, and it was then that a wellwisher sent a telegram to R. B. Cunninghame Graham, who rushed to Glasgow to propose the adoption of Keir Hardie. He failed.

Smarting under the new insult, Hardie now saw for the first time the possibility of a working man's candidate, a Labour candidate, fighting the Liberal Party itself.

'My advice,' he wrote in a miners' newspaper, 'would be that the Labour candidate should be put forward. Better split the Party now than at a General Election, and if the Labour party only make their power felt now, terms will not be wanting when the General Election comes.'

He was using his muscle as a journalist to push through his adoption as a politician. But the Liberal Party didn't take him seriously. Pondering over several candidates, the local association was finally won over by a young barrister, later Lord St Davids. As a consolation, Hardie was offered a chance at the next General Election, and a small salary in the meantime. He was outraged.

With the help of a donation, he fought his own fight. He was miserably defeated, came in at the bottom of the list with fewer than 700 votes. His response was to gather some sympathetic friends and found the Scottish Labour Party. It was a poor and ineffectual affair, but that probably didn't worry its founder too much. We can sense that he enjoyed being a voice in the wilderness. And it started something, because it was not the Labour Party, it was the *Scottish* Labour Party, and Hardie was as eager to throw off the trammels of English political bosses as he was for socialism.

The Scottish Labour Party achieved nothing. It was small, and shrill, and fruitless. The workers simply didn't want to know about it. It did scatter some small seeds which would grow slowly, almost outside of the political arena, into a nationalist idea which started rising in strength as a political force long after Keir Hardie was dead. By the 1920s, Home Rule for Scotland was a respectable plank in the platform of Labour politicians. They never found the power, or the time, or perhaps the practical inclination, to do anything positive about it, and maybe the idea was more sentimental than real. But it wouldn't go away, and in time it was taken over by other people and acquired momentum as a political force in its own right. For this Keir Hardie may fairly be given the credit, or the blame.

In the meantime, the slightly soured propagandist was whisked out of the Scottish scene to make history. In London, there was a split in the West Ham Liberal Association, and the rebel faction invited Keir Hardie to stand against the official Liberal candidate. How that fight might have gone, nobody can guess. It never happened, since the Liberal man died during the campaign, and his supporters had no choice but to rally behind the Labour runner, knowing that at least he would support them in the House rather than their enemies.

And so James Keir Hardie, a Joshua come to Jericho, confronted Westminster with the sound of trumpets.

Since he had lost the Scottish connection, he joined with others in transforming the Scottish Labour Party into the Independent Labour Party, to bring socialism to English, Scots and Welsh alike.

The long-term ambition of the new party was to win Parliament. Its short-term tactics were to irritate the Liberals, and put up hopeless fights against them at elections, to split the progressive vote and demoralise them.

However, as the organisation matured it concentrated on actually getting Labour representatives into Parliament, and in the long to-and-fro strife of the twentieth century, it succeeded. More than that, and perhaps even more satisfying to its first chairman, it pushed the great Liberal Party into the outskirts of British politics. Modern British Liberals may well think their long-dead colleagues in North Ayrshire, preferring a baronet to an ex-miner, served their party very, very ill.

Maybe it is a very Scottish thing that, having made his mark, the prophet began to fade from the scene. He was not re-elected for West Ham in 1900, but five years later he returned to Parliament for the Welsh constituency of Merthyr Tydfil. He did not leave a big impression on the House. He died in 1915, of a broken heart, it is suggested. World War I had broken out, and some members of the Labour Party had even joined the War Cabinet in defiance of the movement's pacifist ideals. Wherever the party was going, he had lost touch with it.

Hardie is dismissed elegantly and cruelly in an essay published by Donald Carswell in 1927 in these words:

> Common sense Keir Hardie had not, any more than he had the salt and salacious humour by which a merciful Providence has redeemed Scotsmen at large from being the dreariest race of prigs west of Suez . . . Sincerity he certainly had, and good intentions, but as his sincerity manifested itself in a petty fanaticism, and his good intentions usually took a spiteful turn, the value of these qualities is subject to a large discount.

Maybe, maybe. Hardie's seminal achievement and his legacy to Labour politics is not to be discounted, and nobody in Cumnock will ever accept a breath of criticism of the man or his works.

The next rebellious Scot to assault, and to charm, British politics was decidedly a man with plenty of that salt humour that Carswell missed in Keir Hardie. The 'beloved rebel', James Maxton, even charmed his bitterest political enemies as he ploughed a straight furrow towards the promised land of socialism, peace on earth and universal brotherhood. So radical reform in Scotland threw up three commanding figures who resembled one another in practically no respect except political conviction: the dashing aristocrat Don Roberto, the prickly Christian ex-miner Keir Hardie and Maxton, the man with the gift of tongues, once described by Winston Churchill as 'the finest gentleman in the House of Commons'.

Jimmy Maxton, who led the Independent Labour Party through troublous times, and later into the political wilderness, was born neither to land and wealth nor to grinding poverty. His father James was a schoolmaster. Young James, his brother John, and his sisters Jessie, Annie and Ada, all followed father into the profession.

He was an intelligent youngster growing up in a well-regulated family devoted to learning, and doing all the proper things, like winning a prize in Scripture at Barrhead Free Church in 1900 at the age of fifteen, and a bursary to Hutcheson's Grammar School; a useful athlete who went to Glasgow University, joined the Lanarkshire Rifle Volunteers and the University Unionist Association. He even worked for the Tory candidate in the university's rectorial election.

But in arguments with fellow students, he moved intellectually to socialism, joined the Barrhead branch of the Independent Labour Party in 1904 and taught Marxist philosophy at evening classes in his native villiage of Pollokshaws. By the age of twenty, this rebel had found his destiny. And already he had the quality (the recent vogue word was 'charisma') that irresistibly attracted attention. He was slender, gaunt and sallow, with long black hair, a born performer with masterly timing and the knack of dominating any audience, and he made his impression on the Cranston's Crowd. This was a group of the new Labour enthusiasts, a generation after Keir Hardie, who met endlessly in Cranston's Tearooms in Glasgow, endlessly drank tea and endlessly shattered the universe to bits and remade it to the heart's desire.

The place was suitable. It was built to the design of Charles Rennie Mackintosh, the Glasgow architect who led the art nouveau revolution. The tea was also essential. Thirty years later, when I first encountered the ILP, the buoyant comrades were still swallowing gallons and gallons of tea. It was as if the revolution was to be swept into being on a tidal wave of tea.

The ILP, certainly the ILP in the vicinity of Maxton, was never a dour, dogged spearhead of a cheerless Armageddon. It was savagely angered by poverty and injustice, and irrepressibly cheerful and optimistic. In 1910, when the Cranston's Crowd were plotting the future, it didn't have a lot to be cheerful about. World War I was just round the corner, and the courage of the faithful was to be stretched to twanging point. But they would bear it.

The ILP, then and later, was also never a monolithic structure like the Bolsheviks. The general aim of socialism brought together an electrifying variety of opinions and intellects, maybe unique in political history. John Wheatley (whose son is now a High Court judge) was a devout Roman Catholic. F. C. Young was an Anglican clergyman. James Barr was, and Campbell Stephen had been, Presbyterian ministers. George Smith was a loquacious atheist. John S. Clark was a lay preacher.

There were committed Marxists and incredulous anti-Marxists, revolutionists, gradualists, social democrats, quasi-communists, devoted family men and free-love enthusiasts. In later years, some teachers dragged in Freud to be synthesised with Marx, thus adding to the confusion and the intellectual entertainment.

All these people worked happily enough together to bring about the new society, and although it didn't happen as they planned, it did happen now and then in a way, since they created a new society among themselves, sharpening their minds on the dialectic. No political party has ever been more varied, more literate or more politically sophisticated than the ILP. These were the Red Clydesiders, whose very name was a threat to all established law and order.

When war broke out, the Labour parliamentarians who joined the Cabinet supported the Defence of the Realm Act, a blanket law designed to enforce patriotism and conformity at all costs, and particularly among socialists and pacifists. The ILP group insisted on remaining both, and they became isolated from the national Labour movement because, according to one observer, 'Glasgow was a place where patriots were on the way out'.

They fought against the eviction of soldiers' wives who couldn't pay increased rents, they opposed conscription. The British Government actually deported three of them to Edinburgh to silence them. Jimmy Maxton, a lifelong pacifist, lost his job as a schoolteacher for declaring himself a conscientious objector, and was facing internment. He forestalled the authorities by inviting a prison sentence with a speech on Glasgow Green against war and any war effort. He exhorted the audience to strike, down tools, and hamper any production of munitions. Since policemen were taking notes of his speech, he repeated it for them.

He was arrested, and bail was refused. As Lord Ormidale, the judge, said, 'This offence is grave, dangerous, cowardly and of the most outrageous nature.' When he came up for trial with other subversives he pleaded guilty and was sentenced to a year's imprisonment in Calton Jail.

The government was right to be afraid of the Red Clydesiders. Their message of uncompromising socialism and pacifism was finding a response. Even before the war ended, the socialist May Day demonstration of 1918 attracted the biggest crowds in the history of the celebration.

In the General Election of that year, Jimmy Maxton stood in Bridgeton, against the Coalition candidate McCallum Scott, and was defeated by 10,887 votes to 7,860. Even that size of minority showed the influence of the ILP propaganda throughout the war. Four years later, in the same constituency, the figures were: Maxton, 17,800; Scott, 10,188.

From then until his death in 1946, Maxton virtually owned the electors of Bridgeton. The local saying was that they didn't have to count the ballot papers, only to weigh them. The reason wasn't just political. Maxton was there, people could speak to him and even touch him, and practically anybody who did speak to him fell under his spell. In my own experience, not many people *liked* Maxton. They either didn't know him, or they loved him. His charm, I am going to suggest, was not spurious or professional. He himself was in love with people.

His political career, in retrospect, doesn't seem very important. He never served in a Government, he never put through radical laws. He was elected Chairman of the ILP in 1926, but already the Labour movement was heading for fission. The ILP was affiliated to the Labour Party, but both groups were beginning to find the company uncomfortable. In simple terms, the Labour Party was devoted to the practical business of parliamentary power, and the ILP was concerned with creating the long-term strategy for an ideal Britain, and with being the conscience of the movement; often a noisy and awkward conscience.

The whole movement had the political tide running against it anyway. In 1931 the National Government called an election and Labour was massacred, its 300 seats cut to 52. Only three ILP members survived, including Maxton. In the next year, the two groups separated permanently, and Maxton led the ILP out into the cold.

Well, not exactly the cold. The faithful who stayed with the party never lost their cheerfulness, their variety or their conviction that the People would one day suddenly turn to them and hoist them into power. In the meantime, since the day was not imminent, they could devote themselves to preaching the pure doctrine (or the seven and seventy pure doctrines) of Socialism and brotherly love. They went on doing this, and consuming torrents of tea until, after Maxton's death, the party simply melted away. The leader they adored had led them out of Egypt and up a dead end. In plain political terms, they had been disastrously wrong.

But it is still not possible to dismiss Maxton. He cut a wide swathe. His influence on people inside and outside his party was prodigious.

Unlike Keir Hardie and Cunninghame Graham, Jimmy Maxton took easily to the parliamentary trade, enjoyed the ritual and the tradition, and became one of the greatest of parliamentarians. When he rose to speak, the benches started to fill because, whatever he said, he was incapable of being a bore. Whatever he said, it usually mattered. A political opponent said that, no matter how much he enjoyed Westminster, he never for a moment forgot the poverty and hunger of the slums and the burden of justice he had taken on his shoulders.

In his early days he was suspended when a Tory minister declined to act on evacuating slum children from an area raging with infectious disease. Maxton accused the minister of murder, and refused to apologise or withdraw. In later years he had the skill to be just as damaging without infringing the rules of the House, and he used his skill.

In World War II, with his colleagues John McGovern and Campbell Stephen, he stuck by his unswerving pacifism, and regularly attacked Prime Minister Churchill. The two men privately enjoyed a mutual regard and affection, for the reason that nobody could hate the Member for Bridgeton, and he was incapable of hating anybody else.

It is reasonable to assume that his presence in Parliament, and his whole life of propaganda, helped to influence the Commons' attitude in World War II to pacifists and dissenters, and even to the poor and underprivileged. If he was a political failure, he was not nothing.

What Maxton brought to the public life of Scotland, and Britain, was himself. He emanated his own magic. When I think of some of the figures in world politics who have actually achieved what they set out to do, and shudder at the sight—Attila, Hitler, Stalin—I am willing to say that the odd Scottish system of failing to win the goal, and doing something better on the way, isn't at all a bad system.

Maxton's failure was a triumph of a kind. The triumph of his contemporary James Ramsay MacDonald was a tragedy. Or perhaps tragedy is too important a word. It was a spectacular voyage to nowhere. MacDonald won the glittering crown, but his head lay uneasy under it. He knew where he was going, and got there; and proved the theory that the worst thing that can happen to us is to get what we want.

Ramsay Mac is remembered too as one of the great political speakers of his time and, like the predictable Scot, he came from nothing. He was born in 1866, in the little town of Lossiemouth, without a father. Maybe his illegitimacy was the extra incentive to his pursuit of greatness. Or maybe he just had the stuff in him.

He had to leave school as a boy to work on a farm, but his teacher was so concerned at the loss of such talent and energy that he got the lad back into school as a pupil-teacher. He was an obsessional reader and student, and soon outgrew the limitations of Lossiemouth and went to London at nineteen to seek his fortune.

He was already politically committed to the Left. He was also tough and resilient and prepared to starve if necessary. One legend has it that he managed to survive in London on oatmeal sent from home. This legend is so hoary, so persistent and so improbable in Scottish history that it may even be true.

His first professional passion was science, but he fell ill before he could complete a science course, and became a journalist. In his twenties, he was invited to take charge of the *Labour Leader*, the weekly propaganda paper of the Independent Labour Party. Two years later he met Margaret Gladstone, a niece of the great Lord Kelvin; they fell madly in love and married. It was a Cinderella story. The poor boy had found his Princess Charming, the princess was rich and his material troubles were over. Margaret was also a political enthusiast, and founded the Women's Labour League. She died young, at forty-one, but by that time James was well launched on his way to the top.

He was elected to Parliament in 1906, and a few years later was the leader of the Parliamentary Labour Party. With World War I, he was out of Parliament, and spent some years in the wilderness, but came back in 1922, as leader of the Opposition. In the election of 1924, no single party had a majority in the Commons, and Mac-Donald was invited by the King to form a minority Government.

Unlike many of his fire-eating comrades, he did not bristle at the sight of privilege and power. He represented the working class with complete sincerity but he quite liked the upper classes, and found himself overwhelmed, as he himself said, by the king's gracious attitude on their first meeting. King George had a private apprehension that a Labour Government would sweep away the colourful old traditions of Parliament, but the new Prime Minister, without consulting the party, felt able to reassure His Majesty. MacDonald's colleagues were shattered to see him next day on his way to court, dressed in high-class finery with a lot of gold braid and a sword.

They were even more scandalised by a report that Alexander Grant, an old school friend and now a wealthy biscuit manufacturer, had given him a present of £30,000 in shares in the company, and a Daimler car. They were incensed when Grant received a baronetcy in the next Honours List; but in fairness it must be stated that the honour had already been put in motion by the previous Government. Whatever the details, the important thing is that in the intoxicating atmosphere of power, Ramsay MacDonald steadily drifted out of touch with the radical traditions of left-wing Labour. He had a natural talent for compromise, and this is by no means a bad thing in practical politics; but political enthusiasts usually see such a talent as a grave sin.

He didn't favour the 1926 General Strike for instance, and to passionate Labourites that event was regarded as separating the sheep from the goats. The strike was heroic in its way, dramatic in its way, and in the end a failure. This might seem to vindicate MacDonald's opposition to it, but it widened the gap between him and his old friends. His personal charm still worked, all the same, and during the electoral ups and downs of the next few years he kept his position as leader.

Still, the gap widened. Increasingly, MacDonald seemed to prefer the company of the Tories, and when the Labour vote slumped disastrously in the 1931 General Election, the Tories were content to let him carry on as Prime Minister of the 'National' Government, although his so-called National Labour party had only a handful of MPs.

He had got to the top. In fact, ordinary non-political people in Britain were very happy with Ramsay MacDonald. He was a convincing Prime Minister, slender, handsome, with a splendid shock of white hair, an earnest candid gaze and a fine command of language. The Scottish burr, the richly rolling R sounds, were extra evidence of integrity and honesty. (This notion still persists among English people. When, decades later, commercial television arrived in Britain, a lot of advertisers plumped for commercials using Scottish accents, which were believed to convey an impression of incorruptible honesty.)

But behind the convincing front, Ramsay MacDonald was more and more a hollow political figure, kept in place, if not in real power, by the people who were supposed to be his political enemies. More and more, his rich oratory too was a hollow thing, full of sound and fury and signifying very little. In his latter days he was capable of gripping an audience by sheer technical skill and nothing else. In cold print, his speeches are like colourful dressing for an empty window.

He lingered on as a colourful Scottish figurehead during the Royal Jubilee celebration of 1935, and was then quietly replaced by Stanley Baldwin as Prime Minister. In the next election he was trounced by

Mannie Shinwell, another of the Red Clydesiders, and was out of Parliament entirely. He was able to regain a seat in Parliament at a by-election, but by then he was a lonely, lost figure with all his real, or imagined, success behind him. He died in 1937; some say of disillusion.

For years afterwards the very name Ramsay MacDonald meant Traitor to enthusiastic Labourites, particularly in the ILP. It is hardly fair. He had great talents and great charm, and it is doubtful if he ever consciously betrayed his principles. He was ambitious, and he achieved some of his ambitions, and somehow went astray with consciously good intentions.

MacDonald honestly believed in compromise. He was never a socialist in any extreme sense, and had no liking for left-wing passions such as nationalising major industries. His vision of an ideal Britain was one in which the worker got a decent share of the national wealth without sweeping away the capitalist process.

There were some Conservatives, in fact, who were more radical. Harold Macmillan, usually regarded as an arch-Tory, was in favour of nationalising electricity and insurance during his early days in Parliament, and once described his own front bench as a collection of disused slag heaps.

Macmillan does not qualify as a native Scot, and he certainly was not the poor farm boy who made good, though part of his entertaining posture in politics was the suggestion that he was the son of a poor crofter. His grandfather was certainly an impoverished farmer on the Isle of Arran, who cleared out to England and founded a successful publishing company. By the time Harold was born, in London, the Macmillans were a solid, wealthy family who could send the boy to Eton and Oxford and give him the polish of the total aristocrat, English-style. His very accent, his bland conviction of his own rightness, often drove socialists to blind fury.

He did not go astray. He enjoyed politics, he enjoyed being Prime Minister, he enjoyed power without being bowled over by it. He was the Unflappable. Vicky the cartoonist christened him 'Supermac'. On one occasion, at a single stroke, he sacked practically his entire cabinet and brought in a completely new collection. He coined the electoral slogan: 'You never had it so good.'

All in all, he doesn't belong in a gallery of archetypal Scottish politicians. On the other hand, every Scot is an archetype of his own. You may hate him, as long as you fear him.

On that basis, Supermac qualifies as a Scot.

DERRING-DO

(Some Bonnie Fighters)

THE OUTSIDER hoping to analyse and quantify the force of Scottish nationalism would be well advised to study rhododendrons or golden eagles or something equally simple. If he conducts a survey on nationalism he will get a contradictory conclusion every day for a year or more.

In one sense, it is a yo-yo phenomenon. Political support for a nationalist crusade rises and falls. In recent decades, voters have rushed to boost the fortunes of the Scottish National Party, have rushed just as fast to desert the party's candidates, rushed back, rushed forward. Standing for public office under the SNP banner is a stimulating, rather than a soothing, hobby.

In modern times, there arose the Scottish Covenant movement, which collected a million and a half signatures in favour of reviewing the position of Scotland inside the United Kingdom. The Government in London deliberated briefly on this event, and decided that, if ignored, it would go away. But in any country which feels aggrieved, and especially in Scotland, there will always be a supply of romantics who are ready to make a spectacular gesture and, if possible, shake governments to their foundations. The need brings forth the hour, and the hour, the man. This is the tale of such a man, a tale of breath-catching peril and arduous adventure, of triumph and anticlimax, of national shock and national hilarity. Nobody gets shot at and nobody gets injured, but the excitement is genuine; and gentlemen in Scotland now a-bed shall think themselves accursed they were not there, and hold their manhoods cheap while any speaks that strove to save the Stone of Destiny.

It all began in 1295, when Edward I of England gave his support to a puppet monarch for Scotland, John Balliol, the Toom Tabard (empty coat) of Scottish history. Edward presumed too much, and Balliol made an alliance with France against his overlord. Edward was livid, and bursting with Plantagenet pride. He took an army into Scotland and smashed all opposition, and loosed his victorious

The River Clyde has always dominated the consciousness of Glaswegians: (*above*) 'Off down the Water' a postcard view *c* 1902; and perhaps it was to escape from scenes like this that drove them out of the city. But note the billposter for the summer pantomime (*The Mitchell Library, Graham Collection*)

(*left-above*) Harry Lauder, the only internationally famous Scottish comedian, imposed his Scotland on the English-speaking world with arrogant aplomb; (*right-above*) regarded by many professionals as 'the daddy' of them all, and revered by the Glasgow public, Tommy Lorne's genius lay in his presence; (*lower*) an undated photograph of the 'Comet', presumably taken in the mid-nineteenth century (*Glasgow Herald*)

troops on an orgy of massacre. Within a few months, Balliol sur-
rendered the throne to the English king.

Edward marched his men to the north of Scotland to demonstrate
his power. On the way back, he paused at the Abbey of Scone in
Perthshire, where, as an arrogant afterthought, he had the Stone of
Destiny picked up and transported to London.

Now the Stone of Destiny was, and is, heap big juju to every Scot
with a sense of history. It was on this piece or rock, or on a seat above
it, that Scottish kings had sat to be crowned throughout three or
four centuries, and the kings of Dálriada for centuries earlier. Legend
has it (a wild thing in Scotland, legend) that it was the very stone on
which Jacob pillowed his head when he dreamed of the ladder to
Heaven. And in taking it to England, Edward was symbolically
removing the true, the anointed, seat of Scottish kingship. Clearly,
when the thing was installed in a throne at Westminster, any man
crowned on that throne would hold Scotland in thrall.

It didn't work out exactly in that way. After Balliol came the
doomed liberator William Wallace, and after Wallace came Robert
the Bruce, and with Robert the Bruce came the independence of
Scotland, Stone or no Stone. When the two countries reached an
uneasy peace a few generations later, by the Treaty of Northampton,
a clause was included that the Stone would be returned to Scone.

Somehow, it never happened. And it rankled. After the two
kingdoms were united, under James VI of Scotland and I of England,
it no longer seemed to matter. Nevertheless, it still rankled. Honour
was unsatisfied.

Now we move through the centuries to our own, and to the time
when the London Government was loftily ignoring the aspirations
of half the Scottish electorate to a review of the England–Scotland
relationship. One young man in Glasgow, talking half in jest to his
friends about the plight of the Covenant movement, suddenly
conceived a masterstroke of propaganda. He would bring the Stone
back to Scone, he would dare all and brave all to strike a blow for
Scottish nationhood.

He was Ian Hamilton, a university student in his twenties; and
from his own reminiscences, we get the impression that he was
prepared to swoop on London singlehanded if he had to, and rush
north with the precious relic in his arms. He cannily discussed the
plot with another student, a young man of some influence, who
encouraged him but eventually drew back from the scheme. Hamilton then plunged into the perilous business of organising a cabal;
and the main peril of that job is that other people have to be ap-

proached, and any one of them might be the man who will expose the plot. More than one, in fact, listened to his vague plans and decided to have nothing to do with it, and he became more and more anxious that the secret was passing into the hands of people who were not committed to it.

But it would be a poor day in Scotland when a patriot couldn't rally a few stout-hearted comrades for a scheme of such dramatic craziness. Virtually penniless, Hamilton found a businessman prepared to subsidise the plan, and one by one recruited the rest of his team: Gavin Vernon, Kay Mathieson, and Alan Stuart. Kay Mathieson, pretty, petite, and working as a schoolteacher, seemed a very unlikely conspirator, but she gave the conspiracy the advantage that nobody suspects a pretty girl of anything but innocence. Gavin Vernon, now successfully settled in Canada, was ideal conspirator material, tough, energetic and reckless. Stuart, a gentle and thoughtful young man, actually volunteered, and was nearly turned down till he revealed that he could get a car.

Hamilton spent a little of his small subsidy on a reconnaissance trip to London, where he joined a group of tourists on a tour of Westminster Abbey and cased the joint. The tour guide was happy to answer all his questions, and he saw the Stone with his own eyes and estimated its size. It was sitting under a simple wooden throne, and to remove it would involve the removal of one piece of timber. He calculated that this could be done without damaging the throne, because he was particularly anxious that there would be no disrespect to treasured artifacts, and no damage to things or persons.

He was delighted that the Westminster authorities were thoughtful enough to publish accurate charts of the abbey, for the convenience of intruders. The layout of the place burned itself into his brain.

When he went back to Glasgow, his plan was practically complete. He was still worried about the weight of the prize, and decided to consult an expert.

The expert was Robert Gray, a popular figure in local Glasgow politics, a city councillor who was in business as a monumental sculptor; and an enthusiastic Scottish Nationalist. Bertie Gray fell into the spirit of the thing with pleasure, took the young man to a corner of his premises and showed him something startling: a replica of the Stone of Destiny. It had been carved for a previous conspiracy that never happened, with some idea of switching the duplicate for the real thing, but the plan had never matured. The weight was about 450lb. The stone was about 27in by 17in by 11in, and although it was not a trifle, it could certainly be lifted by two or three fit young men and taken to safety.

The operation was the predictable mixture of drama, comedy and farce. During the Christmas vacation of 1950, the four plotters travelled to London. They had two cars. During the early evening, Ian Hamilton joined the tourists in the abbey again, drifted away from the group and hid himself until everybody had gone and the place was locked. When he judged he was safe, and got up to explore, a door unexpectedly opened and he was challenged by a startled watchman. He played the innocent and said he had got lost, and the watchman saw him off the premises.

Later, sitting in one of the cars with Kay to keep watch on the abbey, he was approached by a policeman and challenged. The young people acted the part of scatterbrained lovers. Ian didn't even know the registration number of the car he was sitting in, and babbled that it was a hired car and another friend had all the papers; which was true. The constable might have questioned his right to be at the wheel, but the others turned up in time, and the police were apparently satisfied.

All this time, Ian Hamilton was bristling with burglary tools under his coat; and they finally managed to force their way into the abbey in the small hours. They got the Stone, but a piece of it broke off while it was being manhandled. It was now Christmas morning.

An ingenious element of the plan was that they would head for Dartmoor, while road blocks would presumably be springing up in the other direction, on the road to Scotland. In fact, they took the Stone to Kent, in the south east of England, and hid it in open country.

It was the juiciest news item of Christmas Day, and a shockwave went through Britain. Some people were shocked into fury; others into guffaws. The Dean of Westminster denounced the taking of the Stone as a 'sacrilegious and senseless crime'. A private citizen—in Scotland—offered a reward of £1,000 for the capture of the miscreants. One of the quartet, recalling the pursuit of Bonnie Prince Charlie, was fairly sure that if Scots wouldn't sell one man for £30,000, they wouldn't sell four for a mere £1,000.

To anyone with a nose for a secret and living in Glasgow at the time—and especially the West End of Glasgow, in the university district—it was a period rich with excitement and glee. The secret, of course, was not a total secret. Several people had wind of the plot in advance, and many others had powerful suspicions. It just happened that everybody who knew, or thought he knew, joined the conspiracy as accessory after the fact.

Newspaper reporters who managed to reach the conspirators decided to keep their discoveries on ice until the game was played out, except for one man who came near to exposing Kay Mathieson. I remember conducting a reporter and a photographer from *Life* magazine to an apartment to meet two of the plotters, for what turned out to be a festive interview, also suppressed until the time was ripe.

Police forces, in London and in Scotland, seemed to be running in aimless circles; but it is possible to surmise that, in Scotland, some officers were not actually frantic to catch the villains too soon.

The quartet drew up a solemn and dignified petition to the king, denying any subversive or anarchical motives and justifying the return of the Stone to where it belonged by treaty. In the end, a face-saving formula was devised, by which the Stone would be taken to Arbroath Abbey and delivered into the keeping of the Church of Scotland.

Arbroath was peculiarly appropriate. It was there, in 1320, that the Scottish nobles in council had drawn up a declaration of the nation's independence of all other powers and principalities, and even took a firm line with the Vatican. 'It is not for glory, riches or honour that we are fighting,' said the declaration, 'but for liberty alone, which no man loses but with his life.'

The precious object was driven to the abbey at Arbroath and deposited there. It did not pass into the keeping of the Kirk. The forces of law swooped on it and whisked it back to Westminster.

The whole undertaking may seem pointless in view of that. The storm had subsided in the teacup, and nothing was changed. But for most Scots, it was a wonderfully cheering exercise. Something, however obscure, had been proved, even if it was only the ability of a few determined young people to rattle the complacency of government and baffle established authority.

And there remains the impious conjecture about the identity of the Stone. If it could be duplicated once, it could be duplicated again. Are there any vagrant pieces of the true Stone hiding in locked drawers in Scotland? Is the entire Stone in somebody's cellar?

The idea is absurd.

Well, fairly absurd.

32

THE
INNER SCOT

―――――――

ALL THE turbulence—poetic, political, piratical—is often explained away by the odd things the Scots put into their mouths. Human beings are what they eat.

About one beast there is no mystery, except the mystery we have invented for the puzzlement of outsiders. There are straight-faced tales of the breeding and the hunting habits of the haggis, in which it is hard to tell whether it runs, or swims, or flies; and legends of invaders being driven back across the border by flights of anthropophagous haggises rising out of the heather. They are exaggerated.

Certainly strangers approach the haggis with caution and confusion, and many Scots never come near it stone sober. For some, the encounter is strictly a once-a-year undertaking, at a Burns Supper where it is essentially the main course. The bard himself ennobled it in the Address beginning,

> Fair fa' your honest, sonsie face,
> Great chieftain o' the puddin-race! . . .
> Weel are ye worthy o' a grace
> As lang's my airm . . .

So it becomes a mystery and a ceremonial. At the Supper, it is carried in in state to the dining room, preceded by a piper. These details are crucial. The chosen orator then faces it and delivers the Address and, suiting the action to the words, brandishes a sharp knife and plunges it into the thing. At the finish, he gives a sizeable dram to both piper and chef. The slashed remains of the haggis are then piped out of the room, to be returned as individual portions.

Nevertheless, it is possible to eat haggis privately, secretly if you like, without the intervention of Robert Burns or deafening music. There are some people who do not scruple to sample the dish on non-holy days, as if it were just food, taken from hunger and not from reverence. It is very good.

In Burns's time, as you may find by reading the Address in full, it was humble peasant fare, about the cheapest source of meat protein available, and it was a home-made affair. Today, most haggises come from factories or at least from professional butchers; but for anybody far from such a source, it can still be concocted in any domestic kitchen.

The ingredients are two pounds of oatmeal, a pound of chopped mutton suet or something similar, a pound of lamb's liver, two cups of meat stock, a sheep's heart and lights, a chopped onion and a hefty dash of salt and pepper, both white pepper and cayenne pepper.

The liver, heart and lights are boiled and chopped up fine. The oatmeal is toasted till crisp, and the whole collection is mixed up and stuffed into the stomach of a sheep (the stomach first having been removed from the sheep). The air is squeezed out of the stomach, which is then sewn up tight, pricked here and there with a needle to prevent explosions, dropped into boiling water and boiled gently for about five hours.

It goes well with the traditional Burnsian accompaniment of mashed potatoes and mashed turnips. There is no need, and little incentive, to eat the sheep's stomach. The filling is what matters.

Haggis should be eaten hot, otherwise it congeals rather drearily. If it seems heavy to the palate, it is deliciously lightened by a sprink-ling of neat Scotch whisky. According to the poet, it produced a race of men whose very tread made the earth tremble. That may, of course, have been partly the result of the whisky.

Scotland's cuisine tends to match the unassuming merits of the haggis. It is not what international *bons vivants* would classify as *haute*. It developed in a country with a relatively low mean annual temperature, where food was designed to keep out the cold or, as the Scots phrase has it, stick to the ribs. It is all worthy of respect and even joy.

There is no aristocratic tradition of cooking in Scotland. There are virtually no great virtuoso names in its history. The dishes that delight the discriminating native are demotic, recipes handed from mother to daughter; though Mary Queen of Scots is credited with the invention of 'petticoat tails', which are rather boring little flat cakes of flour, butter, sugar and milk, sometimes spiked with cara-way seeds. The great, and fascinating, mass of Scottish foods is cottage-kitchen stuff, and we are not ashamed of it.

Outside Scotland, porridge is often a highly offensive experience, and its original purity should be defended against alien modifica-tions. It is wonderfully simple to get it right. Oatmeal is dripped steadily with the left hand into a pot of boiling water while the right hand stirs with a wooden stick, or spurtle. The proportions are about one volume of meal to four of water, though some people like it thinner, or thicker. When the two elements are thoroughly wed, and not likely to get lumpy, a pinch of salt is added; or, for my money, several pinches of salt. The brew is simmered, and occasionally stirred, for twenty minutes or so.

The exact time is a matter of instinct, experience and taste. The meal should be cooked without being taken to the point where it is gluddery, a childish word that needs no translation.

There are rituals, even superstitions, about how to eat porridge. Some people serve it in soup plates and then eat it with a spoon which they have already dipped into a separate dish of milk. Others like to pour the milk into the side of the plate and watch until the whole helping detaches itself from the surface of the plate and forms a floating island. Some people insist on eating it standing up, a custom that probably goes back to unsettled clan times when lunch was likely to be interrupted by unwelcome visitors waving claymores. The custom has an interesting echo of the Passover.

Alien races brutalise this magnificent Scots dish by heaving sugar over it; or syrup, or even jam. To the Scot, these practices have all the allure of eating anchovies with chocolate sauce.

This is not a cookery book, but we may look at a few recipes just to illustrate the range of pleasures available. I hesitate to look at seaweed soup, but it is certainly very Scottish, though variations are found in other maritime areas of western Europe, and especially among the Celts. Seaweed soup is made of milk, mashed potatoes, a little butter, pepper and lemon juice; and a cup of seaweed, which has to be washed and simmered for several hours beforehand. The soup itself is cooked for about twenty minutes and then beaten up or homogenised. It is rather terrible, but terribly terribly good for nearly everything.

Potato scones, on the other hand, are unalloyed delight. They are among the delicacies exiled Scots dream about and ask visiting friends to smuggle to them. Again, they are easy enough for any fool to make at home. Take half a pound of mashed potatoes, a couple of ounces of flour, three tablespoons of melted butter and a liberal pinch of salt. Mix the potatoes with the butter and salt, and then mix in as much flour as the mess will absorb without drying up. Roll the stuff flat, prick it all over, and cook each side once on a griddle.

The tattie scone can be eaten cold. It can be eaten straight off the griddle with butter spread over it to melt. It can be re-fried to go with bacon and eggs. It is a joy in any form. Theodora Fitzgibbon, author of the mouthwatering cookbook *A Taste of Scotland*, says it can be spread with honey or syrup. It can, if you really hate the potato scone.

Cock-a-leekie is by any reckoning the king of soups. It wants a boiling fowl, some chopped bacon, a dozen leeks, simple herbs to taste, salt and pepper and *a quarter pound of cooked prunes*.

Boil the fowl to produce stock, separate it into bones and flesh and put both back into the stock along with most of the leeks and the bacon. When it is pretty well reduced, get rid of the bones, add the chopped prunes and the rest of the chopped leeks, and cook it again for twenty minutes.

Cullen skink. Well, if cock-a-leekie is king, cullen skink is at least consort. Its basis is two pounds of smoked haddock, which is lightly boiled for five minutes or so, filleted and simmered again with a sliced onion. In the next stage, a pint and a half of milk is added and brought just to the boil, and then cooked mashed potato is added to thicken the mixture. Last of all, a succession of small knobs of butter are dropped in, salt and pepper, and there is a dish fit for a queen; or a ploughman.

All is not savoury, of course. The Scot has a sweet tooth. In fact, working-class Scottish children often grow up with an incurable craving for sugars. The dental record of the nation is appalling. In spite of this glum reflection, it is reasonable to sing the glories of Black Bun, since it is rarely seen except at Hogmanay, and therefore cannot be blamed for the year-through incidence of caries and the alarming prevalence of false teeth among quite young natives.

Black Bun is fearsome. It is a dense mixture of roughly the same specific gravity as platinum, encased in a short paste jacket. The jacket is made from half a pound of flour, a quarter pound of butter, a touch of cold water and half a teaspoon of baking powder. The solids are mixed with enough water to make a firm paste, which is rolled out very thin and used to line a greased cake tin. What remains will be used for the top. Now for the imposing contents.

Two pounds of raisins, three of currants, half a pound of blanched chopped almonds, three-quarters of a pound of flour, half a pound of sugar, two teaspoons of allspice, one of ground ginger and one of ground cinnamon; a touch of cream of tartar, half a teaspoon of baking powder, a gill of milk. A dash of brandy, or even whisky, does not go astray.

Everything except the milk is mixed together, and enough milk is added to dampen. It is then put into the jacket, a film of paste is stuck on top. Prick the top all over, shove a few skewer holes from top to base and bake slowly for three hours. Black Bun can be made in plenty of time for Hogmanay and stored away in an airtight tin. It can be made the previous Hogmanay, in fact.

Even the names of other native dishes roll deliciously off the tongue: Howtowdie, hairst bree, speldings, Atholl brose, cabbie-claw, skirlie and het pint. One more proletarian dish simply must be honoured, because it is deep in the psyche of the Scot, and especially the Glasgow Scot. The mutton pie is as essential a snack to him as the hamburger is to the American. Both are fine. The mutton pie is just . . . it is the pie above all pies, and like the tattie scone, it is the theme of desperate dreams among natives scattered to the Americas and the antipodes. There is nothing, anywhere in the world, even slightly like a mutton pie.

It enters the consciousness of the Glaswegian early in life, because it can be bought hot, or cold, and eaten at either temperature; and it contains nearly every vital element the Glaswegian needs for survival in a hostile environment. Little restaurants serve it with baked beans, or chips, or both. In its great days, between the wars, it was purveyed across counters in multi-storeyed paper bags, each tier separated by a sheet of cardboard through which rich juices percolated. It was the pie of all pies, the total meal, the thing that might well have made all the difference when Scott failed to reach the South Pole. Captain Oates would never have stumbled out into the snowy wastes to die a hero's death if his commander had had a few Glasgow mutton pies in the tent.

The pie also goes with the national lunacy of football. It is sold, hot, at any football ground with any self-respect. It is even possible that the continuing loyalty of fans to the Partick Thistle football club in Glasgow is rooted in the quality of the mutton pies on sale at the club's ground. Partick Thistle mutton pies are certainly high-class mutton pies.

And there are wide variations in this legendary comestible. They are concerned with moisture, aridity, protein content and seasoning. Conscientious pie-men slave over hot ovens to find the ultimate balance of solidity and piquancy, and it is a search for truth that will never end. If the reader suspects that this chapter is going somewhat insane over a snack, the reader is right. There is a restaurant in Toronto, Ontario, which is growing rich by reproducing the mutton pies of yore for second-generation Scots. There is no other item of nutrition that carries a tenth of its mystique.

Well, the pie is circular. It has an outside and an inside. The outside is constructed of hot-water pastry, which contains four parts of plain flour to one part of shortening—usually animal fat—and two parts of water; plus a dash of salt. You boil the fat and water together. Then pour the hot mixture into the salted flour, mixing constantly. The result should be a squidgy material, which is kneaded on a floured board and rolled flat.

The next step is vital. It is a process which nowadays, in the commercial pie business, is done by a machine; but here and there in Scotland you may find butchers who insist on 'raising' the pie by hand, which adds some tangible superiority. What the domestic aspirant does is lay the pastry flat and, in the middle of it, place a jug or a jar about three inches across, work the pastry up the sides of the jar to a height of two or three inches, leave it to firm, and take the jar away. Another flat piece of the pastry is saved up to make a lid.

What goes into this container is finely minced lamb or mutton, spiked with salt and pepper, Worcestershire sauce, chopped onion, maybe allspice, maybe nutmeg, maybe nearly any seasoning the cook dreams of. It is no use being specific about this. Some people like bland mutton pies, some people like incendiary mutton pies, and the range in the middle is enormous and created to permit self-expression. Add some meat stock to soften the mixture agreeably, and put it into the case, fit the lid, pinch it all together and bake it in a slow oven for forty or fifty minutes.

It can turn out disappointingly. Switch the ingredients about a bit, adjust the Richter scale of the seasoning, and try another one. If eating a hot pie in the comfort of indoors, it is quite pleasant to pour a little beef stock on top and let it soak through just before biting into it. The ideal mutton pie would be strong enough to hold together, but on the verge of being damp and floppy. On the other hand, there are aficionados who like it nearly hard; or cold; or smothered in chutney.

There is certainly nothing to touch the Scottish mutton pie. Charles of the Ritz never devised such a delight.

But then, he wasn't a Scotsman.

33

A SPLASH
OF COLOUR

I NEVER MADE a mutton pie. I never saw Shelley plain, but I have danced with Margaret Morris, and if I am lucky I will again. Apart from the vigorous and unquenchable charm of the founder of the New Celtic Movement, the experience was a link with a rich past. I had the same feeling of revelation and reassurance when I once met a man on a Clyde paddle steamer who in his youth had known a man who is *his* youth had worked in a Dundee newspaper where he was able to befriend a struggling old poet named William McGonagall.

Meg Morris had, and has, her own place in history. The Celtic Movement was originally inspired by her ideas of free movement in dance, and she demonstrated it triumphantly in England and France. She is also the widow of J. D. Fergusson, one of the towering figures in the Glasgow School of painters, and his life in turn links the recent past with other giants like Katherine Mansfield and Middleton Murry and Picasso and Charles Rennie Mackintosh.

The Glasgow School, as befits any new Scottish institution, was a band of rebels that sprang up spontaneously as a reaction to the domination of the correct academic painting that Scotland knew at the turn of the century. Prissy Edinburgh artists, probably a bit alarmed, called them the wild men of the west. It was the wild man who won in the end.

'By painting,' Fergusson said, 'I mean using oil paint as a medium to express the beauty of light on surfaces. What we used to call in Scotland "quality of paint"—with solidity and guts!—not drawing a map-like outline and filling in the spaces, with an imitation of the colour of the object, with the paint.'

Beyond the artistic quality of the Glasgow School however, Fergusson is still an absorbing study simply as a man, and a lover, because his life, as told by Meg Morris, is a continuing romance. And, refreshingly for Scottish stories, it is full of happy endings and luminous glimpses of that lost legendary time when artists happily starved in Parisian garrets and met round open-air tables on the Boul' Miche to reconstruct the universe.

Born in 1874 in Leith, John Fergusson had a happy, secure childhood with two brothers and a father and mother he adored. His mind sometimes wandered at school because he preferred the window to the blackboard, but he was interested in language, he rode a bicycle, he was a useful sailor and could hold his own in a punch-up. Some people might say he had a deprived childhood, since he had nothing to rebel against. His mother encouraged him to draw, and he knew that art would be his life; but he was put off by the drudgery of an art school course and decided to teach himself.

In Paris, he became the traditional Francophil, and soaked himself in French painting with his friend S. J. Peploe, another of the wild men. Other expatriates gathered round them to form a colony. They met regularly at a restaurant which must have been like a set from a romantic movie, with a plump landlady and a pretty young waitress who mothered them and were understanding with credit when they were short of money. Middleton Murry arrived and asked J.D. to be art editor of a new magazine. Katherine Mansfield came to meet the group. They went to the Russian ballet, they painted, they had a marvellous time.

They found themselves in set-pieces from that romantic film. Fergusson once started to sketch a plump woman on the beach at Paris-Plage. She got up to go away, but on seeing him sketching she offered to sit till he was finished. 'I know how important these sketches can be,' she said. 'My husband is an artist. I am Madame Renoir.'

In 1913, Margaret Morris visited Paris with her dancers for a theatre engagement, and called on Fergusson with a letter of introduction. He opened the door a crack and asked her to come back later, as he was in his bath. Luckily, she did come back later. Fergusson attended her show, enjoyed it, and arranged for her to dance at the studio of a wealthy Polish woman, who in turn offered the young dancer the use of the studio while she was in Poland.

By the time Miss Morris went back to London, the acquaintance had developed to the point where Fergusson could write jokey letters from his new location at Cap d'Antibes exhorting her to come and join him.

They were not entirely jokey. 'At nights,' he said, 'we'll sit before the fire or play bridge, or talk golf. I'll sleep on the sofa. There's a key to your room, so the whole thing's in order . . .' And later:

> I know lots of men who are really first class shipmates, help one
> to win prizes, keep one from being drowned . . . Do you suppose
> I want you because you can do all these things better than my

men friends? Not damned likely. You may do all these things indifferently, even badly, but when you add sexual attraction to them, I prefer you. Which is a very roundabout way of saying that while still being male, if I like you and you say you don't want to do a certain thing—then that thing ceases to exist so far as our relationship is concerned . . .

She went to Cap d'Antibes, of course, a lonely undeveloped paradise in 1913. It was a bold step for a girl in the straitlaced atmosphere of the time, but it was entirely idyllic. She went back to London to work on a new ballet, but they wrote endlessly and exchanged experiences, and he offered to design the costumes for her new production. She went back to Antibes in the following summer and was astonished when a gendarme told her there was a war.

She managed to get back to London, and J.D. followed her. He was greatly taken with her school and her little theatre, and designed scenery and costumes out of love. The 'Club' attracted a galaxy of interested talents—Augustus John, Epstein, Wyndham Lewis, Ezra Pound, Leon Goossens and others. J.D. and Meg observed the proprieties—he lived on his own, and had his meals at the flat Meg shared with her mother, aunt and a woman friend.

He spent some time in Scotland, and Margaret ran a summer school in the West Country. She was concerned that he was just young enough to be conscripted, and he didn't particularly want to be killed, because he was organising an exhibition. A friend suggested that he might become a war artist, and arranged a meeting with a colonel at the War Office. When the colonel asked him how much he wanted the job, J.D. said that he was worried about the army uniforms because he didn't like khaki. The colonel regretted that the uniforms couldn't be changed to suit the artist, but suggested that the navy might be more congenial.

'Blue is my favourite colour,' said Fergusson, and spent the tail-end of the war quite happily at Portsmouth.

After the war, now positively together, they returned to Paris, at the same time as a Fergusson exhibition was opening in New York. He organised an exhibition of Scottish artists in Paris, with the blessing of Prime Minister Ramsay MacDonald. In Margaret Morris's exuberant biography of J.D. the Paris days sound like careless rapture, and in a way they were, since the work was going well and they were together. But they were still barely making a living, and lunch was often literally a loaf of bread, a jug of wine, and thou. It was not important. They were a golden couple, living on sheer talent and energy and affection.

At the outbreak of World War II, they moved to Glasgow. Glasgow, said J.D., was the most highland city—Edinburgh was a suburb of London. And in Glasgow, the prophet had honour in his own country. And so did Meg. It is possible, of course, that they were honoured at home because they had already proven themselves abroad. In any case, distinguished people recognised them, unknown people came to sit at their feet.

In 1950 they started making an annual pilgrimage to France. In 1961, J.D.'s strength began to fail, and Meg employed a nurse to tend him. One evening Meg found him asleep, looking healthy and relaxed, and took his hand. He gripped her hand, then loosened his grip. He was dead.

J.D. spent almost ninety years pursuing his vision, bringing honour and standing to Scottish art, and making crowds of friends. It was a good life.

34

DRUNK
WITH WORDS

THE LOWLAND SCOTS speak English. This statement will be denied by English people who get totally lost in the sound of Scots-English. But we should remember that some local English dialects are quite opaque to people bred in other English localities. Conversation in Newcastle, in the north east of England, is a long way from small talk in Cornwall in the south west.

Scots-English, all the same, is a thing of its own, as the old makars tried to insist. Language patriots today are sad at the extinction of the old tongue, under the onslaught of radio and television from England, they are sad at seeing all dialects in Britain being homogenised. Not least of these mourners is David Murison, who has spent most of his life compiling the *Scottish National Dictionary*, in an effort to preserve the good Scots tongue on paper at least, before it vanished completely from speech. It is a magnificent and monumental work, and Dr Murison is worthy of high honour in the annals of Scotland.

The picture may not be completely black. In country districts in Scotland they persist in speaking a reasonably rich form of Scots, and even in the cities the overheard speech is recognisably something different from 'standard' English.

The difference is not just a matter of accent. Scots has its own vocabulary, even if it is shrinking. Dr Murison has pointed out that *The Dictionary of the Older Scottish Tongue* and the *Scottish National Dictionary*, taken together, contain over 50,000 words particular to Scots. Very few of us have a vocabulary that size in any language.

The complicated rules of pronunciation in Scots-English make it a fiendish challenge to impersonators. Scotty in the television series *Star Trek* is obviously trying to live up to his nickname, but to Scottish viewers he sounds like an awkard patch-up of American-English, Irish-English and Scots, speaking a tongue that was never heard on land or sea, and certainly never in Edinburgh.

Other English-speaking peoples usually pick up a weird caricature of the Scots tongue, and imitate it by rolling their R sounds wildly and spluttering over guttural sounds. In fact, there are so many Scottish dialects that there is no such thing as a simple Scottish dialect. We speak as we speak, all differently. Our language will probably survive in some degree because those Scots who have passed beyond the pathetic snobbery that thinks of proper Southern English as proper and respectable, are still getting fun out of their quaint northern diction.

We love to hear of a shop assistant shouting to another shop assistant, 'Have we ony Bolognese forbye Heinz, Samantha?' (Ony=any; forbye=as well as). We enjoy the cry of a Glasgow bus conductress—'Come oan, get aff!' (Come on, get off. There is no contradiction, because 'Come oan' simply means 'Behave your-selves'.)

I was enchanted by a waitress, somewhat thrang and taigled (busy and frayed), who declared after the soup course, 'I'll take your follows now.'

When it is only a matter of pronunciation, there are some rudimentary rules. In Scots, down becomes *doon*, cow becomes *coo*, brow becomes *broo*. But to make it complicated, pound becomes *pun;* and clown remains as clown.

Bread becomes *breid*, and head becomes *heid*, and dead becomes *deid*. But fed remains fed, bed remains bed, and if you refer to a dead loss, dead remains dead.

The vulgar Scot drops final *g* sounds, as did the English aristocracy of some generations back (huntin', shootin' and fishin'). Illiterate Scots who are desperate to sound proper often tend to over-correct this failing, and refer to oranges and lemmings. Or they mix proprieties and improprieties in such statements as, 'Ai was jist pitting the kettle on for to bile.'

The essential difference from standard English is still a source of many private Scottish jokes. Sometimes we turn the joke on other people, as in the true tale of a Scot in a London bus, who was asked by the conductor if she owned the suitcase under the stairs. She admitted this and the conductor then said, 'You left a pie on it.'

'I've got nothing to do with the pie.'

'You left a pie on it!'

It was minutes before the passenger realised that the Cockney conductor was trying to say, 'You'll have to pay on it.'

Scots in the entertainment business often milk the obscurities of speech in such gambits as:

'Yaffa yat? Whit yat yaffa?' (Are you off a yacht? Which yacht are you off?)

Or:

'Whaurra brar?' 'A brar's ower err.' (Where is the brother? The brother is over there.)

Or:

'Achawa url skite ra bunnet affye.' (Go away or I shall knock the bonnet off you.)

An innocent American tourist who wanted to learn a Gaelic toast with which to dazzle his friends back home was taught painstakingly to pronounce, 'In Ecclefechan, craws flee erse-wise tae keep the stoor oot their een.' (In Ecclechan, crows fly backwards to keep the dust out of their eyes.)

In spite of the homogenising influence of the media, Scots words survive, at least among the older natives: *aiblins* (maybe), *gleg* (cross-eyes), *scunner* (sicken), *blether* (talk nonsense), *clishmaclaver* (stupid gossip) and at least scores more of those 50,000 mentioned by Dr Murison. It is quite possible for two Scots, in the company of English-speaking foreigners, to conduct a private conversation aloud and give nothing away to eavesdroppers.

And, against all the superficial trend, Scots has an irresistible fascination for versifiers. The study of the tongue is a book in itself (and David Murison has written the best short book for interested students: *The Guid Scots Tongue*, Blackwood, 1977). The important thing is whether it is really dying out, or has merely gone slightly underground and is able to poke its head into view when it chooses. The answer may lie in a successful literary hoax a few years ago, when a television performer launched the poetry of Ebenezer McIlwham, the Bard of Whifflet West, and started a hunt for the enigmatic McIlwham and his other works, which had to be published in book form to satisfy an eager public.

Even Scottish readers found McIlwham a taxing job, partly because, when he ran out of authentic Scots words, he didn't scruple to make up a few of his own. I make no apology or explanation for including a sample of work by this elusive modern makar. Readers who are baffled by the language may well enjoy reading it aloud as nonsense.

Days Lang Syne

Ah weel mind the oor when ah jouked in the stoor
And raked through the midgies for lucks
And blithe I hae gane wi' pals o' ma ain
A hantle o' splay-fittit nyucks

Ah, little we thocht as joyfu' we wrocht
That life maun gae chund'rin' awa'
That straucht as an arra rins Time's guidy-barra
As straucht flees the corbie, or craw

We spurtled the glaur wi' ba's made o' taur
That sair pu'ed the oose oot your ganzie
And fair had a baur, stealin' hurls on a caur
And roon aboot Mary ma Tanzie

We dined on a lotty soordook and a tottie
And graipled a black-currin bun
When syne we were fu' we cried hooch aye the noo
And aiblins we fell aff the grun

Ah, youth was the drooth in the sooth o' the mooth
And a dunt wi' a tacketty buit
Noo ah maun licht the leerie, and lukk oot ma peerie
Ah'm no' a' that auld even yit!

Ebenezer McIlwham lives; or at least somebody lives, and the
verses keep appearing to entertain fellow Scots and puzzle everybody
else. As I have said elsewhere, one of the legitimate functions of the
Scots is to confuse the rest of the world.

35

JOY
UNCONFINED

FOR INSTANCE, the Edinburgh International Festival of Music and Drama is one of the great improbabilities that preserve cynical Scotsmen from despair, and also illustrate the thrawn Scottish passion not to accept anything without examining its teeth, haggling, and prophesying that no good can come of anything.

In the light of old Scottish history, the idea of drama springing out of the grey stones of Edinburgh, and being accepted as respectable, is quite far-fetched. But old Scottish history, and new Scottish history for that matter, is a parallel tale of totally opposite and irreconcilable impulses. By the year 1947, drama and music had taken a fair grip of the stern Presbyterian Scot's psyche.

Even before World War II, the country had acquired its own symphony orchestra; or to be more exact, the rowdy lowbrow city of Glasgow had acquired its own symphony orchestra, which it was generous enough to call the Scottish Orchestra and give lesser towns a share of. It was nevertheless a Glasgow product, and played under such conductors as Barbirolli, Szell, Solti and Beecham and provided a rich diet of the world's great music for hordes of Glaswegians.

There were, of course, even among the seething aesthetes of Glasgow, the required proportion of philistine rebels, as there would be in Pittsburg or even Salzburg. One citizen at least could be heard muttering darkly that people attended symphony concerts merely to be seen and admired, since no sane person could enjoy such stuff. The orchestra thrived regardless, and especially throughout the war. The lively arts treated wartime Scotland as a renaissance, in fact. The Citizens Theatre sprang up in Glasgow, there were thriving repertory drama companies in Perth and Dundee, commercial repertory drama played to big houses in Glasgow and Edinburgh, culture was fairly bouncing in all directions.

All the same, with the war scarcely over, it was an act of boldness, almost foolhardiness, to thrust Scotland on to the international charts. In 1947, wartime rationing lingered on. Even clothes were rationed. Edinburgh might be—indeed, Edinburgh was—one of the most beautiful cities in Europe; but it was the capital of a punch-drunk country, grey with scarcities and suffering from a sore identity problem. Who would want to visit such a place?

Everybody.

Edinburgh's recklessness was compounded by the decision to make a bold show of everything. Side by side with the festival, it organised a brash exhibition of Scottish stuff and called it Enterprise Scotland. Sensible Scots recognised that both undertakings were doomed; that life was real and life was earnest and that the nation should go into mourning, or something equally grim. Both the festival and the exhibition took off like rockets.

After all the years of isolation from the European mainland and the western world, Edinburgh looked round to find its streets bubbling with exotic foreigners, looking fit and well-fed, speaking in strange tongues, and goggle-eyed at the sight of a great city *en fête*.

This could not be allowed to happen, of course, without further prophecies of doom. The sheer cost of the operation gave douce Edinburghers dark nightmares. Their money was being spent in huge subsidies to bring highfalutin bands and opera singers, actors, artists and other mountebanks into the capital, to flaunt their cash and jam the hotels and bars and make life quite unsettled.

The net profit of the festival, compared with the subsidies, is prodigious. More important, the net amount of fun is incalculable, and Edinburgh is the ideal setting for such fun. Even Glaswegians admit that.

Where else in Scotland, or anywhere, is there a main street with a precipice towering over it, and a genuine castle atop the precipice? At night, the floodlit castle hovers in the air like one of Disney's better visions. It is magical.

The street itself is ablaze with coloured light. Well, the street *was* ablaze with coloured light for several festive years, until perplexed representatives on the city council realised that the lights cost a lot of money and decided to dilute the colours and cut down on the voltage. In truth, the cost is not important. What is important is that the prospect of a great many people having free pleasure is offensive to the dark God worshipped by small Scotsmen.

There was a period, in fact, when the city council realised it had been trapped into Babylonian excesses, and retreated in tight-lipped panic. During the early years of the festival, Scottish law kept a tight hand on the legal hours of drinking, on the philosophic principle that while it might be oppressive to forbid the populace to take a glass of something before 10pm, it would be flagrantly sinful for anybody to have a dram at one minute after. Still, a lot of these foreigners were used to more decadent ways, and some of them might even be impelled to drink after the curtains had gone down on the drama and the conductors had wrapped up their batons.

With misgivings, but a reasonable show of international bonhomie, the council decided that a properly constituted festival club might be set up to accommodate those outlandish social impulses, and provide even alcoholic relaxation for the deviants within the gates. The thing was so novel, so Continental, so redolent of social liberation, that native Edinburghers joined the club in large numbers and had a whiff of whisky and freedom.

As the early years passed, this dread fact penetrated to the minds of the local rulers, and the ancient Edinburgh spirit reasserted itself. John Knox strode the horizon once more and 'the drink' was banned. All very Scottish.

In recent times, the spirit of the people, as opposed to that of the master class, has been seduced by foreign travel and the easygoing habits of alien lands, and in a national upsurge of libertinism, quite ordinary pubs may now open all day and till orgiastic hours of the night, whether the festival is on or not. In a mere thirty years, the public social face of Scotland has changed, and Edinburgh's with it.

Let us not be too hard on Edinburgh's city fathers and mothers, one of whom once objected publicly to outright pornography in the festival drama (Shakespeare). As I have mentioned elsewhere, the wild poetic uninhibited Scots have a tendency to elect inarticulate mediocrities to rule them. For all I know, California may have the same habit. What matters is that, led by ordinary citizens and the energetic strolling players who invade their city, the rulers have been dragged into the seventies and eighties and almost believe that fun is legitimate.

Edinburgh is a splendid place to be at any time of the year. During the three weeks of the International Festival of Music and Drama, it is quite enchanting. Mary Queen of Scots would love it. Given a few moments to adjust to present reality, John Knox would too.

36

AND
GALLIMAUFRY

A FEW YEARS ago I was driving a Mini on a single-track road
through a wild glen in Argyllshire, acting as pathfinder for a
Californian family in a big Ford. In the driving mirror I saw that
my American friend had misjudged the width of the tarmac and
put both nearside wheels in the ditch. I stopped, and started to walk
back to assess the disaster, but before I got there, another car
travelling in the other direction also stopped. Five men leapt out of it
and galloped towards the stranded car.

They were all shortish men in working overalls, and there was
something both purposeful and conspiratorial about them. They
seemed to be acting in concert without needing to talk. When I
caught up with them, their leader—some men are unmistakably
leaders, and this was such a one—was brusquely ordering my
American friends out of their car, and they got out. He was not a
man to quibble with. While they stood on the road, wondering
what the hell was coming, the leader was crouching in the ditch,
peering at the wheels, and his four handers were scouring the hillside
and carrying great boulders down to the road. They rammed the
stones under the wheels and manhandled the stuck car back on to
the road.

The leader then glared at my friend, and nearly snarled, 'That's
no way to drive on this road. If you don't watch these corners you'll
be in real trouble next time.'

The whole operation had taken less than five minutes. The five
got back into their car and shot away at high speed. My American
friend, quite shaken, said, 'My God, what a country! If I had been
in California and these five guys had made a run at my car, I would
have been fumbling for a revolver and praying. He was quite angry,
wasn't he?'

'Ah, we're a dour people, a dour people,' I said. The reason why
I relate the story is that it is brief and trivial, and not the kind of stuff
that goes into history books. At the same time, the flavour of a

country is composed of small inconsequentialities. The day-to-day trivia mean as much as the great sweeps of history.

When I taste this country from the inside, the little things often have the strongest tang. There is, for instance, the strange affair of my friend Torquil, who was working away from home and living in an old-fashioned hotel in Perth. As a resident, he was legally entitled to drink all day and night, which he proposed to do. Torquil, it must be admitted at once, had a drink problem; or as he confessed himself, his drink was other people's problem. Around midnight, he found himself in the little lounge bar, with the proprietor and two respectable businessmen.

'Let me put it this way,' he told me later. 'I was smashed, I was boring and I was obnoxious, but I couldn't think of anything to do about it.'

The others did think of something. The landlord produced Torquil's room key, and the two other guests shouldered him up two storeys, put him in his room and dumped him on the bed. They then left to go downstairs for some civilised conversation and moderate boozing.

Left alone, Torquil felt slightly miffed. He scanned his room, which he had never seen before, and as he said, he scanned it with the clear analytical eye of the practised drunk. A curious object by the window caught his eye, and he lurched over to inspect it. It was a patent fire-escape mechanism, consisting of a reel of rope bolted to the floor, with a harness on the end of it, and a dial which could be turned to the body weight of the user. Without a moment's hesitation, he put on the harness, turned the dial to 175lb, and launched himself out of the window.

'It was one of the great sensations of my life,' he told me. 'Free fall. Marvellous. Obviously, there was some kind of spring-loaded brake thing incorporated in the gismo, and I slowed up and landed like a feather on the street outside. I unclipped the harness and it sort of flew back up and vanished into the bedroom.'

Straightening up and assuming a profound dignity, Torquil then strolled into the hotel and entered the little lounge. The proprietor was startled to see him, but not nearly as startled as the two guests when they arrived a couple of seconds later. As he recalled, they stared at him as men stare at ghosts, retreated from the lounge and were never heard of again.

True, many of the curious components of Scottish life have an association with 'the drink'. In the old days, not all that long ago, Scottish law took the firm and totally mistaken view that if drink were available all the time, everybody would be drunk all the time.

Pub opening hours were rigidly limited by statute, and the Sabbath was inexorably dry, except for hotel residents or people described as 'bona fide travellers'. These were people far from their home towns, and planning to go even farther. This regulation produced the odd paradox that if, say, Charlie visited a friend twenty miles away, they could both go into a local hotel and Charlie could enter his name and address in a book and drink himself insane before driving home, while his friend was legally barred from the tiniest sip of alcohol.

The scene, then, is an elegant apartment in Edinburgh, and the *dramatis personae* are two poets and a very eminent Scottish barrister.

The sparkling conversation was losing its shine because the drink had run out. The poets bewailed the vicious law which prevented them from having another swig unless they left the city entirely. The barrister announced that they could all go out and have a dram, absolutely legally, without leaving Edinburgh at all.

Now these poets had a long and passionate experience both of whisky and of the prohibitions surrounding it in Scotland, and they were willing to lay a fiver that it couldn't be done. The barrister consulted a railway timetable and summoned a taxi, and all three were whisked to the main station, Waverley. There he bought three return tickets to Haymarket, the little main-line station barely a mile away at the other end of Princes Street, and well inside the city limits. The trio boarded a train on its way from London to Glasgow by way of Edinburgh, went into the buffet car and each had a large whisky which lasted comfortably for the three-minute journey to Haymarket. The barrister consulted the timetable again, they crossed to another line and caught the main-line train from Glasgow to London via Edinburgh, on which they had time for another sensible modicum of alcohol on the way to Waverley.

The barrister collected the fiver. The trains, in effect, were not in Edinburgh, or subject to Edinburgh regulations. They were legally in the position of ships at sea, beyond the three-mile limit where anything goes. The Scots have a genius for inventing strange laws, which in turn call forth the nation's other genius for coping with them.

When civil aeroplanes were getting bigger and bigger, it became clear that the main runway at Prestwick airport was too short for the giants of the future, and the town council had a long and anxious meeting on the problem. Unfortunately, a main road ran along the end of the runway. The choices were to reroute the road, or tunnel it under the runway. Rerouting the road was a lot cheaper, the tunnel was enormously expensive; but if aircraft got even bigger, the road might have to be rerouted again in a few years.

A new councillor, a lady of firm decision, listened to all the arguments with some impatience, and pointed out that if a tunnel cost so much, it would be better to build a bridge.

Local councils provide quite a lot of the essential quiddity of the Scots, though it's true that such bodies can be fun anywhere in the world. When Glasgow planned the great Exhibition of 1911, one visionary councillor proposed that the city should import a dozen gondolas from Italy and have them cruising up and down the river Kelvin as a picturesque attraction. Another councillor scented an exorbitant bill for these foreign folderols, and suggested that since there was plenty of time available, they should import two gondolas and let them breed.

The same people are, however, capable of genuine resource, and even flashes of inspiration, in modern times. A committee of the Glasgow Council recently convened to discuss and vote on some issue of such critical importance to the city that everybody has now forgotten what it was. What they do remember is that there were two rival political groups involved, and that Group A, realising it had a majority of one, pushed the meeting to a vote before anyone else should turn up. Group B, however, had an ace in the hole with which to make civic history; and it was literally a hole.

It numbered among its faithful the smallest councillor in the city. The committee room had a big open fireplace—luckily with no fire in it—and the dimunitive member was able to hide in the chimney and burst out, like the demon king, when the roll was being called. You don't get that kind of fun in the US Congress, and certainly not in the Kremlin.

Even in the field of crime, the picayune cases may have a piquancy lacking in the *causes célèbres*. A modern desperado certainly put Glasgow high in the league of ludicrous capers when he held up a bank just round the corner from his home. He wasn't only a near neighbour, he was on nodding acquaintance with the bank staff. He got the cash, all the same, and trotted outside to the getaway vehicle, which was possibly the only bright yellow moped in the city.

It refused to start. A couple of workmen saw his plight, and in the true Scottish tradition gave him a push. He was so grateful that he gave each of them a huge fistful of banknotes before he wobbled homewards. The law caught up with him in about fifteen minutes, sitting in his parlour with the money spread on a table, and looking vague.

The Glasgow Underground (or Subway) is one of the city's legitimate prides. Its history stretches back to the turn of the century when it first operated on the rope traction system. An enormously long cable was pulled round and round the circuit by a mechanical winch, and drivers propelled their trains by working a metal claw which grabbed the cable and then released it at the stations.

This method was possible because the Underground has only a simple circuit; or rather, two circuits side by side running in opposite directions. In time they were converted to electric power, they have now been realigned and modernised. As well as being fast and efficient, the Underground is also rather cute. Glaswegians don't need to ask for a toy railway set for Christmas because they already have one.

The Underground does seem an eccentric choice as a getaway car, since it always comes back to where it started. But another enterprising bank robber saw its potential. He actually got away from the bank in a car, but cars can be identified and chased. He dumped it and shot down into the subway to lose himself in the commuter crowds.

With him, he had the loot, and a shotgun cunningly wrapped in brown paper so that, to the casual observer, it looked exactly like a shotgun wrapped in brown paper. A conductor had a quiet word with the ticket collector at the next station, and the police intercepted the train, fairly incredulously. The fleeing master criminal could hardly believe it either.

Nearly everybody in Paisley writes poetry. In hot weather, Scottish urchins scrape melted tar from the street, mould it into a ball round the end of a length of string, dip it in water to harden it, then whirl the string and hurl it straight up in the air. They then scream, 'A taury ba'!' and crouch, waiting for it to smash down on their skulls. A Highlander, on declining a lift from a friend, was warned that the bus wouldn't arrive for half an hour. 'Och,' he said, 'it'll not take me long to wait half an hour.' There is a hill in Ayrshire, the Croy Brae, where a stationary car with its brakes off will run upwards.

It is all very odd and inexplicable, a country where anything can happen, and usually does, though not necessarily punctually. You name it, and a Scotsman has done it; or has thought of doing it; or has done something else even odder.

They are a strange, ordinary, delightful and exasperating people. The world would not be the same without them.

BIBLIOGRAPHY

BARKE, James, *The Song in the Green Thorne Tree*. A novel of the life and loves of
Robert Burns. Collins, 1947

BARRIE, James Matthew, *Peter Pan*. Penguin, 1970
A Window in Thrums 1896. Scholarly Reprints, New York, 1978

BAXTER, J. W., *William Dunbar*. A biographical study. Edinburgh, 1952

BIRBECK, J. J. and HENRYSON, Robert, *Robin and Makyre*. A Scot's pastoral written
in olden times. Edinburgh, J. J. Birbeck, 1955

BLAKE, George, *Barrie and the Kailyard School*. English Novelists series edited by
Herbert Van Thal. Andrew Barker, 1951

BOSWELL, James, *Journal of a Tour to the Hebrides with Samuel Johnson*. London, 1928.
Life of Johnson. Six Volumes edited by George B. Hill and L..F. Powell, with
Boswell's *Journal of a Tour to the Hebrides*. Oxford University Press, 1934

BREWERS, *Dictionary of Phase and Fable*. Cassell, 1970

BROWN, George Douglas, *The House with Green Shutters*. Holmes McDougall, 1974

BROWN, Jennifer M., *Scottish Society in the Fifteenth Century*. Edward Arnold, 1977

BRUCE, Robert V., *Bell: Alexander Graham Bell and the Conquest of Solitude*. Victor
Gollancz Ltd, 1973

BUCHAN, John, *The Thirty-nine Steps*. Pan Books, 1967

CARLYLE, Thomas, *Sartor Resartus: lectures on heroes: Chartism: past and present*. 1890

CARSWELL, Catherine, *The Life of Robert Burns*. Chatto and Windus, 1930

CHAMBERS ENCYCLOPEDIA. Newnes, 1972

COMRIE, John D., *History of Scottish Medicine*. London, 1932. 2 Vols 2nd edn, 1976.
Reprint of 1932 edn. A.M.S. Press Inc, New York

CRAIGIE, Sir William and AITKEN, A. J., *Dictionary of the older Scottish Tongue*. (The
defininitive work for the period before 1700.) University of Chicago Press,
1929

DAICHES, David, *Sir Walter Scott and his World*. Thames and Hudson, 1971
Stevenson and the Art of Fiction. Folcroft, 1951

DARLING, Grace and David, *Stevenson*. Contemporary Books, 1977

DONALDSON, Gordon and MORPETH, Robert S., *A Dictionary of Scottish History*.
Edinburgh, Donald, 1977

ELLIOT, Charles, *Poems of Robert Henryson*. Clarendon Press, 1974

FAY, Charles R., *Adam Smith and the Scotland of his Day*. Cambridge, 1956

FITZGIBBON, Theodora, *A Taste of Scotland*. Scottish traditional food; period
photographs specially prepared by George Morrison. Dent, 1970

GIBBON, Lewis Grassic, *A Scots Quair*. Hutchinson, 1974

GRAHAM, William, *The Scots Word Book*. Ramsay Head Press, 1977

HOGG, James, *Private Memoirs and Confessions of a Justified Sinner*. Oxford English
Novels. Oxford University Press, 1969

HOME, John. *Tragedy of Douglas*. Edinburgh 1823. p.ph.; Festival Souvenir
Number of Galliard. Edinburgh, 1950

HOUSE, Jack, *Square Mile of Murder*. Chambers, 1961. Molendinar Press, 1975

INNES of Learney, Sir Thomas, *The Tartans of the Clans and Families of Scotland*. Johnson and Bacon, 1971

KINGHORN, A. H., and LAW, A. (ed), *The Poems of Allan Ramsay and Robert Ferguson*. Scottish Academic Press, 1974

LINDSAY, David, *Ane Satyre of the Thrie Estates*. Edinburgh Festival Version by R. Kemp. Edinburgh, 1951

LUDOVICI, L. J., *Fleming: Discoverer of Penicillin*. Andrew Dakers, 1952

MCALISTER, Gilbert, *James Maxton: The Portrait of a Rebel*. John Murray, 1935

MACDIARMID, Hugh, *Robert Henryson*. Selected by Hugh MacDiarmid. Harmondsworth, 1973

— — *Henryson*. Poet to Poet Series. Penguin, 1973

— — *William Soutar*. Collected Poems edited by Hugh MacDiarmid. Andrew Dakers, 1948

— — *Knox, Calvinism and the Arts*. (in John Knox Edinburgh) Ramsay Head Press. 1976 (New Assessments)

MCNEILL, F. Marion, *The Scots Kitchen*. Its lore and recipes. Blackie, 1974

MACKIE, Albert D., *The Scotch Comedians: from the Music Hall to Television*. Ramsay Head Press, 1973

MACKIE, J. D., *A History of Scotland*. 2nd edn. Revised and edited by Bruce Lenman and Geoffrey Parker. Allen Lane, 1978

MACKIE, Robert L., *A Short History of Scotland*. Oliver and Boyd, 1952

MACLEAN, Fitzroy, *A Concise History of Scotland*. Thames and Hudson, 1970

MORRIS, Margaret, *The Art of J. D. Fergusson*. Blackie, 1974

MUNRO, Neil, *The New Road*. Blackwood, 1969

— — *Para Handy Tales*. Pan Books, 1969

MURISON, Dr David, *The Guid Scots Tongue*. Blackwood, 1977

NAPIER, John, *A description of the admirable tables of Logarithms* (Mirifici Logarithmarum anus descriptiv). Translated by E. Wright. 1618, Facsimile edition

NICOLAISEN, W. F. H., *Scottish Place Names*. Batsford, 1976

PREBBLE, John, *The Darien Disaster*. Secker and Warburg, 1968

— — *The Highland Clearances*. Secker and Warburg, 1967; Penguin, 1969

— — *Culloden*. Penguin, 1967

— — *Glencoe*. Penguin, 1968

PRICE, John V., *Tobias Smollett—The Expedition of Humphrey Clinker*. Studies in English Literature No. 51. Edward Arnold, 1973

RAFFERTY, John, *One Hundred Years of Scottish Football*. Published to mark the Centenary of The Scottish Football Association. Pan Books, 1973

RINTOUL, D. and SKINNER, J. B., *The Poet's Quair*. An anthology for Scottish Schools, London, 1950

ROUGHEAD, William, *Classic Crimes*. Cassell, 1951

The Scottish National Dictionary. Edited by W. Grant and D. Murison. Scottish National Dictionary Association, 1970

SMOLLETT, Tobias. *The Expedition of Humphrey Clinker*. Wood engravings by D. Harris. The Folio Society, 1955

SMOUT, T. C., *A History of the Scottish People*. 1560-1830. Fontana, 1972

STEVENSON, Robert Louis, *Dr Jekyll and Mr Hyde*. Dent, 1962

WHITLEY, Elizabeth. *Plain Mister Knox*. Skeffington, 1960

INDEX